THE *In*[illegible] SLIP MADIGAN

The Flamboyant Coach Who Modernized Football

Dave Newhouse

To Ben—
A Blue Hen forever.
Dave Newhouse
5-23-19

SJP
St. Johann Press
Haworth, New Jersey

ST. JOHANN PRESS

Published in the United States of America
by St. Johann Press
P.O. Box 241
Haworth, NJ 07641
www.stjohannpress.com

The paper used in this publication meets the minimum requirements of the American National Standard for Information Sciences—Permanence of Paper for Printed Library Materials, ANSI/NISO Z39/48-1992

Composition and interior design by Susan Ramundo
(susan@srdesktopservices.com)
Cover design by G&H Soho Inc., Elmwood Park, NJ
(ghsoho.com)

ISBN 978-1-937943-48-6

Manufactured in the United States of America

DEDICATION

To the memory of Jack Wendell Jones, who planted the seeds of a writing career long ago on an Air Force base in far away France.

—D.N.

CONTENTS

FOREWORD

by George Seifert

San Francisco 49ers coach, won Super Bowls XXIV, XXIX

During the present period of sports in our country, rules rule. Slip Madigan's energy, innovative ideas, business savvy, and football genius would have run into a wall of NCAA laws and college administrative suppression. That's the beauty of the Slip Madigan story.

His coaching time took place during the era of "The Old West" of football. Anything goes, as long as it works, and winning became the narcotic for Slip Madigan's power.

We all love the story about a person who has the gall to be the best. It motivates our horizon. Gosh, they named a school for him before he became the coach at SMC: St. Mary's College (Slip Madigan, Coach)!

When I was a young coach, my buddies and I would talk about the characters of our time: Woody Hayes, Bear Bryant, and Duffy Daugherty. The stories about those coaches, their characteristics and successes, proved to be the energy for our dreams.

Coach Slip was trying during this period of economic turmoil—the Depression—to "make a buck," and he also made history.

Theodore Roosevelt once made a speech where he stated: "Far better it is to dare mighty things, to win glorious triumphs even though checkered by failure, than to rank with those timid spirits who neither enjoy nor suffer much because they live in the gray twilight that knows neither victory nor defeat."

President Teddy Roosevelt and Slip Madigan were of the same mold. Heck, in today's world, Slip Madigan could run for President!

PROLOGUE

by Sonny Dykes

Southern Methodist University football coach

I hadn't heard of Slip Madigan before, but it's guys like him who put football on the map. His ability to create a story was pretty unusual, yet that allowed St. Mary's College to make its mark in the football world.

The barnstorming thing when they went to New York to play Fordham was awesome. It was a game back then where coaching made a difference. Slip was flamboyant, and he wasn't afraid to try things that were unusual, to go against the conventional wisdom. That's what made him successful. St. Mary's was an outsider, and an underdog.

I thought I had a full plate as a head football coach, but Slip had a buffet—coaching football, basketball, baseball, track and field, and boxing. Plus he was director of physical education, or what is now an athletic director, when he got to St. Mary's in 1921. He had to be incredibly versatile.

But you could gain an advantage back then by thinking outside the box. Slip was able to do that. He came up with an idea, and it took others five, six years to catch up. With today's technology, you put something in the playbook you think is unique, and people catch up really fast.

Slip was creative enough to where his teams weren't the biggest or strongest or fastest, but he gave them a competitive advantage.

In my mind's eye, I could picture myself coaching back then. I think it would have been fun. Loading your team on a train and traveling across the country is pretty fascinating to me. To do the things he did, and meet the people he met, that would have been a blast.

Like I said, he knew how to coach, how to create ideas that were unique, and how to motivate his teams to score huge upsets. He just knew how to create a story.

ACKNOWLEDGMENTS

In the basement of Ed Madigan's home, the same home in which his famous father, Slip Madigan, once lived, there are scrapbooks up to ten inches thick stacked in three piles. Those scrapbooks, from 1910 through 1939, contain almost daily information about the elder Madigan's life as both athlete and coach. In that same basement, a nicely furnished rumpus room, there are photographs of Slip Madigan, the coaching celebrity, with famous people who gravitated toward him, from sporting arenas to Hollywood to the White House.

From that invaluable repository of data, written and visual, comes the genesis of this book about an extraordinary individual who modernized, and glamourized, the world of football. Slip Madigan had a vivid imagination and a technical mind. His name may not be as recognizable as Fielding H. Yost, Amos Alonzo Stagg, Pop Warner, Knute Rockne and Bob Zuppke, the early legends among football coaches. But no coach impacted football more so than Madigan, and no coach ever lifted his school to improbable heights quite like Madigan at St. Mary's College in California. The documentation is all there in those scrapbooks.

Without Ed Madigan, his wife, Carol, and sons Fred and Edward, this book would not have been possible. Without George Guppy, the conduit, the process would not have even begun. George Baljevich contributed mightily to the text, as did Dick Underhill, Allen Nichelini, Jr., and Pat Smith, sons of St. Mary's Gaels who played football for Slip Madigan. Lise Peters, widow of venerable journalist Nick Peters, generously provided valuable historic data from her husband's vast memorabilia collection. Patrick O'Brien and Kevin Donahue added pertinent information, and D. Ross Cameron graced the test with excellent photography.

Much gratitude goes out to Andy Jokelson for his excellent editing of the manuscript, and to John Christian of the Hayward Area Historical Society, keeper of the *Oakland Tribune* clipping files, for furnishing information pertinent to this book project.

To David Biesel and St. Johann Press for their belief in this book.

The author also thanks his wife, Patsy, for the umpteenth time for her endless patience, and his son, Casey, wife Michelle, and grandchildren Callan and Campbell for their love and support.

INTRODUCTION

Football coach, promoter, showman, innovator, raconteur, hustler (but not huckster), celebrity-magnet, wartime military officer, architect, mentor, giant-killer, and giant-maker—there was only one Slip Madigan.

"I'll tell you," said Ed Madigan, "the mold was broken by my dad, and there's been no one like him in football since."

There was no one like Slip Madigan before Slip Madigan either. If he weren't real, you'd think he was fictitious. He didn't invent football, but he changed the way America thought about the game. He was the first mainland coach to play a football game in Hawaii, actually two games back-to-back, in 1922. He was the first football coach to travel coast-to-coast for a game, by train in 1930 to play Fordham. He built St. Mary's College into a national football power and one of the country's biggest football draws, even without a campus stadium. And while other teams wore standard cotton and khaki, Madigan dressed his team in silk.

"He was one of a kind," his son emphasized.

He was, indeed. Madigan played for Knute Rockne before becoming the "Knute Rockne of the West." Madigan was a Notre Dame teammate of George Gipp, and the Gipper benefitted from the blocking of the Slipper. Madigan originated college football on Sundays, and he was a pioneer of night football. He built two unbeaten teams at St. Mary's in spite of a miniscule student body. He knocked off a national champion on its own turf, and he won his only bowl appearance. And he alone was responsible for relocating his school to a new campus site, through finances accrued by his football teams. A smart businessman as well as an innovative coach, he received a percentage of every football ticket sold. After leaving football, he became a millionaire in construction.

"Anything my father touched, he achieved," the son noted.

Ed Madigan continued to describe his indescribable father in 2016, exactly fifty years after his passing. And the son's memory hadn't faded one iota. But, then, how does one easily forget such a unique father?

"An incredible man," the son said, "the son of Irish immigrants, captain of his high school football and baseball teams in Ottawa, Illinois. Dad had three college scholarship offers: Dartmouth, Notre Dame and a small school in Illinois. Whether it was Wheaton or Knox, I can't remember, but he was a very intelligent man, almost on the genius side.

"Speaking to that, he went into the Navy in World War I as a seaman and ended up an officer. He was fantastic in mathematics and navigation. He started at Notre Dame in architecture, but the dean told him he couldn't study architecture and play football. Dad said he had to play football, because he was on scholarship. So he switched to law, which wasn't then a post-graduate degree."

At that precise moment, as the younger Madigan was being interviewed at St. Mary's, the school his father put on the map, noon arrived and the bells of St. Mary's chimed twelve times, a ringing heard throughout its campus and across the surrounding Moraga hillside.

"Very apropos," the son said of the harmonic familiarity before continuing. "My father went into coaching as a means to an end. After graduating from Notre Dame, there weren't too many opportunities. He already was married, so he got into coaching and the rest is history. From coaching he went into business, becoming a successful homebuilder. He used his law studies on the business side of football, arranging contracts and creating the gate at football games."

The son isn't sure if his famous father had a photographic memory, "but he was very good at remembering names. He also used his architecture background from Notre Dame after coaching, drawing all the homes he built. He had a big drawing board in the back of our house, and he'd sit there for hours drawing houses and apartments."

Slip Madigan—he was tagged "Slip" from ice-skating falls as a kid—passed away at 69 in the Spanish-styled home he bought in Oakland in 1932, directly across from the Claremont Country Club golf course. Son Ed and wife Carol live in that same home, having raised two sons, Edward and Fred. That's three generations of Notre Dame alumni in one family:

Slip, Ed, and Edward. Fred, a University of California at Berkeley graduate, doesn't feel ostracized living in a house of Fighting Irish, but not altogether fighting Irish. After all, his mother is a Cal alumna, not to mention his two aunts, Slip Madigan's daughters.

Slip was born Edward Patrick Madigan, while son Ed was christened Edward Eugene Madigan. "My mother and dad had a stillborn son before me whom they named Edward Patrick Madigan II," said Ed. "So they named me Edward Eugene Madigan after Father Eugene Burke, a Holy Cross priest at Notre Dame who introduced my father to my mother. Father Burke also got my dad his first coaching job in Portland. I named my oldest son Edward Patrick Madigan II after my father.

"My father didn't fail at anything he put his mind to. With his business background, he partnered with Transamerica, one of the biggest business corporations in America. They recognized his skills. During World War II, he was director of the Smaller War Plants Corporation, involving seven western states, a congressional appointment. Dad told me that some of the congressmen didn't feel a football coach could run such a big political and corporate identity. But he did a good job."

In Slip Madigan's various pursuits over a lifetime—from coaching football, to a wartime officer ranking, to building a housing empire, the outcome was always positive. Failure was not an option. He had the golden touch. Midas could have learned from him.

"If my father hadn't showed up," said the son, "St. Mary's probably still would be the little school on Broadway (Street) in Oakland. The other local Catholic schools, Santa Clara and University of San Francisco, had bigger campuses, so their coaches didn't have to do as much as my father, coaching five sports and being the athletic director, too."

Slip Madigan interrupted his Notre Dame education to serve in World War I, though without seeing combat. He served on a destroyer in New York Harbor. "He always kidded that it was better to fight in a war where you have clean sheets at night," said the son. "But he was so successful, he was asked to stay in the Navy after the war. He said, 'Can I become admiral?' They said, 'No, you didn't go to Annapolis.' So he said, 'I want out.' He was asked to go back in World War II, but he said only if he could be a line officer. He was turned down again."

Slip Madigan didn't always get what he wanted, but he wouldn't settle for anything less. Thus he served in only one World War. However, his eighteen months of military service meant that he would have two head coaches at Notre Dame: Jess Harper his first two varsity years, and Knute Rockne as a senior. Madigan played center at only 156 pounds. Though light on the scales, he was a tough two-way Irishman for the Fighting Irish, blocking and knocking bigger men on their backsides.

"Dad borrowed a lot from Rockne when he went into coaching, by using the Notre Dame box, or shift, flexing the ends and putting a man in motion," said the son. "Rockne told him that if he wanted to make it big in coaching, he'd have to look east for recognition. My dad took him up on that with those train trips."

Rockne was famous for his locker room oratory, "but my father was a much better speaker than Rockne. Well, he had a better voice, in fact a wonderful voice. He loved to sing Irish tunes. When I was a boy, he'd sing me to sleep with 'Tura, Lura, Lura.' His voice was so strong that you could hear it across the St. Mary's campus. He didn't even need a loudspeaker."

The son grinned, remembering the dramatic locker room speeches his dad and Rockne created in exhorting their troops to victory. "I died a few times if you believed my dad's pre-game speeches," Ed Madigan laughed. "A couple of dad's players from the 1920s, Bill Murphy and Toots Casper, told me this one story. They saw my dad in the hallway, filling up a bottle with tap water, before telling the team, 'This is holy water.' Then he went around blessing the players. Bill and Toots kept their mouths shut."

Slip Madigan was a great orator. Rockne gave classic halftime talks; Madigan gave legendary halftime talks, although not as publicized as Rockne's. "He had a kind of magic," said one of Madigan's former players, quarterback Lou Ferry. "Even the most cynical veteran players were ready to run through the walls after he finished talking."

That, of course, depended on the thickness of the walls. "When Buck Shaw coached at Santa Clara against my dad," said Ed Madigan, "the two teams would be in the Kezar Stadium locker rooms at halftime, with only a wall between them. My dad's voice was so loud that Buck told his players, 'I'm not going to say anything. Just listen to what Slip is saying, and that's what you're going to be facing in the second half.'

"My dad was flamboyant, but I'm not sure where he got his flamboyance. It wasn't from his father, who worked in the brick and glass factories in Ottawa, Illinois. Flamboyance was just dad's nature, because it was so natural. But he wasn't a braggart. He always said, 'Self-pride stinks.' And he was very religious; he seldom missed Mass."

That flamboyance, sometimes, was predetermined. Slip Madigan put on a show. He yelled at the game officials, calling them "horse thieves." He removed his hat and crunched it, kicked it, and stomped on it, while hearing opposing fans shouting, "Sit, down, Slip!" "He'd need a new Borsalino (hat) every week," said his son. "He wanted to make football exciting, to give the fans and the press something to talk about."

"That hat was on the field as much as we were," said fullback Andy Marefos. Madigan was half-coach, half-performer, making sure the fans got their money's worth. "Sit down, Slip" was a stand-up performer.

Madigan's Gaels galloped over the Rose Bowl-bound University of Southern California "Thundering Herd," 13-7 in 1931, the same year that USC was the national champion. The game was played in Los Angeles, but St. Mary's "home" attendance at 60,000-seat Kezar Stadium in San Francisco sometimes ranked as high as second nationally behind USC, which played at the 90,000-plus Los Angeles Memorial Coliseum. Madigan, with a tiny campus enrollment compared to the huge student bodies of his opposition, somehow found ways to win the big ones, although it eventually took a huge toll on his health.

Those Gaels were fast and fashionable. Their uniforms seemed designed by Paris courtiers, not Army surplus. The Gaels, whose colors were blue and red, wore red, white and blue uniforms. Pigskin patriots. Or, occasionally, they'd wear green pants and jerseys with gold harps on their chests, as Madigan was Irish to the core. And creative to the core, though lacking enough students to form a marching band, he recruited high school kids and union workers, anyone who could play an instrument in tune, to come join the St. Mary's band. A baton-twirling high school girl then led the band onto the field. Madigan raised the money somehow to dress the band in the classiest uniforms, made out of genuine silk, just like his football uniforms. He always went first class.

Madigan dressed himself accordingly. He wore a suit, overcoat, tie and scarf to accompany his Borsalino on the sideline. Surrounding himself with celebrities, he needed to look sharp himself. Madigan and his Gaels met President Herbert Hoover at the White House after knocking off Fordham in 1930. President Franklin Delano Roosevelt invited Madigan to a reception at his home in Hyde Park, N.Y. Madigan hobnobbed with such Hollywood types as Robert Taylor, Errol Flynn and Pat O'Brien. Bing Crosby and Bob Hope sent Christmas cards to the Madigan home. Babe Ruth attended St. Mary's games. Famed New York restaurateur Toots Shor always managed to find a table for Madigan in his ever-crowded establishment. No football coach had more celebrity.

"Dad always said he knew everyone from the big house to the White House," said Ed Madigan. "He had a very good presence and a great smile. He had these watery blue eyes, and dimples. With his nice features, he greeted people like he'd known them all their lives. Dad was very outgoing, and he made people feel comfortable. When he entered the room, you knew someone important was there. His personality made him a magnet.

"He was a moral man, and very loyal. But he was a fighter. My mom, when they were dating, went to see him play for Notre Dame. He got thrown out of the game in the first quarter for fighting. She married him anyway in 1917. He came from five brothers, and he was the defender of the family. My dad had a quick temper, but once it was over, it was over. But he had a glare. You only had to look at him to know what was up. He was like that either on a football field or in his own home. George Canrinus, who played for my dad, told me this story. While getting ready to face USC, with all its stars, at the Los Angeles Coliseum, George said: "We looked at USC on the field, and then we looked at your dad on the sideline. We were more scared of him. And we won the game."

Slip Madigan snapped the football for Notre Dame with an accurate aim and unlimited grit. "He was quick, and he was rough," his son learned. "Playing against Washington & Jefferson, he intercepted a pass at his linebacker position. He saw a great player from that era, Fats Henry, coming at him. Dad thought he could outrun Fats every time, but Fats knocked him into the bench. That's how dad got a bad knee."

Then Madigan went west and raised St. Mary's from infancy to manhood. He coached his last game at St. Mary's in 1939, and all because the little school he turned into a giant decided not to renew his contract. "I suspected from the start that it wasn't steady work," he told the press with equanimity in spite of his firing. Ever the forward thinker, he had prepared himself for that outcome by negotiating a sweetheart deal with the Christian Brothers that, in addition to his modest salary, gave him ten percent of the gate at every home game. Thus during the Great Depression, he became one of the highest-paid coaches in the land in 1936 by accepting a $38,324.15 settlement from his gate-percentage deal. And so he departed St. Mary's with a huge chunk of change, deservingly so, considering what he had left behind.

By 1939, though, St. Mary's College officials had grown tired of hearing that the "SMC" on the hill overlooking the campus stood for "Slip Madigan College." Well, could that be denied? "The brothers felt dad was bigger than the school itself, which was true," said his son. "When football was over, it was over. It was time to go. He became ensconced in his new career."

After leaving football for good in the mid-1940s, Slip Madigan built a thousand residential structures, according to his son, in Contra Costa County. "The billboards read 'Slip Madigan's homes,' and that meant you were getting a good home," said Ed Madigan. The son currently oversees his father's homes and apartments, with the help of his own two sons, Slip's grandsons. Slip Madigan's legacy lives on as a builder of solid structures, either on a football gridiron or inside a housing tract.

And a century later, there is evidence, though rather spooky, that Slip Madigan still is keeping a close eye on the school he made famous.

1

The Ghost of St. Mary's

Slip Madigan died in 1966, but he didn't go away, not entirely. He continues his looming presence over the St. Mary's College campus, even though he stopped coaching the Gaels way back in 1939. And what form of looming presence might that be? Well, do you believe in ghosts?

Steve Jacoby certainly didn't believe in ghosts until one autumn day in 1983. Jacoby, a defensive lineman for St. Mary's after it resumed football at the Division III level in 1970, had endured a tough practice session, and was naturally fatigued. He decided to take a nap before showering inside Madigan Gym. So he grabbed a wrestling mat, pulled it onto the basketball court, and quickly fell asleep.

Awakening several hours later, he discovered that he was not alone. Above the bleachers, he spotted a human form pacing back and forth, apparently in distress. Concerned as much as curious, Jacoby called out, "Hello, up there." There was no response; the figure continued pacing.

Jacoby's senses sharpened by what he believed he was seeing, he stood up and moved in for a closer view. Night had fallen by then, and moonlight shone through the gymnasium windows, framing the bleacher figure, who wore a dark suit, a topcoat, scarf, and a gray dress hat—a Borsalino?—that had seen better times.

"Hello, mister," Jacoby spoke again, still without evoking a response. The figure took a few more steps, then suddenly vanished, even though there is no exit atop the bleachers. Shaken by the experience, Jacoby left the building as fast as he could, wondering who'd believe him if he explained what he had just seen. He wasn't so sure himself. It happened in Madigan Gym, but that couldn't have been Madigan, who died seventeen years earlier. Or could it?

Slip Madigan did wear a suit, topcoat, scarf and Borsalino when he coached St. Mary's to national prominence in the 1920s and 1930s. And he often thrashed his Borsalino while attempting to fire up his football teams and their fans, usually by showing disdain at an official's ruling.

We know about "Marley's ghost," "The Ghost and Mrs. Muir," and "Ghostbusters," but "The Ghost of St. Mary's?" Now, students singing "The Bells of St. Mary's" on campus is one thing, but what if ol' Slip is ringing those bells in accompaniment? Jacoby isn't the only one on the Moraga campus seeing such a ghost. Other St. Mary's students have spotted an apparition through a window of Madigan Gym as they strolled past the building under a full moon. Spooky, indeed.

Yet Madigan's image doesn't have to be seen or identified to believe that it's actually him. George Baljevich, a former St. Mary's athlete and assistant basketball coach, experienced two instances where he felt Madigan's ghostly presence inside Madigan Gym.

"It was 1970, and I had just been hired by Bruce Hale, the new St. Mary's basketball coach," said Baljevich. "Bruce was a carpenter, and he already had done some work making the old gym, which had been around since 1930, look better. Bruce and I then decided to paint the keys on the basketball court, where the Gaels still played their games in the 1970s. We painted each key red, then we were both startled.

"I'll never forget it. It was 4 p.m. on June 5th. We were at the south end of the gym under the basket. Bruce took the paint and the roller, put them in the equipment room, locked it up, and we started taking the masking tape off the key. Suddenly a door to the equipment room started banging. They were Dutch doors, and the top door kept banging back and forth. We could see into the equipment room, and we kept listening to the banging, banging, banging of the door. Something strange was happening.

"Bruce looked at me, and I looked at him. And it was, like, who moves first? We went out to the hallway, and we saw the top door continuing to bang back and forth. The bottom door was secured. Finally, the top door stopped banging. Nervously, I said, "You go in first, Bruce." But we decided to walk in together, and all we saw was the equipment. That was enough. I said, 'Let's get out of here right now.' And he said, 'yeah.'

"I was a little scared because I'd never had anything like that happen to me. I was the type of person who thought that people who believed in UFOs were, well, out there. But it was a warm summer day, there was no wind, and nobody was in the gym but the two of us. Finals were over, school was out. A new athletic director had been hired, but he wouldn't be there until August. So to whom do we report this? Bruce tried making a little joke about it. He asked me, 'Do you think John Wooden is painting the key at UCLA?' But I think Bruce was a little scared, too."

Was it Slip Madigan banging the door? St. Mary's colors are red and blue, and possibly he was angered that the key was being painted red, not blue. Or was he protesting the hiring of Hale, an alumnus of Santa Clara, St. Mary's biggest rival? Regardless, the whole incident was eerie.

Ten years later, in 1980, the larger, brand-new Albert Rahill Pavilion had replaced Madigan Gym as the Gaels' basketball arena. Baljevich had returned for a second run as assistant coach. Late one January evening, he was in his Rahill office, doing some work. About that same time, a Gaels football player was preparing to take a shower with his girl friend at Madigan Gym. But before any hanky-panky occurred, all fifty showers in the locker room came on simultaneously. The player tried to turn off one of the shower knobs, and couldn't. Something weird was happening.

"The player came over to my office," Baljevich recalled, "and said excitedly, 'I can't turn the showers off.' I went over and the fifty showers were still on, even though not one of them had been turned on by human hand. A maintenance guy said there was no way that fifty showers could have turned on at once. Maybe one or two, but not fifty, and nobody had tinkered with the main plumbing in front of the gym. That was another Madigan ghost story that went around the campus."

Was moral Slip, a strict Catholic, wreaking his wrath at the thought of his showers being used for immoral purposes? Or was he irate that Madigan Gym strictly was a basketball facility, when his football teams had practiced in that gym on rainy days? He had the gym built purposely high so that his Gael gridders could practice punting indoors.

Yet another ghostly story surfaced at St. Mary's, involving a safe in the administrative offices at Madigan Gym. The door to the safe was removed for repairs that, reportedly, would take several days to accomplish. But, mysteriously, the door was back in place the very next day. And the combination to the safe no longer worked. Well, this was the very safe that Madigan kept his gate receipts from St. Mary's football games. Perhaps he disliked anyone tampering with his safe, so he returned the door in its usual place and changed the combination.

"I hardly ever told those stories," Baljevich said, "until a book came out: "They Did It Every Time: The Saga of the St. Mary's Gaels," by Randy Andrada. I've never heard of ghost stories on any other campuses. But, then, I guess, no other school had a coach quite like Slip Madigan."

Not a ghost of a chance. There has been no other football coach like Madigan, either in spectral or human form. Henry McLemore of the United Press marveled that the Gaels' silky attire in the 1930s seemed "patterned after the formal dress coat of a high-ranking French Army officer." From what Steve Jacoby saw, the ghostly Madigan was dressed GQ style, minus the rumpled fedora.

Madigan believed in style, convinced that if his teams looked resplendent in their uniforms, they would play just as classy. But was he still watching over Gaels football after he left—better than the Gaels watched over themselves? Their Oil Bowl trophy from 1946, earned from beating Georgia Tech, 41-19, was lost, mysteriously, for decades. Then it was discovered buried in the Madigan Gym basement. St. Mary's needn't have worried. Slip's ghost was guarding it all that time.

When Baljevich was a St. Mary's freshman in the 1950s, part of his initiation required his carrying a rock up a hill that overlooked the charming rural campus. He would add his rock to those that formed the "SMC" on the hillside, and then paint the rock white. The "Slip Madigan College" reference bears accuracy, because St. Mary's College wouldn't have become nationally recognized without Madigan. No other football coach had a bigger impact on a college; his football team, by itself, grew the campus—moved it, too—during his coaching years, 1921 to 1939. And he's still hanging around? Who is that figure inside Madigan Gym?

St. Mary's College first opened its doors in 1863 in San Francisco as a diocesan college for boys, a combination of high school and college. The school's first mover and shaker was the Most Rev. Joseph Alemany, the first archbishop of the See of San Francisco. But the archbishop was dissatisfied with the archdiocese's operation of the college, and so in 1868, St. Mary's was turned over to the De La Salle Christian Brothers.

More change was afoot in 1889 when the college moved across San Francisco Bay to Oakland, locating at 30th and Broadway in a building known affectionately as "The Brickpile." In 1892, St. Mary's fielded its first football team, following the lead of neighboring Stanford University in Palo Alto and the University of California in Berkeley. But it was the Presbyterian Academy and Divinity School, located near The Brickpile, which spurred St. Mary's into gridiron action. The perfectly named PADS approached St. Mary's for some weekday games. Its invitation was accepted, though cautiously, because the St. Mary's kids knew nothing about football. The PADS even loaned them uniforms as further inducement. St. Mary's didn't fare well against the PADS, but they did win one game that first season, defeating Oakland High School.

A year later, St. Mary's raised enough money to purchase fifteen uniforms—canvas jackets that laced up the front with flannel pants, but without helmets and shoulder pads; too futuristic. In 1896, fittingly the year Edward Patrick "Slip" Madigan was born in Ottawa, Illinois, St. Mary's and Santa Clara commenced playing each other in football, often heatedly, in "The Little Big Game." However, their heated rivalry had its roots back in the 1870s, when their first baseball game ended in a brawl. In its early existence, St. Mary's primarily was known as a baseball school. Future Hall of Famer Harry Hooper, part of the celebrated Boston Red Sox outfield of Tris Speaker, Duffy Lewis and Hooper in the early 1900s, earned an engineering degree at St. Mary's.

In 1920, the University of California decimated St. Mary's in football, 127-0. St. Mary's accumulated sixteen yards of offense, completed one pass, and managed a single first down against Cal's "Wonder Team." St. Mary's promptly cancelled the rest of the schedule. Brother Gregory, FSC, St. Mary's president, began looking for a new coach, stating, "A college or university that does not appear on the sports pages of the newspaper is out of the running. The boy coming to college selects his school largely because of its athletic prowess." Ah, the athletic tail wagging the academic dog, though hardly an original concept.

The following winter, St. Mary's hired Madigan to coach its football team, but also its basketball, baseball, and track and field teams, thereby eliminating any possible slack time. "I could be just the Christmas present St. Mary's is looking for," he confidently told Brother Gregory. Following his graduation from Notre Dame in 1920, Madigan had gotten a job teaching and coaching at Columbia Preparatory in Portland, Oregon. Columbia hadn't won a football game in 1919, but under Slip's guidance, it was 6-2 in 1920 with four shutouts. A Christian Brother visiting the Oregon school was naturally impressed with Slip's achievement and encouraged him to seek the St. Mary's job. When Slip lost to Cal, 21-0, in 1921, it was a remarkable improvement of 106 points from the year before. Madigan always considered that game his biggest coaching achievement. Brother Gregory knew at that moment he had hired the right man. Madigan produced a 4-3 winning record that first season, with only a seventeen-man roster culled from a campus enrollment of one hundred and thirty-five males. St. Mary's barely lost to Stanford, 10-7, in '21, one more highlight for the promising Madigan.

St. Mary's then was known as the Saints, and Madigan one day would attain saintly status on the bucolic four hundred and twenty acre campus in hilly Moraga, a suburban community ten miles east of Oakland and twenty miles east of San Francisco. The innovative Madigan changed the look of college football, implementing blackboard "chalk talks," spring football practice, and a training table. He scouted teams, not a universal concept at that time. He closed practices, which was unheard of as well. Here was a man to be admired, and imitated.

And what worked so splendidly in South Bend, Indiana—the "Notre Dame shift"—would also work wonders in Moraga, California. Madigan introduced Knute Rockne's offense not only to the Bay Area, but also to the West Coast. In that shift, a forerunner of the "single wing," the quarterback became a blocking back, lined up several yards behind the guard. A halfback lined up similarly between the tackle and end. The other halfback and fullback lined up side by side four to five yards back of the center. This system was built for speed, fitness, and deception, not brute strength. With

St. Mary's small roster, they would have to outthink opponents, since they couldn't overwhelm them.

"You saw the Rockne influence in the way Madigan organized things, with his entrepreneurial ventures and his marketing pizzazz," said College Football Hall of Fame executive director Bernie Kish. "He even out-Rockne-ed Rockne!"

Geroge Baljevich agreed with that analogy: "Slip was an innovator, a great recruiter, and a businessman. He studied architecture and law at Notre Dame, and he was good at mathematics, so he figured out percentages quickly. He was a ticket seller, travel agent, and promoter. When the team traveled by train, the press had their own Pullman car with a bar. Slip made sure he got a percentage of the gate, and so he left St. Mary's with a big payday. But he, indeed, put St. Mary's on the map."

In Madigan's second year at The Brickpile, 1922, his Saints held Stanford to a scoreless tie. Stanford was so flummoxed by that outcome that it wouldn't play St. Mary's again until 1927, when St. Mary's stunned a Rose Bowl-bound Stanford team, 16-0, coached by Pop Warner. Little St. Mary's had arrived! And Madigan was left Pop-eyed, excited by his own success, humbling a coaching legend. Thoroughly embarrassed, Stanford promptly dropped St. Mary's from its football schedule through 1950, when St. Mary's dropped major-college football.

Madigan was selected to the College Football Hall of Fame, the Bay Area Sports Hall of Fame, and the Helms Athletic Foundation. He attended only the Helms event; the other two honors came posthumously. He left a legacy at three institutions: Ottawa (Illinois) High School, Notre Dame University, and, mostly, St. Mary's College. In truth, he built St. Mary's with a coaching whistle and sideline guile.

That 1927 victory over Stanford brought St. Mary's instant national exposure; some Catholic conversions, pundits noted, took longer. But a 26-7 milestone win over Cal in 1926 brought with it a new nickname. Sportswriter Pat Frayne's lead paragraph the next day in the *San Francisco Call-Bulletin* read: "The Lone Horseman and the Galloping Gaels trampled the Golden Bears of California on Saturday in a flurry of speed and strength. . . ." Madigan, the Horseman mentioned by Frayne, applied for a copyright on "Galloping Gaels" within a year. Madigan enjoyed his Gaels being called the "Notre

Dame of the West." Along that same line, *Oakland Tribune* sports editor Art Cohn often referred to Madigan as the "Fifth Horseman." Only Slip wasn't horsing around; his Gaels were in full gallop on the gridiron by 1926. And St. Mary's College was on the move, literally, because of Madigan's rocketing success.

The Brickpile was St. Mary's home until 1928 when it was damaged by fire. Rather than rebuild in Oakland, the Christian Brothers executed a land grab in Moraga, relocating the school in cow country. Without the financial windfall reaped through Gaels football, the move wouldn't have been feasible. With lumber trains passing by campus, students had an alternative means of transportation. Then with the Great Depression of 1929, St. Mary's faced bankruptcy, but avoided that fate with its purchase by Archbishop John Joseph Mitty. Bankruptcy re-appeared on campus in the mid-1930s, preceding the beginning of the end of the dynamic Slip Madigan era. Football couldn't save St. Mary's forever.

St. Mary's College resumed football on a lesser scale in 1970, but gave up that endeavor in 2004. The only football played on campus these days is touch, or rugby. But the school's gridiron aura hasn't died, largely because of the looming specter of the miracle man who made it all happen so long ago.

"The dream of alumni is to bring back the Madigan era," said former St. Mary's professor Ron Isetti, who has written a book on the school's three-century history. "The Madigan ghost still haunts the campus, at least in the minds of a lot of alumni. The ghost is there."

At that ghost of a chance, the sound of laughter is heard from behind the bleachers in Madigan Gym. Who is up there, anyway?

2

The Overland Express

Certainly, Slip Madigan had put St. Mary's College squarely on the map with some memorable victories in the 1920s, however with only one negative: It was a West Coast map. Never one to be thought of as myopic, Madigan had a much grander vision. He wanted the nation to know about his mighty little school and its fearless football team.

So he contacted his old coach at Notre Dame, Knute Rockne, about how to expand his horizons. And Rockne gave it to him straight: "Slip, if you want to be a success, you've got to go to New York City."

Amazingly, Madigan had created a phenomenal success story in the shortest amount of time, beating USC, UCLA, Oregon, Santa Clara, Stanford and even California in the 1920s. But in Rockne's sage opinion, St. Mary's College was a stranger on the East Coast.

The status and popularity that Madigan sought so badly awaited him in the Big Apple, and he was eager to take his first big bite. So following his unbeaten and once scored-upon season in 1929—that score coming in the very last quarter of the very last game—he scheduled East Coast powerhouse Fordham in 1930 at the Polo Grounds.

But being Slip Madigan, he wasn't merely going to show up and play a football game. Not Slip the consummate showman. He turned that football trip into an extravaganza—a cross-country train trip with well-heeled alumni and well-oiled media along for the ride, providing fresh newspaper copy daily. Madigan supplied the copy, plus the food and drink, resulting in a revolutionary trans-continental gridiron expedition. Of course, he charged the alumni for coming along. How else to pay for vittles and the libation? As his final stroke, Madigan arranged for a White House visit with President Herbert Hoover on the way back home. Imagine, the Gaels and traveling party, getting an audience, or at least a photo shoot, with the leader of the free world. As the master impresario, Madigan arranged the White House visit. Even our nation's 31st president couldn't refuse him.

And so Madigan, thirty-three of his players, plus alumni, faculty, and sportswriters, boarded a train at the Ferry Building in San Francisco and headed toward the East Coast. There was so much excitement about this unprecedented trip that one St. Mary's alum told his wife that he was going to buy milk and bread, then see the St. Mary's party off, and be right back. He was pulled on the train and didn't return home for two weeks, but was saluted as having gone the extra mile, or miles, in terms of loyalty to his school.

Madigan, the ultimate coach/tour guide, arranged for his players to have a "gym car," so they could exercise en route. They also got off the train to practice at various spots Madigan had picked out. At each stop, they drew curious crowds, interested in catching a glimpse of this new age of college football: A team traveling cross-country to intersectional games rather than being restricted to regional contests. Rockne took his Notre Dame teams west to play USC, but that was South Bend to Los Angeles. Madigan was traveling ocean to ocean, San Francisco to New York City, for a non-bowl-type football game, something unheard of before 1930. He was always one step ahead of the crowd.

The world was changing in 1930, one year into the Great Depression, with the introduction of Mickey Mouse, Hostess Twinkies, the chocolate chip cookie, night baseball (Independence, Kansas), the Motion Picture Production Code (restricting sex, crime, religion and violence on film), and, more seriously, the formation of the German Socialist Labor Party and the establishment of the Communist Party of Vietnam. Haile Selassie was crowned emperor of Ethiopia that same year, yet another educational topic to discuss on this cross-country excursion. For to be away from school a full two weeks would mean lost time in the classroom. But Madigan made sure proctors traveled with the team to assist the players with their studies on a fast-moving train. Ah, studying physics in Arizona, New Mexico, Texas. . . .

The remaining train cars were filled with hilarity, libation, and newspaper stories to be written. Madigan arranged for the sportswriters to travel at no cost, including food and drink. He knew the value of publicity, and so he treated the press as family. He provided interesting quotes, and many a highball. Madigan had the most congenial relationship imaginable between a coach and sportswriters. They seldom wrote a bad word about him. He could do little wrong in their eyes, and he wasn't adverse to a highball himself. Thus the train trip to play Fordham became known as "The World's Longest Bar."

But this wasn't entirely a happy trails adventure, because fearsome Fordham waited at the end of the trail. The Rams hadn't lost a game in two years, receiving strong consideration as the best team in the East. A Baltimore journalist, Tom Thorp, wrote, "Major Frank J. Cavanaugh's fighting Maroons should not experience any great amount of trouble in defeating the representatives of St. Mary's College on the Polo Grounds gridiron this weekend. The West Coast collegians are not as strong as last year." As proof, noted Thorp, Cal lost, 7-6, to St, Mary's in 1930 before Cal lost, 74-0, to USC. Cavanaugh, the Fordham coach and World War I hero known as the "Iron Major," was proudest of his rock-solid linemen: "The Seven Blocks Of Granite." The Rams, reputedly, had the best line in the country, and odds makers decided that line play was all the Rams, or Maroons, required to vanquish St. Mary's.

Madigan sent his only assistant coach, Vincent McNally, ahead to scout visiting Fordham's 13-0 victory over Detroit Mercy, which hiked the Rams' record to 5-0. They had earlier defeated the University of Baltimore, 73-0, Holy Cross, 6-0, New York University, 7-0, and West Virginia, 18-2. So the Rams had given up nine points in five games. McNally joined the traveling party in Chicago with a scouting report to present to Madigan, who was anything but intimidated.

"Knowing the East as I do," he told the Bay Area press, "I see no reason why the Gaels shouldn't ride roughshod over Broadway next Saturday night." Madigan was given to dramatic quotes, but he also made his players available to the writers, not at all fearful of how they might be quoted. And end Harry Ebding predicted, confidently, "We'll carry the football reputation of the West Coast football with us, and next Saturday we'll see another Western victory."

As the Gaels drew closer to New York, Madigan didn't slack off in his confidence: "Our kicking game is sufficient to beat Fordham. My reports are that Fordham has a great defense, but the St. Mary's offense is far superior." Whether that information reached Fordham in time to pin the Gaels' quotes on the Rams' locker room wall prior to kickoff is unknown. But, clearly, each team felt superior to the other. However, Fordham was made an 8-to-5 favorite over the upstarts from parts unknown. Where in God's name, New Yorkers wondered, is Moraga? Perhaps in Spain?

Though St. Mary's record was 8-1, Easterners regarded West Coast football as inferior. Thus Fordham fans weren't worried about the outcome. If the Rams needed added incentive, they introduced a new goat mascot, Rameses IV. His predecessor, Rameses III, had been attacked and killed by savage dogs on campus. Rameses IV was a much luckier mascot, having been saved from a butcher's cleaver at the last second. Mascots III or IV, it didn't matter: Fordham felt Ram tough.

Madigan sent his public relations man, a student named Will Stevens, to New York a week early with a thousand dollars in cash and some bootleg whiskey in a satchel to woo the city's sportswriter literati, including heavy hitters Damon Runyon and Grantland Rice. Stevens persuaded Runyon to write about the Gaels by taking him to dinner, then convincing him that the Gaels ate raw meat. Stevens ordered uncooked steak for himself in order to prove his point. "I was never so sick in all my life," he said later, "but it was worth it." Indeed. Runyon, no vegetarian himself, wrote a column about the carnivorous Gaels.

When the St. Mary's touring party arrived in New York City, Madigan arranged for the team to stay at the posh Westchester Country Club, while putting up the alumni at the Vanderbilt Hotel in Manhattan. Slip was asked: How much is St. Mary's traveling budget? "It doesn't cost any more to go first class," he replied, cheerily. He threw a press party in New York City that combined, as some wag described it, "the most spectacular features of an old-fashioned Irish wake and the last days of Pompei." Well, Madigan was Irish. He invited politicians, football coaches, various sports figures, the New York press, including Runyon and Rice, and former heavyweight boxing champion James J. "Gentleman Jim" Corbett, a San Franciscan whose brother had played baseball for St. Mary's in the 1890s. New York journalist Arthur Daley was overwhelmed by Madigan's generosity. "The artful Slip," wrote Daley, "missed no tricks. His pre-game press party in the prohibition era was a social event that drew the flower of American literature for exposure to the Madigan charm. It was no contest. All capitulated and gave him rave reviews even before they had seen the production."

St. Mary's didn't sport a fancy nickname like the "Seven Blocks Of Granite." The best the Gaels could do was the "Blue Ghost Backfield" of quarterback Dick Boyle, left halfback Fred "Mack" Stennett, right halfback Bud Toscani, and fullback Bob Barrett. This nickname was borne out of the Gaels' blue silk jerseys. The ghostly reference: Perhaps, the Gaels backs moved like an apparition. But that day, a new backfield star and his subsequent nickname would emerge for St. Mary's.

A crowd of 65,000 was expected, but only 15,000 showed up for the November 15 game at the Polo Grounds. Driving rain convinced the rest of the ticket holders to stay home and listen on the radio. Back home in the Bay Area, the game was broadcast on San Francisco station KFRC. Madigan had done it: St. Mary's would be heard coast to coast. God bless you, Knute Rockne. By halftime, though, many radios were turned off coast to coast as Fordham took a 12-0 lead. The Rams' Johnny Tavis scored on a lateral pass, then Jimmy Murphy caught an 18-yard touchdown pass from Johnny Fisher. Fordham failed on each conversion attempt, but it didn't seem to matter. The Blue Ghost backfield had all but disappeared. If Madigan was a showman, those in the press box scoffed, his show was hardly ready for Broadway. His team came across as a second-rate act. West Coast football must be a charade, the carping continued, for this cross-country train ride just derailed.

St. Mary's locker room was in a state of shock at halftime. Faces were crestfallen, spirits defeated. Madigan had to find a way to inspire them. "Tick, tick, tick," he started off, emulating a clicking telegraph key. "The news is crossing the country that the Gaels are failures. Tick, tick, tick." Then he recited his favorite inspirational line: "'The fighting human heart is made to win.' Do you hear me, men? 'The fighting human heart is made to win.' Now who will fight for old St. Mary's?" Madigan held his breath. "I will," shouted a voice from the back of the room. Angelo Brovelli, a third-string sophomore halfback, spoke up. "I will, coach."

Legends are born in an instant sometimes, especially in New York City, the capital of legend-makers. Angelo Brovelli was about to become Ruthian. The Gaels didn't break down the locker room door in returning to the playing field that day, but they clearly were a different team in the second half, spearheaded by Brovelli's bulk and bravado. He hurled his 182-pound frame at "The Seven Blocks of Granite," chipping away at their impregnable might, carrying tacklers for chunks of four, five and seven yards. Suddenly, the Gaels had solid footing on a muddy field. With a new conviction, they began chipping away at the Fordham lead.

Then Madigan sprung a surprise. With the Rams braced for yet another Brovelli smash up the middle, Stennett dropped back and threw a 14-yard touchdown to Dick Sperbeck. Harry Ebding kicked the PAT off the sloppy turf. Turnovers then took over the game. Stennett was intercepted, but Boyle picked off a Murphy pass and returned it 36 yards to the Rams' 42. Stennett was picked off again before the third quarter ended, by which time the helmetless Brovelli was carried off the field with a concussion. He had rejuvenated the Gaels with 41 tough yards on 11 carries in sloggy conditions. Ebding then intercepted Murphy's quick toss to put the Gaels in scoring position, and Boyle banged over from a yard out. Ebding again converted, and St. Mary's led, 14-12. Whatever chance Fordham, suddenly in a defensive mode, had of mounting a comeback was silenced when Bill Beasley intercepted a Murphy pass and raced 62 yards for the touchdown that clinched a 20-12 victory for the resilient Moragans with the fighting human heart.

The biggest practitioners of prevarication can be politicians or football statistics. The numbers of the St. Mary's-Fordham game told a big lie. Fordham led in rushing yards, 165 to 59, in passing yards, 133 to 74, and in first downs, 13 to 8. Fordham was intercepted four times, and St. Mary's had six passes picked off. Fordham won the stat sheet, but St. Mary's won the second half and the ball game. The St. Mary's traveling contingent was ready to party hearty. Slip-hip hooray!

It's unpredictable how legends begin. Although Brovelli spoke up at halftime, ready to step in and save the Gaels, he already had appeared in the first quarter, and he didn't play at all in the fourth quarter because of the concussion. But his inspired effort in that third quarter had the legend creators working overtime. "Some writer asked me if Brovelli had a nickname," Will Stevens recalled. "Well, he didn't have a nickname. He was only a third- or fourth-stringer. I was stuck. Then I remembered a movie with Ronald Coleman called 'The Dark Angel', about a blind man who married a blind girl or something. Brovelli's dark hair and complexion made him perfect, and from my head out came 'The Dark Angel of the Moragas.'" The nickname registered instantly. Slip Madigan had the most creative publicists, too.

"What a man," New York scribe Sid Mercer wrote of Brovelli. "There hasn't been one like him since Jim Thorpe and Ted Coy used to take whole lines for yards." Jim Thorpe? If Brovelli had played a full game instead of one quarter, the comparison might have been made about Bronko Nagurski. The famous sportswriter, Paul Gallico, was equally verbose in his praise of Brovelli: "He was the frightenest feller I ever did see on a football field anywhere. He played without a headgear, and in the third period, he put on one of the greatest individual displays of won't-be-licked, won't-be-stopped, won't-quit-wriggling-until-they-stop-me I have ever seen. He started tearing that Fordham line apart. . . ."

The press crowded in to hear from the newly christened Dark Angel himself. "They just jump on and I take 'em for a ride, I guess," Brovelli said of tacklers in general. "You can't beat the old pick and shovel for conditioning. I did plenty of manual labor for fifty cents an hour. You get used to heavy loads, and it isn't so hard then to scramble with two or men on your back." So a rock-breaker broke down the "The Seven Blocks of Granite." As for playing without a helmet, he said, "They come down over your ears and eyes, and don't have much padding anyway. Your hair is as much protection." Perhaps an angel sat on the Angel's, or Angelo's, shoulder. That helmetless concussion could have been worse.

Fordham's fourteen-game win streak had ended against the motivated men of Moraga. The *New York Times* dissected the result: "The Californians' attack, puny throughout the first half, now showed a bristling spearhead in the person of Angelo Brovelli, a bareheaded curly haired thunderbolt who carried the ball on four successive plays from the Fordham 41-yard line to the 19-yard line. Never again did Fordham manage to get its ground game working as it had in the first half. Then the Gaels caught Fordham napping by putting the ball into play without making the backfield shift. The Gaels showed a versatility of attack, forward passing on first down. The bugle sounding taps to initiate the coronation ceremony (of Fordham's new mascot Ramses IV) likewise sounded the death knell of Fordham's victory wave."

Madigan was ecstatic at what his Gaels had achieved in the country's media center. "The finest lesson ever taught in or out of the classroom was given by the St. Mary's team and its players individually against Fordham," he told the Gotham press. "Every member of our team will leave school with the idea firmly implanted that life can be conquered the same way that a little fighting spirit will carry them over the top. They never would learn that in the classroom. They taught themselves to depend on their own resources and their own wills." This victory, he felt, could fuel a lifetime. The Eastern sporting press hadn't ever interviewed a football coach comparable to the colorful Madigan.

Brovelli had left a powerful impression as a one-man battering ram against the Rams' crumbling defense. But no running back does it alone. Brovelli, as good as he was that day, needed blockers. And lineman Bill Fischer cleared holes by moving a difficult obstacle. "I was trying to block All-American 'Pistol' Pete Wisniewski straight ahead in the first half," said Fischer. "He was 220 pounds and tough, so I couldn't move him. I tried a new technique in the second half—'logrolling' my man. I'd take a step back and let Pistol Pete charge whichever way he wanted to, and I just pushed him in that direction. Brovelli could cut off my block and go the other way."

St. Mary's stunning upset stirred the nation's interest in the Galloping Gaels. Rockne was correct: It was all there for Madigan in New York. Copeland Burg of the International News Service wrote: "From Maine to Mineola, they are bowing to Slip Madigan's Blue Ghosts, who slipped through the fog and murk of the Polo Grounds on Saturday afternoon to turn back unbeaten, untied Fordham, 20-12." Under a foggy, murky autumn sky, the Blue Ghosts rode again . . . not this day. Grantland Rice preferred a less fanciful lead to his game story that afternoon.

Having conquered the East, Madigan and his players, plus their entourage then headed to the White House, where President Hoover greeted then joyously. "I am mighty glad that you have come to this section of the country to help me uphold the reputation of California," he told the team. Hoover, an Iowa native but a Stanford graduate, might have regretted making that statement because he wouldn't be re-elected in 1932. Fordham is a New York school, and Hoover might have lost the New York vote with that quote. It all adds up in politics, just as it does on a football scoreboard. But those in St. Mary's traveling party, Democrats and Republicans alike, who upon observing the President and the coach together, thought Madigan was more presidential.

"It's my wonder week," Madigan said as he boarded the train. Before getting back to California, he had added a new passenger: A ram. Back in the Bay Area, he told everyone that it was Rameses IV, for some of his Gaels had kidnapped Fordham's mascot. That "heist" was played up in the press, complete with photographs. It was all a ruse. Fordham still had the real Rameses IV. But being poor sports, Fordham sent it to a New Jersey stockyard for slaughter. There would be a Rameses V when the Gaels returned to New York in 1932. Fordham already was demanding a rematch. Madigan agreed, but only if there was a $10,000 guarantee to cover the Gaels travel expenses. Fordham quickly agreed.

The "Slip Madigan Fordham Special" arrived at a San Francisco train station to a huge celebration. Thousands attended a parade in the Gaels honor. A gala reception also was held at Oakland City Hall. Clarence "Nibs" Price, the coach of the California team that handed the Gaels their only loss that year, sent the following telegram: "Slip, congratulations on your wonderful victory." Pop Warner, the Stanford coach who lost to St. Mary's in 1927, then cut the Gaels from Stanford's schedule forever, sent no telegram. Pop was a known curmudgeon. Ten years earlier, St. Mary's had lost 127-0 to Cal. Now teams were scared to play the Gaels.

Fordham showed St. Mary's proper respect by "promoting" the Iron Major. Coach Frank Cavanaugh signed a new two-year contract to continue coaching the Rams, giving him the opportunity to get even with Madigan. Thus a new rivalry was born. Fordham and St. Mary's, starting in '32, would play each other annually through the end of Madigan's coaching reign in Moraga, and even beyond, albeit not yearly.

Those Gaels, who beat Fordham in their first meeting, supposedly weren't as strong as they were the season before, 1929. The Gaels went undefeated in '29, albeit with one tie, and they came within a point of being unbeaten in '30. The letdown in both cases, the tie and the one-point loss, occurred against Cal. A pundit had previewed St. Mary's '30 prospects thusly: "The goose hangs high at Moraga this season. Coach Madigan's material will be as good or even better than last year. California is the only team that will trouble the Gaels." The *San Francisco Call-Bulletin* projected that "New York is beginning to wonder about the St. Mary's team it will see against Fordham. New Yorkers were told that St. Mary's is better than the Stanford team that beat Army two years ago, and New Yorkers felt that Stanford team was the best ever put together." And New Yorkers always feel they are right, regardless of what the rest of the country is thinking.

Madigan greeted sixteen lettermen that season. Stennett, Ebding, and Boyle were back for a third year. Barrett loomed as the logical choice to replace the graduated Cal Pritchard at fullback, but Madigan talked up a young kid from Porterville, name of Brovelli. Speaking of backfields, new rules restricted the use of the Notre Dame shift, which Madigan, a Notre Dame alumnus, installed at St. Mary's for the purposes of power football. What prompted this restriction: Schools that didn't use the shift refused to play teams that shifted. Madigan called the ruling unfair to players and fans, but his complaining fell on deaf ears. So he schemed anew to keep St. Mary's football competitive.

It would seem unthinkable in today's society to coach an undefeated football team with just one coach, but that's what Slip Madigan accomplished in 1929. He was a one-man show. But in 1930, he added the luxury of an assistant coach, Vincent McNally, himself a Notre Dame alumnus. McNally's arrival lessened Madigan's overall coaching role. He no longer was responsible for the basketball and track and field squads; those were now McNally's responsibilities. Besides football, Madigan remained in charge of the Gaels boxing and baseball teams.

At a get-acquainted football team banquet, the theme song was "A Girl's Best Friend Is Her Mother," an odd selection since St. Mary's was an all-male institution. Returning in time for the banquet were Ebding, Woody Peebles, Mike Stepanovich and John Lyden, all four straight from Hollywood. They had formed the baseball infield of a prison team in the Fox movie "Up The River." Ebding hit a home run in the movie and struck out the last batter in a

3-1 victory for his team. Ebding even showed pugilistic ability that summer, impressing former heavyweight champion Jack Dempsey, who watched him work out in the gym. Madigan had assembled a versatile athletic roster. Pete Markovich was a medalist in a *Call-Bulletin* golf tournament, while Joe McAlese piloted a bird boat during yacht week at the St. Francis Yacht Club.

Looking at the '30 schedule, which included UCLA, Oregon and Santa Clara, Madigan considered Cal, not Fordham, his toughest opponent. He lobbied to extend fall practice from two to four weeks, noting that only football, of all the college sports, had a limited practice time schedule. His request was denied. He was twenty years too soon.

For the Cal opener, Madigan recruited fifty-five, non-collegian, union musicians to fill out St. Mary's first marching band. There weren't enough St. Mary's students for a band. Madigan dressed the thrown-together band members in school's colors—blue military uniforms with red stripes. He had built a football team out of nothing, so why not a band? His mind always was in tune with what needed to get done.

Madigan scheduled Cal every year that he coached at St. Mary's. During the 1920s, he had a record of one win, one tie, and seven defeats against the Golden Bears. The 1930 opener was played before a capacity crowd of 75,000 in Berkeley. This was a beatable Cal team that would finish the season with a 4-5 record, was shut out four times, and scored in double figures only twice. St. Mary's jumped ahead at halftime, 6-0. Stennett threw a 30-yard pass to Ebding at the Cal 10. Bud Toscani, the original "Italian Stallion," scored from a yard out, but Ebding's PAT kick was low and blocked. That blown point in their very first game would become the Gaels' biggest missed opportunity of the season. For Cal tied the score in the fourth quarter on a 69-yard drive, led by the passing of its standout back, Hank Schaldach, who threw 18 yards to Russell Avery, then 37 yards to Edwin Kirwan, and finally 3 yards to Avery for the tying touchdown. Schaldach then calmly dropkicked the PAT through the uprights for a 7-6 win. Madigan kicked himself the entire autumn for blowing a perfect season in the opener.

Next up for St. Mary's was the West Coast Army, a locally based team comprised of ex-collegians and other inductees. The WCA played college teams up and down the Pacific Coast. The Gaels took out their frustrations from the Cal disappointment on this military bunch, 32-0, at Kezar Stadium.

Two minutes into the game, a blocked punt turned into a Gael touchdown, and the rout was on. St. Mary's received a huge performance from the bareheaded Toscani, who led the Blue Ghosts backfield with some scintillating runs. However, Madigan pulled the bulk of his first string after the first quarter. The Army gridders would have preferred KP duty to receiving such a shellacking.

The Gaels then took on Catholic rival St. Ignatius, a fog-based university that eventually would become the University of San Francisco, with its nickname also changed from the Gray Fog to the Dons. After a scoreless first half at Kezar, Stennett intercepted a Bob Kleckner pass and returned it 15 yards to the Gray Fog's 20. Toscani scampered for 6 yards, and Barrett twisted for 7 more before Stennett squeezed over for the score. Ebding's PAT kick failed again, but it mattered little this day as St. Ignatius was having difficulty moving the football. Barrett then busted loose on a 60-yard run to the Gray Fog 33. Stennett completed passes to Bob Patterson and Ebding to set up Toscani's 4-yard scoring run. Ebding's PAT was good this time, and St. Mary's walked off with a 13-0 win, having outgained the Fog, 183 to 53 yards. Kleckner of St. Ignatius later shifted from first downs to rub downs, becoming the first trainer of the San Francisco 49ers in 1946.

Despite its 2-1 record, St. Mary's was perceived as a dangerous opponent. After covering its shutout of St. Ignatius, a reporter wrote: "No football team on the coast can make any just demand for acclimation until they have disposed of the Galloping Gaels." Knute Rockne made that notion even clearer, declaring in his syndicated column: "None but the brave should schedule St. Mary's for the next year or two." None but the brave, excluding Notre Dame, which refused to schedule St. Mary's; some believed it was because of the close relationship between Rockne and his former center, Madigan. But Rockne, no fool, reasoned that nothing would be gained by beating St. Mary's, but plenty would be lost by losing to the Gaels. Madigan, though, would have jumped at the chance to face his mentor.

Speaking of a titanic matchup, negotiations proceeded toward an USC-St. Mary's showdown in 1931: The Thundering Herd against the Marauding Moragans. USC's rival, UCLA, was next up for the Gaels, in front of 40,000 at the Los Angeles Memorial Coliseum. St. Mary's came out strong with Stennett running 40 yards for a touchdown one minute into the game.

Stennett then turned in a one-man show, passing 21 yards to Toscani for a touchdown and a 14-6 halftime lead. Stennett circled left end on a 10-yard scoring run in the fourth quarter. Stennett was Joe Montana in the 1930s. St. Mary's shut down UCLA's offense in the second half for a 21-6 win. Ebding made one PAT kick and missed two, but St. Mary's was awarded the points anyway because UCLA was ruled offsides twice. Football has progressed light years since 1930, when a miss counted as a make. But Madigan's sideline antics had UCLA followers shouting "Sit down, Slip," three times as often as "Go Bruins."

St. Mary's then engaged Gonzaga, crooner Bing Crosby's alma mater, and stomped the Bulldogs, or Zags, 41-0, before 20,000 at Kezar. Stennett's 15-yard run off left tackle opened the scoring. Stennett then threw a 29-yard pass to Toscani, who followed up with a 17-yard burst into the end zone. Stennett would score once more, and Toscani twice more as the Gaels amassed 367 yards of offense to the Zags' 56. Madigan had built a powerhouse in less than a decade. When critics complained that Gaels football was becoming too important, Brother Leo, the St. Mary's chancellor, said, "The wise man does not take his recreation too seriously. It is just possible that there is something wrong with an age which insists on working at its play, and playing at its work."

The Gaels continued to play at their work, keeping chief Catholic rival Santa Clara off the scoreboard in a 13-0 "Little Big Game" triumph at Kezar. The Gaels' Bob Patterson made the highlight reel—cinematically, as there was no television in those days—with a 95-yard interception return for a touchdown. Stennett then passed 31 yards to Boyle before the latter barreled 16 yards into the end zone. Stennett—a triple threat runner, passer, kicker; Montana wasn't a kicker—pinned the Broncos consistently deep with punts of 63, 34, 51, 54, 47, and 45 yards. He was playing like an All-American, even though he wouldn't become one.

Madigan's defense then wracked up its third consecutive shutout with an impressive 15-0 silencing of the Olympic Club, a San Francisco outfit made up entirely of former college stars. What the Gaels gave away in years, they took back in yards, although the game was scoreless at halftime. Stennett then tallied on a 2-yard run, acquiring a black eye in the process, before Boyle flipped a 1-yard scoring pass to Bill Beasley. St. Mary's Bill

Carpenter then earned a safety by blocking an Olympic Club punt through the end zone. The Gaels nearly matched their stifling defense of 1929 by allowing just 13 points in the first seven games. Few teams in the country were playing better defense.

Fordham, in week eight, would be the only team to score in double figures against the stingy Gaels, who had answered Madigan's pre-season message. He wrote his players that summer to report in superb physical condition, because in Slip's dramatic wording, "From the rock-bound shores of Maine to the beaches of sunny California, the Saint Mary's Gaels are about to make history." The reference, of course, was to the Fordham trip in Week Nine. He didn't forewarn the players about meeting the President on the same trip, because he didn't want to give them too much to think about too early.

Madigan's finest coaching job that season actually occurred a week later against Oregon. After traveling across the country and back, then being feted on both sides of San Francisco Bay, the Gaels still had one opponent left: Oregon. Madigan needed to clear their heads of the national adulation they had acquired. So he held some tough practices prior to facing the Ducks. He also needed to squeeze in time for coaching, because newspapers everywhere began clamoring for interviews, wanting to know about his entire life. Ever accommodating, and ever the ham, Madigan understood the needs of reporters. And he needed them, so he made himself available, though it meant longer hours, and less time with family, and having to sleep in his office. The price of his increased fame, and the advent of his health concerns.

Somehow, St. Mary's managed to edge Oregon, 7-6, before 30,000 at umbrella-like Kezar. Stennett threw a 50-yard touchdown pass to Boyle, and Ebding kicked the PAT for a 7-0 lead at halftime. Johnny "Dutch" Kitzmiller then threw a scoring strike for the Ducks, but his PAT kick was errant. Oregon had a second touchdown negated by a penalty, and the Gaels managed to end the season with the same score that they started the season with, only reversed.

St. Mary's was 8-0-1 in 1929, and 8-1-0 in 1930. The '29 team had one touchdown scored against it, while the '30 team surrendered only five touchdowns in nine games, or 3.5 points per game. The main difference between the two teams: the '30 team was more famous. "The Dark Angel of the Moragas" had made that happen at the Polo Grounds.

But while Madigan had succeeded in putting his Gaels on the national radar, a school closer to home was determined to show him who was the true king of the Pacific Coast. Madigan began seeing a Trojan horse in his dreams, a horse chomping on a football, and snorting fire.

3

What Could Have Been

No matter how much success St. Mary's had enjoyed the previous two years—the best back-to-back seasons of the Slip Madigan era—the Gaels couldn't do enough, for some reason, to please the pigskin pundits.

Dink Templeton, the Stanford University track and field coach who doubled as a journalist, wrote of St. Mary's chances against USC in 1931 in the most negative tone: "The Trojan Horde is a team so good that it was awarded the conference championship before the season started. . . . St. Mary's is no better than she has been for the last four, five years. . . . I can't conceive of a team with such a record being able to cope with the power and diversity of Howard Jones' great offensive system of play when manned by players such as the Trojans have in great profusion this year."

So, Templeton opined, why should St. Mary's even bother to show up for the game, when the outcome was ordained in the Trojans' favor? Didn't Madigan, himself, also favor USC to win the Pacific Coast Conference title prior to the 1931 season? And how could the Gaels expect to win anyway without "The Dark Angel of the Moragas?" For Angelo Brovelli was sidelined with knee and ankle injuries. Other Gael regulars had similar medical issues: Pete Danilovich a tender hamstring, captain Ed "Toby" Hunt a sprained elbow, and Elmer Preston a broken hand. Regardless, Jones, the USC coach, remained skeptical, believing the Gaels' injury report to be "Some more of Madigan's psychology."

USC's 1931 team, celebrated as the Thundering Herd, still is rated among the finest Trojan teams historically. Interviewed by Los Angeles sports writers a few days before the game, Madigan said, "I certainly had a tough time convincing them that we're not going to have a strong team. They said they'd heard (Knute) Rockne tell the same story, so they just laughed at me." But, cagily, Madigan, while respectful of the Trojans, wasn't fearful of them. In his biased view, the Bay Area was home to the best college football in the country. Also, why hadn't Templeton and other self-appointed experts recognized the importance of St. Mary's historic defeat of Fordham in '30? "If the boys have the right frame of mind," Madigan told Bay Area sportswriters, "we stand an even chance" of beating USC and Cal, St. Mary's first two opponents.

Even with their significant injuries, the Gaels boarded fifty-five players for the train ride down to Los Angeles. Six hundred St. Mary's fans accompanied the team on the four-hundred-mile trip south, wondering if Madigan's confidence in his Gaels was justified. At kickoff, 80,000 fans, 79,000 of them for USC, anticipated the Trojan Horde ripping the gallop right out of the Gaels, and slowing them to a halt.

USC, as expected, scored first on Gus Shaver's one-foot plunge in the opening quarter. The Los Angeles writers in the press box nodded in agreement that the slaughter was on. The possibility of USC not scoring again that afternoon was inconceivable, the visitors furthered their confidence by trailing only 7-0 at halftime. Those Trojan teams customarily buried opponents in the second half with their depth and talent. However, surprisingly, the second half belonged to Madigan's marauders. Red Sheflin found Toscani running free behind the Trojan secondary and hit him with a perfect 17-yard touchdown pass. Fletcher's PAT kick was blocked, so USC still led, 7-6. Four minutes later, Sheflin was on the mark again, passing 36 yards to George Canrinus for the go-ahead touchdown. Fletcher's conversion kick put St. Mary's ahead, 13-7, thereby taking the thunder right out of the herd, and leaving the 79,000 Trojan fans in disbelief.

And that's how the game ended, St. Mary's 13, USC 7, the biggest upset of the 1931 college football season, and on the opening weekend no less. The Trojans won their remaining ten games, six by shutouts, including a 21-12 victory over Tulane in the Rose Bowl, crowning them as national champion.

So if USC was No. 1 in the country, shouldn't St. Mary's be No. 2? Its upset of USC was strikingly similar to the Fordham contest, in that the Gaels were dominated statistically, but won the battle. USC led in total yards, 277-133 (219 yards by rushing) and in first downs, 15-3. With "their cleats in the end zone," St. Mary's stopped USC short of the end zone in three of the four quarters, thereby corralling the Thundering Herd. Defense was paramount to Madigan.

"He was a defensive genius," said George Canrinus. "He had us blitzing and stunting long before it was common. We didn't have to score much to win." The only numbers that mattered to the Gaels were those on the scoreboard when the final gun sounded. After that USC shocker, the Gaels became the "Moraga Merriwells," named after the fictitious hero, Frank Merriwell, who concocted many a comeback victory. Madigan was gracious toward USC, noting, "We were lucky to win. USC has a great team and will go a long way this season. But I can't help but feel jubilant over the performance of the fighting St. Mary's team. It has always been a fighting team." Here was a fighting team with a fighting heart, resilient to the core, missing several of its key players, yet still subduing the next national champion. The "human heart" that Madigan preached about constantly wasn't ever any bigger for St. Mary's than what was evident on that 1931 afternoon in Los Angeles.

The train trip back to Moraga was obviously upbeat, until the team heard the sad news that two Gaels fans, St. Mary's student Jerome O'Leary and San Francisco businessman E.D. Hughes, were killed in a car wreck after hitting a tree near Paso Robles while returning from the game. Meanwhile, the Gaels' David vs. Goliath football image continued to grow nationally. The *New York Times* wrote: "It distresses me no little that 'little' St. Mary's College of the Pacific Coast is not coming East this year, and will not get a chance to prove that it is the best team in the country. . . . Reading some football scores, I learn that Southern California was upset by 'little' St. Mary's. . . . I do not think much of the characterization, for 'little' St. Mary's has been upsetting some team or another ever since Slip Madigan took charge. . . . So I cannot see where it should be considered cruel and unusual punishment for the Christian Brothers to be knocking off USC." Yet Goliath was felled without a slingshot that memorable day in L.A. Mighty David was getting mightier.

The biggest loss of 1931: Knute Rockne's death in a plane crash. Madigan had lost his mentor. And Rockne had visited Madigan just that year to inspect the St. Mary's campus in Moraga. The two men discussed a game between their schools, but it was only talk. Rockne wanted no part of St. Mary's, for Notre Dame was the nation's Catholic football darling.

A wire service story looked ahead to the second week of the college football season: "In the big game of the day, because of a famous custom of winning and the fate of Notre Dame's new coach, Hunk Anderson, hanging in the balance, the Irish, even without Rockne, have an edge over Indiana. Second in interest is the California-St. Mary's game." Madigan had stated publicly in August that his Gaels had an "even chance" of beating both USC and Cal. This meant a back-to-back double parlay, because the Golden Bears were next up for St. Mary's. And 72,000 packed Memorial Stadium in Berkeley's Strawberry Canyon for their first local look at the Gaels, who maintained their early season surge even without the hobbled Brovelli. But they didn't need Brovelli's powerful running because their passing attack once again was the deciding factor, joined that day by their tough-in-the-trenches defense.

From the Gaels' 44-yard line in the first quarter, Sheflin passed 19 yards to George Canrinus, followed up by a clever deception play, Toscani tossing 25 yards to Sheflin at the Cal 2. Fletcher sneaked over from a yard out, and his PAT glanced off an upright and through the posts for a 7-0 lead. Toscani was regarded as a running threat, but thanks to Madigan's clever game plan, he starred as a thrower this day, connecting with Charley Baird for 27 yards to the Cal 9. Baird then became a thrower, flipping a 6-yard scoring pass to George Canrinus. Fletcher converted more cleanly this time for a 14-0 St. Mary's victory.

How significant was that shutout? Cal would lose one more game in 1931, 6-0 to USC. St. Mary's wouldn't ever have two better wins to start a season, or two bigger wins on successive weeks. What Slip Madigan had accomplished since taking over the disillusioned and deflated St. Mary's program in 1921 was, by 1931, unparalleled in college football during that era. "Little" St. Mary's now was a behemoth.

West Coast Army was the Gaels' third opponent, and the Moragans came out flat, hurting themselves with fumbles that kept the score close in the first half. But Brovelli was back, banging up the middle 17 times for 45 yards and kicking three PATs. Beasley scored on a short run to grab a 7-0 lead before the Army team tied it on a 30-yard pass from Nudgie Gannuzzi to Scooter Enos. Baird then threw a 37-yard touchdown strike to Fred Canrinus, George's brother, and Bill Beasley lofted a 30-yard scoring toss to Gary Vivaldi for 21-7 victory before 25,000 at Kezar Stadium.

Rumors resurfaced that St. Mary's was the coast favorite for the Rose Bowl. Madigan had danced to that tune once before, only to have his toes stepped on, and so he sat this latest rumor out. An undefeated, untied season remained his primary focus. Besides, even though he whipped USC on its own turf, the Rose Bowl committee still favored the neighboring Trojans, largely for attendance reasons. To that myopic committee, Moraga might have been located on the moon.

The University of San Francisco had undergone its name transition from St. Ignatius, though it still was the Gray Fog that encountered St. Mary's at Kezar before a revved-up crowd of 50,000. The Gaels lost some of their September magic that day with fumbling issues, putting the ball on the ground nine times against USF. Brovelli was hard to stop between the tackles before injuring a shoulder that would sideline him for the next three weeks. The Gaels standout against USF was the elusive Baird, who rushed for 159 yards and threw a touchdown pass to Fletcher. The equally impressive Toscani also connected with Fletcher for a touchdown, and St. Mary's escaped the Fog with a 14-6 win.

Though St. Mary's was off its game for two straight weeks, Jock Sutherland, the University of Pittsburgh coach, labeled the Gaels "The best team on the coast, and now looks to go through its schedule without a setback." St. Mary's improved to 5-0, albeit with a third consecutive struggle, in beating Gonzaga, 13-7, before a rained-soaked crowd of 7,000. Toscani scored twice and was equally effective on defense. The Italian Stallion made three tackles on the same goal-line stand, even though knocked out momentarily. To St. Mary's benefit, he stayed on the field, because Gonzaga failed to score, or the outcome might have been different. Toscani rushed for 56 yards, but Baird stole the show again, scampering over the sloppy turf at Kezar for 138 yards.

Prior to the St. Mary's-Santa Clara game the following Saturday, Broncos coach Maurice "Clipper" Smith said, "We're going into this game with the idea that we are playing the national champions." Madigan knew he was being set up by his former Notre Dame teammate, even though a national championship was, indeed, Slip's objective. Well, the Broncos gave him his toughest tussle to date, as the Gaels didn't lock up the game until the fourth quarter. Before then, they trailed twice, and were tied twice. Santa Clara scored first when Anton Judnich threw a 28-yard pass to Gil Dowd. Toscani came right back with a 23-yard touchdown pass to Beasley. But Sheflin lost a fumble to the Broncos' Johnny Paglia, who then scored from the 3-yard line. Toscani evened the scoreboard again on a dazzling 47-yard cutback run. Finally, the Gaels marched 67 yards to capitalize on Baird's 3-yard run for a 21-14 victory played out before 55,000 at Kezar.

The game's post mortem overlooked the Gaels' lost momentum, even with a spotless 6-0 record. "I thought our boys did well in handling the game, and in coming through at the finish," said a relieved Madigan. "That's the greatest St. Mary's team I've seen," said Clipper Smith. "In my opinion, Toscani is the greatest halfback St. Mary's ever had. We did not have enough manpower to compete with the Gaels." Toscani had reached the level of 1920s Gaels hero Jimmy Underhill as a superb runner. "In Bud Toscani," Madigan said, "I have really found a money player. His dash for a touchdown was the work of a tired, crippled athlete in a ball game that had gone against him." Madigan thought as highly of Brovelli, but injuries had reduced the Dark Angel's availability.

The pressure of living up to their press clippings, plus the lofty projections of a national title, began to weigh heavily on the Gaels. Their great expectations collapsed in game seven against the more experienced Olympic Club before 25,000 witnesses at Kezar. The former collegians, still disciplined about football, yet taking the game more lightly, became dead serious upon engaging a potential national champion. "They even stopped drinking that week," said one club member. Two Oregon State alums, Ralph Buecke and Bill Meggett, combined on a 19-yard touchdown pass, and ex-Texas A&M Aggie Dick Black kicked a 30-yard field goal for a 10-0 upset victory—the first shutout of the Gaels since their 1929 0-0 opener against Cal.

There went St. Mary's national title, and there went the Rose Bowl, too, after USC throttled Stanford, 19-0. However, "Little" St. Mary's had little chance, realistically, of achieving either goal. The world is round, the sun rises in the East, Christmas falls on December 25, and St. Mary's football, for all of its achievements, still was a West Coast novelty to national pollsters. The Gaels plummeted further the following week, traveling back to Los Angeles—the height of their earlier ecstasy—and capsizing, 12-0, to UCLA before 50,000. Toscani coughed up a fumble at his 20. The Bruins scored right away on a reverse, Leonard Bergdahl passing to Bobby Decker. Bergdahl later threw 32 yards to Leonard Wellendorf to complete the scoring, handing the Gaels their first consecutive defeats since 1928. Madigan beat up his Borsalino that day.

"This victory was worth waiting for," said UCLA coach Bill Spaulding. "I have always thought that this team had it in them to do something of this kind." Madigan used a twisted analogy to describe his feelings afterward. "The victory over the Trojans was far more gratifying than today's game was disappointing," he said. "I still consider the Trojans the best team in the West. Bill's team outfought mine for three quarters of the game. I never feel badly after losing to a bunch of boys who fight like those Bruins did." Only it was a double loss. O. Hitchens "Dave" Grimstead, 44, St. Mary's revered athletic trainer, died of a heart attack in Los Angeles after that game. His death was attributed to a poison gas attack during World War I. The entire Moraga campus was in mourning.

So how would Slip Madigan turn his devastated Gaels back around? "It is the darkest before the dawn," he said, "and maybe my team will surprise me and put up a great ball game" (against Oregon). He blamed the schedule maker for putting the Olympic Club and UCLA games on successive weekends; only he was the schedule maker. And how, seriously, could the Olympic Club and UCLA be any tougher back-to-back opponents than USC and Cal? The truth is, they weren't tougher. UCLA's talent wasn't anything close to USC's in 1931. Troy wouldn't even play the Bruins, deeming them inferior. And Cal beat the Olympic Club, 6-0. The Gaels, simply, had their sombreros handed to them.

Madigan then used his endless ingenuity to kick start St. Mary's idled engine. "Rameses IV," the perceived Fordham mascot kidnapped by the Gaels the year before, had been living on a Napa farm, grazing in the grass and enjoying himself. Madigan had the ram transported to Moraga to inspire his players. And they needed inspiration because of a season-long injury onslaught, the latest of which was standout guard Bill Fischer, ruled out of the last two games with multiple injuries. Replacing him was an inexperienced Wayne Pendleton. And still no Brovelli. How would suddenly humbled St. Mary's respond next against Oregon?

Just in time, the human heart beat mightily again for the Gaels. Playing before 20,000 at Kezar, they sank the Ducks, 16-0. Toscani was the hero once more, opening the second half with a sensational 95-yard kickoff return for a touchdown. Later, George Canrinus, one half of St. Mary's pass-snagging Canrinus brothers, caught a 29-yard throw from Beasley at the Ducks 1-yard line. Beasley scored from there, and the Gaels defense did the rest. St. Mary's seemed itself again, but Madigan was hesitant. He still needed to be convinced.

"You can quote me," he told the local press. "I've set my cap for Southern Methodist, and I think we'll beat the antspay off of 'em." Antspay? What the heck is that, Slip? Did he mean ants pay, which, translated, is, "bull ants relying heavily on surrounding landmarks, and less on a sky compass in order to navigate during both bright and dark moments?" Did any of that make sense? Maybe to Slip, with his inventive mind, but how do the Gaels play like a bunch of bull ants?

Maybe bullishly, for St. Mary's toughened up again on defense and navigated a season-ending 7-2 win over the SMU Mustangs at Kezar. Beasley's 20-yard pass to Toscani accounted for the game's only touchdown. Twice in the first half, and once more in the second half, the Gaels valiantly held off SMU inside their 2-yard line, with key tackles made by Fischer, Stepanovich and Baird. Fischer wasn't supposed to play, but convinced Madigan that he was healthy enough. Madigan pulled out every stop to get that win, shelving the run and throwing 27 passes, completing 17 during an era when the forward pass was an afterthought, except that afternoon in Slip's ever-creative mindset.

A patriot to the core, and a vocalist of some talent, Madigan sang along with the rest of America as the Star-Spangled Banner became the nation's anthem in 1931. As a believer, too, in justice, Madigan was pleased that gangster Al Capone was sent to prison that same year. Madigan anticipated playing Fordham again in 1932 so his traveling party could see the newly constructed Empire State Building and George Washington Bridge. Madigan, and America, building together.

St. Mary's, to cap off 1931, placed two players on the All-Coast team: Toscani and Fischer. The Gaels finished 8-2, but with no national championship, no Rose Bowl invitation because of USC—and no USC on the Moragans' 1932 schedule. Some smack down.

"We still are smarting under the defeat of Coach Madigan's lads," explained USC athletic director Willis O. Hunter, "and we don't care to repeat the experience. But we must wait another year to even up the score."

The ultimate compliment for St. Mary's: The national champion refused to play them in 1932. USC would schedule weak sisters Loyola and USF instead. But, oh, what that 1931 season might have been hadn't the Gaels faltered against the Olympic Club and UCLA. Slip Madigan had let his biggest opportunity for acclaim slip away.

4

The Boy in Illinois

Slip Madigan isn't the only famous person who lived in or passed through Ottawa, Illinois. Abraham Lincoln was discharged from military duty in Ottawa after serving briefly in the Illini Militia in 1832. The first presidential debate between Lincoln and Steven A. Douglas also occurred in Ottawa in 1858. And in 1910, Ottawa resident William Dickson Boyce created the Boy Scouts of America.

Ottawa was incorporated in 1853 at the same time Lincoln was practicing law in Springfield. Ottawa is west of Chicago at the confluence of the Illinois and Fox Rivers. Ottawa, the county seat of La Salle County, was instrumental in the development of the Illinois and Michigan Canal, which terminates in La Salle, twelve miles farther west.

And Ottawa is where Slip Madigan first put on a football uniform, at Ottawa High School, from which he graduated in 1915. He then went off to Notre Dame, served in World War I, returned to get his degree at South Bend in 1920, and then headed to the West Coast to bring football into the modern age before living out a full life in Oakland, California.

But Madigan's Irish blood ran deep, in fact, all the way across the Atlantic Ocean. "My grandfather, Patrick Madigan, was an immigrant from County Kerry in Ireland," said Ed Madigan, Slip's only son, in June 2016. "Granddad came from Listowel, famous for its race track and two well-known writers, playwright John B. Keane and author Bryan MacMahon. Listowel is a well-known literary town. My grandfather, after coming to

America, worked on the Illinois and Michigan Canal as a laborer. He settled in Ottawa, better known then as the Kerry Patch, all Irish folks. He worked in a glass factory because Ottawa is famous for its silicon glass. My granddad was married in Ottawa to an Irish girl, Honora Kelleher, who was from a town near Listowel."

Grandpa Madigan's story only gets bigger. Slip told his son that grandpa Patrick was a Sinn Fein sympathizer. Sinn Fein is the oldest political movement in Ireland, founded in 1905, and defending the right of Irish people to attain national determination. Sinn Fein is an Irish Gaelic expression for "We Ourselves." While living in Ireland, grandpa Madigan harbored someone from the clergy, was caught by the Irish government, and as punishment was put on a ship to America and told never to return. And he never did.

Patrick Madigan was a common laborer, working in a brick factory. His wife, Honora, bore him five sons. Jeremiah, the oldest, became the police chief of Ottawa. Timothy was next; he worked for Railroad Express and served as an Ottawa councilman. Then came John, who fought in World War I, made the military his career, and rose to the rank of colonel during World War II. After Slip came William, or Bucko, who played football without a helmet, splaying his nose as a result. Bucko became a truck driver and then followed Slip to Oakland.

"I would say my dad grew up in moderate, not poor, conditions," said Ed Madigan. "My grandmother worked as a house maid for one of the wealthiest families in Ottawa. There was wealth in Ottawa because of the brick and sand companies. All five boys were raised in the Catholic faith, and all five had good educations. The canal had a bridge that crossed the Fox River, which froze over during the winter. The boys would skate there a lot. My uncles said my dad got the nickname Slip on that frozen pond, although they all slipped a lot there. Then my dad got into sports. My uncles told me that my dad was the fighter in the family. When there was a fight, he would go defend the brothers. I'm told he was very good with his fists."

Grandpa Madigan would throw a pair of boxing gloves in the living room in front of his five sons, and Slip would get to them first. His brothers wanted no part of him, and neither did his schoolmates. He became known as a scrapper who wouldn't quit. "He wasn't a boxer, but he liked boxing, and he attended championship fights his entire life," said Ed Madigan. "He introduced me to Fred Apostoli from San Francisco, who became the middleweight champion. Apostoli was my boyhood hero. And through my dad, I got to meet another middleweight champ, Tony Zale, a very nice man."

Ottawa was a fighter's town. Billy Papke grew up there before becoming middleweight champion, though unethically. He illegally punched champion Stanley Ketchel instead of shaking his hand before their title fight. A groggy Ketchel lost the match, but regained the title by savagely beating Papke, who later shot and killed his wife, and then killed himself in a murder-suicide. Johnny Coulon, a bantamweight champion, also resided in Ottawa.

Slip Madigan played baseball as well as football at Ottawa High. "He was a good ballplayer, a pitcher," said his son. "My grandfather was a friend of Charles Comiskey, the Chicago White Sox owner. My dad was sent to get instructions from Ed Walsh, the great spitball pitcher. My dad threw the spitter back when it was legal. But he threw his arm out and couldn't play baseball at Notre Dame. He loved baseball, though, and always wore a baseball cap during football practice at St. Mary's."

Slip Madigan began his schooling at St. Columba's Parochial in Ottawa, receiving his first "Certificate of Honor" for perfect attendance in 1909. His high school accomplishments were captured in "The Ottawan," a semimonthly literary pamphlet edited by Ottawa High students. Slip held onto those pamphlets until he died in 1966, and they remain in the possession of his son. Slip demonstrated a literary flair in writing the "Football Team of 1913" summary in The Ottowan. To wit:

"Here is to Read as he sits in his chair, wondering and thinking how he used to hit the air;

"Here is to George Crawford, for he will always win;

"And here is to Ernie, the other Gold Dust twin;

"Here is to Edgecomb, and his two hundred and twenty;

"And health to the two Heibergs, whom Murph calls windy;

"Here is to Hessling and his powerful attack, for Mills has lit it in the middle of his back;

"Here is Park Kimball, for he is mightily built, and many a fellow wishes he had a head like under that gilt (sic);

"Here is to Bill Hart, who in his tackles takes pride, for when he comes to you, you're bound for a slide;

"Here is to Woolbut, the last of them all, but he is mighty fine for falling on the ball."

Madigan was a wordsmith of sorts, though not a future Wordsworth as a poet. He was a football star at Ottawa High, a two-time captain and quite the campus hero. Oledine Wood wrote "The Spectator Goes to a Football Game," which was printed in The Ottawan: "At one point a girl in the stands yells, 'Oh! Slip! Slip! Slip! Slip!' I wonder which Ottawan is in her heart." Madigan, the heartthrob, played quarterback, halfback, and fullback, besides his line play in Ottawa. He also was the kicker. These snippets from The Ottawan chronicle his prep gridiron days:

Ottawa 0, Pontiac 0: "Madigan, the captain, is listed at fullback."

Ottawa 27, Lyons Township 0: "Yentzer replaced Madigan at the pivotal (backfield) position in the fourth quarter."

Ottawa 13, LaSalle-Penn Township 7 (1913): "Madigan, now at quarterback, had a dropkick field goal blocked, but later drove through the line near the goal, but W. Herberg scored. Madigan kicked the PAT."

Ottawa 13, Harvey 0: "Madigan made one PAT, but he dropped the ball on the second."

Ottawa 0, Princeton 0: "In the last quarter, Ottawa worked several forward passes, Madigan to the Herbergs, but it seemed that we could not gain when gains meant scores."

Ottawa 13, Peoria 0: "In the third quarter, the team put on a new steam and carried the ball to the three-yard line, from where Capt. Madigan carried it over on a straight plunge."

Ottawa 7, La Salle-Penn Township 7 (1914): "Madigan made a long end run and succeeded in crossing the goal line, but a La Salle player tackled the ball behind the goal, knocking it out of his hands and recovering on the one-yard line."

Knocking the ball out of one's hands after crossing the goal line would be a touchdown, not a fumble. So this was either an officiating error or a misinformed Ottawa High School journalist. And, finally:

Ottawa 31, Ottawa Alumni 7: "For O.H.S., Madigan gained more ground than any other player. No one was able to get away with any long runs on account of the hard-tackling alumni. The forward pass was used with deadly effect. Yentzer, W. Herberg, Lowe, and Madigan received passes for good gains. This style of offense seemed to baffle the alumni."

The Ottawa football team received solid support from its students, the townspeople, and even the school band, except on one occasion against La-Grange High. We can play football in the rain, the band reasoned, but we can't play instruments so tunefully when there's a downpour. Try playing the school fight song when you might slip and fall while carrying a tuba. So the Ottawa band sat that game out.

Football fundamentals were taught at Ottawa High, but so were the basics of sportsmanship, which didn't go unnoticed by L.W. Smith, the principal of rival Thornton Township. He wrote the following letter of appreciation that appeared in The Ottawan: "Our team came back disappointed to be sure, because they had not won, but with the highest praise for the treatment they had received at the hands of your team and your school. They reported the conduct of the sidelines as, in every respect, ideal. Your team and your school must certainly be in the best spirits of sportsmanship."

But, then, Ottawa High set a high standard for itself in its approach to athletics. In September 1913, its Athletic Board of Control passed a resolution which stated: "That at the end of the football season, honorary letters should be granted to those boys who had played in, at least, one quarter of half the games scheduled, who had not smoked during the football season, and who had trained consistently." No mention was made of drinking alcohol, unless it was complicit with training consistently.

The board might as well have been referencing Madigan, who carried himself with the highest ideals. The Ottawan saluted him as a junior: "Capt. Madigan found his position—quarterback—the one for which he seemed best-fitted toward the close of the season. His pep has meant a great deal for the team. He plays hard, is in the game all the time, and uses his head well in selections of plays. On defense, he plays left tackle, a vital part of the 'stonewall' line, has aggressiveness in breaking through opposing lines, spoiling many plays."

Madigan lined up against Clarence "Fat" Spears of Kewanee High, a weight difference of sixty pounds. "He played everything," Slip recalled. "He was up in the line or playing in the backfield. Fats Spears was all over, and one of the greatest high school players I ever saw. When he brought a man down with a tackle, he smothered him. He was one of the fastest big men I ever saw." In 1930 and 1931, they met again as coaches, Madigan at St. Mary's and Spears at Oregon. Slip 2, Fats 0.

As a youth, Madigan became friends with a French royal family. The family, based in Paris, had financial ties in Ottawa, owning a sand and gravel business there. "The family's name was De La Chappelle, and the father was a count. My dad was best friends with the count's son," said Ed Madigan. "Dad worked for the family, steering a toboggan with passengers. Well, years later, dad got a press pass to cover the 1936 Olympics in Berlin, and had dinner with his French boyhood chum, who was now a count himself." A count who counted Slip as a good friend.

Madigan clearly left his mark at Ottawa High. He was its first two-year football captain, and he played on its first undefeated football team. Pat Frayne, sports editor of the *San Francisco Call-Bulletin*, wrote about Madigan's prep years in 1931, contending that he got his nickname from his "slippery defensive tactics," and not his slippery skating antics. The latter is the truth, though his football defense was, indeed, slippery. Ottawa historians remember him as someone who slipped off blockers to become "one of the hardest hitters in Illinois football."

On Dec. 6, 1914, with World War I at hand, Slip Madigan was the main speaker at his high school banquet at Ottawa's New Clifton Hotel, hosted by the local Board of Education. Since Ottawa High was the only game in town, it received a second banquet, a "football feed," at the Harrison Hotel. And what a feed! Thirty-seven players sat down to a spread of raw oysters, consommé, roasted turkey, sweet potatoes, roast pork, applesauce, cranberry, sherbet, cheeses, coffee and sweets. So how did the teenage Madigan not weigh more than 150 pounds?

Prior to Madigan's 1915 graduation from Ottawa High, The Ottawan had fun with its prominent senior leader: "Edward 'Slip' Madigan, native of Tipperary, listed his Favorite Study as 'Lillian Russell's Beauty Secrets,' and his Ambition to be a Matinee Idol and Movie Actor." The Ottawan also wanted to know "If Madigan realizes that it is quite the fashion 'Dontcheknow' for freshman girls to carry his picture in their locket." Oh! Slip! Slip! Slip! Slip!

The Ottawan then offered this final tribute to its campus hero: "For he's a friend to everyone, and he's held in high esteem. We will not forget E. Madigan, the captain of our team." Ottawa High wouldn't ever forget E. Madigan. In 2009, he was inducted posthumously into the school's hall of fame. Son Ed traveled to Illinois to accept his induction.

After high school, Slip Madigan didn't travel far to attend college, heading just below Illinois to South Bend, Indiana. Notre Dame's entrance requirements, abbreviated, were "as old as Christendom in her insistence upon the education of the whole man. Notre Dame teaches a man not only how to make a living, but how to live. The ideal of Notre Dame is not necessarily to have a large school, but rather to limit the enrollment to students whose character and scholastic qualifications are such that they will really profit from the type of education that Notre Dame offers."

Madigan entered Notre Dame in the fall of 1915. Deacon Jones, the freshman team coach, alternated him at quarterback and halfback. Against Culver Military School, Madigan broke off a long run, but was tackled and dislocated a knee. Not only was his season over, his career was in doubt. But Dr. John D. "Bonesetter" Reese in Columbus, Ohio, re-arranged the knee in such a way that Madigan was allowed to continue playing. In 1916, he moved into the line after showing an ability to spiral the football better than the other centers. He played some guard until settling, permanently, into the center position in 1917. Ironically, his first St. Mary's All-American (1927) was a center, Larry Bettencourt, whom Madigan taught how to deliver a perfect spiral.

Madigan received his first taste of coaching, indirectly, during the Notre Dame-West Point game of 1916. The Irish took a 10-3 lead into the fourth quarter, but lost 30-10. "That taught me another lesson," he said. "No matter how far behind a team may be in a football game, it has a chance before that final gun is sounded." He carried that philosophy west to St. Mary's, where his Gaels rallied for some impressive victories.

Slip's weight hadn't changed much at Notre Dame from high school. He was up to 156 pounds when he squared off against West Point lineman John McEwan, who weighed 200. Slip held his own against the bigger man. By 1917, the United States was at war. Madigan, like other stouthearted young men, was ready to defend his country. But, first, there was Washington and

Jefferson to contend with—a college football team, not the two presidents. Before that game, Madigan contracted pneumonia, but he played anyway, toughing out a 3-0 Notre Dame win.

Madigan then left college to serve Uncle Sam, carrying with him this sage advice from Knute Rockne: "If you are going into the navy, go in it to fight, and to get as much out of it as you can. Don't mix play with war." Madigan listened to Rockne and turned down a chance to play football for the Great Lakes Naval Station in Illinois. He enlisted as a sailor and worked his way up to ensign, operating the transport Herbert K. Oaks. While in the navy, he married his Charlotte. He saw no combat during his brief military time.

"To give you an idea about his leadership skills," said his son, "after he reported for duty at a Chicago pier, he was put in charge of a bunch of troops, and he marched them all the way to the Great Lakes Naval Station. He learned how to be a sailor on a Great Lakes ore carrier. He did so well that he was commissioned as an officer. He remained in the naval reserves throughout his time at St. Mary's."

Madigan returned to Notre Dame in 1919, the second year that Knute Rockne was head coach after serving as Jess Harper's assistant. "My dad never talked much about Rockne," said Ed, "but he used to talk about George Gipp. He said that Gipp could do anything he set his mind to. He was a great gambler, a great card player, a great baseball player, and a great billiards player. He beat a famous professional billiards player, whose name I can't think of, in an exhibition in South Bend. Gipp could dropkick a football 50 yards through the uprights one way, then turn around and dropkick it 50 yards through the uprights the other way."

Officially, Gipp dropkicked a 62-yard field goal against Michigan Western State Normal. His exploits at Notre Dame were that extraordinary. He played the 1918, 1919, and 1920 seasons. His career rushing record of 2,341 yards lasted fifty years, and he still holds the school record of averaging 8.1 yards per carry for a season. He also passed for 1,789 yards, and punted for a 38-yard average—with a larger, bulkier football than is used today. His legend grew with Knute Rockne's famous "Win One for the Gipper" locker room speech. Gipp died at 25 of a throat infection just days after leading the Fighting Irish to victory over Northwestern. Madigan was the Gipper's center in 1919.

Notre Dame became the cradle of coaches under Rockne. The number of college head coaches produced during Rockne's time in South Bend was extraordinary. Just among Madigan's teammates alone, Buck Shaw and Clipper Smith both coached at Santa Clara, Charlie Bachman at Florida, Dutch Bergman at Catholic University, Harry Maher at Georgia, and Jimmy Phelan at Washington and later at St. Mary's. Phelan replaced Red Strader, who succeeded Madigan in 1940.

"My dad was very proud to be a Notre Dame alum," said son Ed. "On St. Mary's train trips back to play Fordham, they'd go through South Bend, so he could show his players the campus. Even when my dad was out of coaching and in the construction business, he kept up that relationship. He always went back to Notre Dame for reunions. He stayed in touch with old classmates. But the reason my dad and Rockne never played each other was something Rockne told him: 'You've got everything to win, and I've got everything to lose if you beat me.' Rockne also said that with all of his players having become coaches, he didn't want to play favoritism."

One valuable lesson Madigan took with him after graduating from Notre Dame in 1920 was how winning projects winning. How else do you recruit top football prospects, and interest alumni and other followers, unless you're piling up victories year after year? Notre Dame was 23-2-1 during Madigan's three varsity seasons, including 9-0 in 1919, Rockne's second year as head coach. And Madigan didn't waste much time at St. Mary's in turning that school into a winner on the gridiron.

Slip might have slipped on the ice as a child, but he didn't lose his balance on grass on autumn Saturdays. He kept his feet under him as a player, and then metaphorically as a coach, stepping up in national stature. He wasn't certain where that ascendance might take him, because he wasn't sure how high St. Mary's would climb. Though he failed to reach the top in terms of a national championship, he came very close, closer than St. Mary's would ever come.

But it can be said that the boy in Illinois rose to the top as a man.

5
One Brick at a Time

Abraham Lincoln was two years into his presidency in 1863 when St. Mary's College was founded. California had been a state thirteen years when some Catholic miners, prospering from gold and silver strikes in the Sierra Nevada, provided the funds that launched St. Mary's College, which initially was located on San Francisco's rough-and-tumble waterfront. Reading and roughhousing, biology and beer mugs, suddenly were unlikely neighbors, an unusual classroom setting. But it was a beginning, regardless, toward higher education.

The college's founding father was Joseph Alemany, OP, a pioneer archbishop in San Francisco. The school remained under his jurisdiction for five years, until he persuaded—with much difficulty—the Christian Brothers, the largest teaching order of the Catholic Church, to assume control. The archbishop had pursued the Christian Brothers, since the school's inception, to step in and take over, but was met with resistance. Frustrated, he traveled to Rome, where his pursuit resulted in success: He obtained a papal edict that ordered the Christian Brothers to administer the day-to-day operations of the fledgling college—a relationship that continues two centuries later. Slip Madigan would have been impressed by the archbishop's recruiting skills.

St. Mary's College wasn't the first college in northern California, just among the first. Santa Clara and the College of Pacific started in 1851, followed by Mills College, a women's institution, a year later. The University of San Francisco began (as St. Ignatius) in 1855. The University of California in Berkeley and Holy Names, a second women's college in Oakland, both opened in 1868, followed by Stanford University in 1891. As for two known southern California colleges, both future St, Mary's opponents, USC began in 1880 and UCLA in 1919.

As San Francisco continued to grow, St. Mary's felt crowded on the waterfront. Thus in 1889, it relocated to a seven-acre site in Oakland, and inside one tall building, i.e., "The Brickpile." Grover Cleveland was serving the first of his two presidencies (separated by Benjamin Harrison) at the time of the move. But by then, St. Mary's already was making its mark in sports. Baseball was its first athletic endeavor in 1872, adopting the Phoenix as its nickname. Long before Madigan turned his teams into a traveling circus, the Phoenix traveled to Philadelphia to participate in a tournament during that city's Exposition. The Phoenix showed its might by tying the Cincinnati Red Stockings, baseball's first professional team (1861), and a juggernaut considered unbeatable, especially against collegians. Thus a tie felt like a win.

St. Mary's success on the baseball diamond continued into the 1900s. Besides Hall of Famer Harry Hooper, Joe Oeschger also was a St. Mary's student before he pitched in that historic 26-inning 1-1 tie against Leon Cadore in 1920. Oeschger of the Boston Braves and Cadore of the Brooklyn Robins both, remarkably, went the distance. Oeschger gave up nine hits and Cadore fifteen before the afternoon game was called because of darkness. The two men lacked by one inning of pitching the equivalent of three baseball games in one day. There were no pitch counts, obviously, in those days of extraordinary mound endurance.

Thus St. Mary's was a baseball factory long before its success in football, sending a number of alumni into professional baseball. Brother Agnon McCann, FSC, was quite the coach in his priestly garb, hitting fungoes and warming up pitchers. For twelve straight seasons, from 1901 to 1913, St. Mary's reigned as champion of the California-Nevada College Baseball League. Its 1907 team won twenty-six games, lost none, and tied once. Its 1912 team upset the world champion Boston Red Sox. College or pros, it didn't matter. St. Mary's attitude was "Bring 'em on."

St. Mary's entry into football was 1892, with a rocky start against Santa Clara, losing 46-7 to its rival in 1896, and 57-0 in 1898. It was difficult convincing St. Mary's students to turn out for football, not only because the student body was small, but also because the game was played brutally in its infancy. Players wore no helmets, thereby risking concussions. Few rules existed, thus leading to a barbaric climate. For that reason, in 1899, St. Mary's banished the sport, joining many schools nationally in switching to rugby as a more civilized alternative.

St. Mary's returned to football in 1915, and in 1917 produced an 8-1-1 record under coach Russell T. "Babe" Wilson. Excitement abounded at The Brickpile that year as St. Mary's defeated USC, 7-0, and then shocked California, 14-13—St. Mary's only win over an Andy Smith-coached Cal team. The St. Mary's Saints, as they were known then, recorded five shutouts in 1917, declaring themselves the Pacific Coast champion. But with World War I raging in Europe, and America needing fighting men, St. Mary's enrollment was reduced, by two thirds, to seventy-one students. Thus its undermanned football team in 1920 lost 127-0 to Cal. St. Mary's finished that game with ten players and an eleventh on a stretcher. St. Mary's administration cancelled the rest of the season, wondering how to somehow restore its gridiron integrity.

Meanwhile, in Portland, Oregon, Slip Madigan's debut as a football coach was successful that same fall, lifting Columbia Prep to a 6-2 record. Columbia beat Commerce, 27-12, to establish itself, and then whacked Jefferson, 33-0, to close out the season. Houston Stockton scored two touchdowns and kicked three field goals in the finale. "Madigan found a green squad of candidates," analyzed The Oregonian, "when he took up his duties at Columbia, but the football team was one of the best turned out in several years. . . ." Madigan wasn't long for Columbia. Informed of a college opportunity in Oakland, he showed up for an interview at St. Mary's brimming with confidence. Brother Gregory, the college president, was sold quickly, but said, "You'll have to coach everything. You'll even have to collect tickets. But you're hired. Now go make St. Mary's a winner, son. Oh, you open with Cal."

With thoughts of 127-0 in his head, Madigan signed a three-year contract at an annual salary of $1,200. He didn't show up at St. Mary's empty-handed; he brought along Houston Stockton. The *Oakland Tribune* welcomed the arrival of Ed "Flash" Madigan. Knute Rockne sensed big things were ahead for St. Mary's. "Madigan," he said, "is the best coaching prospect Notre Dame has had in three years. He knows football from A to Z. He is a consistent and conscientious worker, and will be a credit to any institution that secures his services." But as confident as Rockne was regarding Madigan's potential, the Rock couldn't have known just how difficult it would be for his protégé in the very beginning. Rockne didn't have to coach four sports and serve as athletic director, and perform maintenance duties on the side.

"I suited up a dozen high school players to sit on the bench, so we wouldn't look silly in Berkeley," Madigan said thirty years later, looking back on the 1921 season opener. "I couldn't use them if I wanted to. I had them sit for window dressing, what you call the 'long bench' these days. Actually I had 13 men (available). Stockton was my one extra backfield man, and he had boils and couldn't play. Doc Silva, the quarterback, came up with a charley horse. He limped off the field, but I waved him back in as I didn't have a man to replace him. He hobbled around the best he could; the quarterback was a key blocker then."

Madigan's arrival at St. Mary's, though newsworthy, was hardly the newsiest event of 1921. Adolph Hitler became Fuhrer of the Nazi Party. Warren G. Harding was inaugurated as the twenty-ninth U.S. President, while a future President, 39-year-old Franklin Delano Roosevelt, was diagnosed with poliomyelitis. Communist parties were established in Czechoslovakia, China, Spain and Italy, which also welcomed the National Fascist Party. The first radio broadcast was heard on KDKA in Pittsburgh, and the first Miss America, Margaret Gorman, 16, was crowned. And a race riot in Tulsa, Oklahoma, led to thirty-nine deaths.

Not until 1926 would St. Mary's have enough players to field a freshman team. During Madigan's nineteen years at St. Mary's, substitution rules were stringent, regardless of squad size. After a substitute entered the game, he had to play the rest of the quarter before he could come off the field. Madigan was forced to mix and match, unlike Rockne's well-stocked Notre Dame teams. Rockne sometimes started his second unit to absorb the impact of an opponent, and then put in his fresh first unit for the second quarter. It was the late 1920s before Madigan had enough players to emulate Rockne's strategy. By then, Madigan had two teams named for his centers, Armand Seghetti and Woody Peebles. The Seghettis played the first and fourth quarters, the Peebles the second and third. Finally, in the 1950s, free substitution became the norm in college football.

Besides being overworked in the athletic department, Madigan also taught history, economics and government. Fellow professors at St. Mary's regarded him as an academic, not as a "moonlighting" coach. Madigan also was a one-man maintenance crew. With his Stephens automobile, he not only paid for its gas, he hooked a grader to the vehicle and dragged the practice field, missing a chuckhole here and there. Madigan and Brother Lewis, a faculty member, kept the grass cut. With games to coach, classes to teach, and exams and term papers to grade, Madigan needed a thirty-hour day. His "home" basketball games through 1928 were played at Kezar Pavilion in San Francisco, requiring additional travel. As the baseball coach, he received a welcomed "bonus" for his madcap work schedule. St. Mary's baseball alumni, in 1927, started a fund to purchase him a new auto, seeking donations of $1 to $10. Enough money was collected to buy him a new Buick, which wasn't needed, by that time, to drag any playing surfaces.

"St. Mary's rise to the football heights," Madigan said years later, "was not due to any expert coaching ability or business management, which I might have fostered due to our frugality. Why, I was even the team shoemaker (while his wife and mother-in-law sewed up uniforms). I used to buy regular street shoes, without cleats, because shoes were cheaper that way. I put the cleats on myself with a hammer and nails. And (graduate manager) Louis LeFevre and I always carried football tickets in our pockets. We never overlooked an opportunity to sell them. I also opened a sandwich shop across from the school, to add to my income. My wife ran the shop; her mother was the cook."

Madigan had to cover every angle to get his sports programs off the ground. This meant courting the sporting press. "Even if I didn't like the guys," he said, "and even if I didn't realize they had a job to do, and were doing it the best way they knew how, I'd remind myself that the cubs of today are the sports editors, the city editors, and managing editors of tomorrow. Who wants to have an editor mad at him?" So he embraced sportswriters as well as any football coach ever has, and likely better. Those ink-stained wretches weren't used to such regal treatment.

In 1921, Madigan's first year, he couldn't scrimmage because he didn't have enough players. In addition, the practice field sloped, boulders were everywhere, and he used sawdust to cover up the chuckholes. Mostly, he thought of this herculean task he had undertaken, beginning with 127-0 Cal. Perhaps the size of St. Mary's bench, with high school juniors and seniors acting merely as props, made coach Andy Smith's Bears slightly nervous. Madigan's own players demonstrated tremendous heart, battling the "Wonder Team" tooth and nail. Cal's Crip Toomey was the difference-maker, scoring on a short plunge and later on a 70-yard punt return. Cal gained more yards, 162 to 31, and more first downs, 12 to 8, but walked off California Field with a hard-earned 21-0 victory. "The comparative lower score (from 1920) was not an indication of a weaker Bruin eleven, but of a stronger St. Mary's team," the *Daily Californian* student newspaper reported. "A new coach, several new players, and the increased interest of the alumni had worked marvels with the Saints team." Has any other football team, college or pro, ever improved by 106 points against an opponent from one season to the next? Madigan's debut was utterly amazing.

"St. Mary's must be handed a flock of credit," reported the *Oakland Tribune*, "for the excellent showing that they made against Andy Smith's men, for the boys of coach Madigan had been figured to take a much worse beating . . . the showing of the Saints has set all the boys to talking." Stanford was next up for St. Mary's, so Madigan and LeFevre scouted its 41-0 win over the Mare Island Marines.

"In preparation for the game with Stanford next Saturday in Palo Alto," the *San Francisco Examiner* noted, "coach Edward 'Slip' Madigan is driving his men to the limit, and is making last-minute changes. The shifting of 'Chief' Black, the big Indian fullback, to right end, and placing Clarence Lane, world's champion swimmer, at right half, with Houston Stockton at fullback, adds speed to the team." The *San Francisco News* reported: "Coach Madigan has practically, singlehandedly, turned the school football crazy. Madigan is a live wire. He has a voice like the crack of the whip, and when he says something, everybody jumps. From the time the first string trots out on the (practice) field until they leave, the ball is kept continually on the move, and it moves fast."

Stanford wasn't yet a gridiron force after playing in the first Rose Bowl game in 1902—a 49-0 loss to Michigan, a blowout that was shortened to three quarters for merciful reasons. But, Stanford looked more formidable in 1921 than St. Mary's, strictly from depth. The Saints put up yet another strong fight and lost by another respectable margin, 10-7. St. Mary's took off from there, winning four of its five remaining games—14-0 over Nevada, 46-0 over the Mare Island Marines, 20-7 over the Olympic Club, and 68-0 over the Santa Maria Legends, while incurring a 20-0 loss to the Pacific Fleet—the greatest turnaround in West Coast football history. Who else finishes 4-3 a year after losing 127-0? Say, that Madigan fellow must be a miracle man.

"St. Mary's has probably the best team turned out by the local college in the past four or five years," the *San Francisco Chronicle* noted, "and without question a team possessed of the greatest fight a college team has been known to show. St. Mary's is indeed fortunate in having Edward P. Madigan, an all-around athlete, a fighter, and a true sportsman, as their coach." Shifting from fall to winter, he had a winning basketball season, too. Then moving into the spring, his baseball team won the league championship, beating Cal, 4-2, in Berkeley. Madigan also was such an important addition, academically, that St. Mary's experienced its largest freshmen enrollment in 1922.

Madigan was making do with what he had, leading to adjustments on the fly, a technique he learned from Rockne. "Why that Rockne is a marvel," he said, "He's the greatest of them all. Why I've seen him make an end out of a guard right in the middle of a ball game. What a psychologist he is." Only Rockne had more players to move around, making for much easier adjustments. Sometimes Madigan wished he could play himself, although he admitted using "some Notre Dame ringers" once, and getting away with it. Oh, that slippery Slip.

Madigan, as a history teacher, saw history happening right before his eyes. In 1922, the Lincoln Memorial was dedicated, Rebecca Felton of Georgia became the first United States female senator, and the Teapot Dome Scandal led to Secretary of the Interior Albert Bacon Fall becoming the first cabinet member sent to prison, for accepting bribes from oil companies. And, closer to home, the California Grizzly Bear became extinct. But not the University of California Golden Bear, which continued to feast on the football team from The Brickpile.

St. Mary's opened the 1922 season against the University of Arizona in Tucson. The *Oakland Post-Enquirer*'s Al Santoro wrote of the opener: "For the first time, Madigan's Saints go into a fray with one of the strongest elevens. The Oakland collegians, however, are slightly handicapped for the lack of practice. A drenched football field made workouts impossible." And so the Saints began the 1922 season with a handicap, losing to Arizona, 20-3. Cal poured it on St. Mary's this time, 49-0. The Saints played Stanford to a scoreless tie, and beat U.C. Davis, 19-7, and Santa Clara, 9-7, on a last-second goal line stand. The Saints then lost to Nevada, 20-13, and the Olympic Club, 28-7.

That same 1922 season, the football world got its initial look at the peripatetic Madigan. He took his team to Hawaii aboard the SS Maui for a Christmas Eve game against the Hawaiian All-Stars, a 10-6 St. Mary's win, and a New Year's Day contest against the Pearl Harbor Navy, which prevailed, 14-6. That Christmas Eve contest marked the first time an American college played football in Hawaii—a first, though, by a matter of hours. For on Christmas Day, the University of Hawaii beat visiting Pomona College, 25-6. But did St. Mary's suffer from island fever? For it finished 3-5-1 in 1922, Madigan's last losing record for seventeen years.

But 1922 brought yet another Madigan first—a radio broadcast of the Saints-Nevada game from Reno. The entire St. Mary's student body and many of the Brothers gathered in the gymnasium at The Brickpile, listening to the play-by-play. History continued to change off campus in 1923. The Walt Disney Company was founded. President Harding died of a heart attack, succeeded by Vice President Calvin "Silent Cal" Coolidge. Vladimir Lenin suffered a third stroke and retired as Chairman of the Soviet Government. Pancho Villa was assassinated, Yankee Stadium opened, Louis Armstrong made his first recording, "Chimes Blues," and Mount Etna erupted in Italy, leaving 60,000 homeless.

Madigan was beginning to show the public, and the sporting world, what was brewing inside his fertile mind. "The first secret of success," he offered before the 1923 season, "is to keep your mouth shut. I'm a superstitious Irishman; what happens twice happens three times." This superstitious Irishman loaded his roster with Irishmen: O'Grady, O' Brien, O'Rourke, Conlan, Kelly, Rooney, Lorrigan, Corrigan, Collins, Tobin and McVay. Relying more on the pluck, not luck, of the Irish, the Saints improved to 4-3-1. That pluck was most evident against Arizona, which led 20-2 in the fourth quarter, when St. Mary's scored three times for a stirring 22-20 season-opening victory. Cal's Wonder Team then steamrolled the Saints again, 41-0, but they recovered to knock off U.C. Davis, 42-7, the Mare Island Marines, 48-0, and the Multnomah Club, 27-6. A 10-10 tie with Nevada was followed by two close defeats—9-6 to the Olympic Club, on three Clyde King field goals, and 10-9 to Santa Clara, the Broncos last win over St. Mary's until 1936.

In his fourth season, 1924, Madigan launched his first successful team, coinciding with the year's biggest football story—Red Grange of Illinois scoring six touchdowns against Michigan. That year also saw the founding of IBM and Metro Goldwyn Mayer, J. Edgar Hoover becoming the FBI director, and two college students, Richard Loeb and Nathan Leopold, Jr., murdering Bobby Franks, 14, in a thrill killing. But Madigan was as interested in creating history on the football field than teaching it in his history class.

Without one senior on the 1923 team, everybody was coming back in 1924, including the "Pony Backfield" of Jimmy Underhill, Leo Rooney, Hugh "Ducky" Grant" and Louis "Dutch" Conlan. However, it was fullback Red Strader who became the team's horse, receiving St. Mary's first All-America recognition, named to the third team in '24. The Saints had turned the corner on talent in only four seasons. Madigan showed he could recruit as well as coach. He defeated a club team, Agnetian, 7-3, and an American Legion team, 21-0, to get things rolling. Next up was Cal's Wonder Team. Only the wonderment was oozing out of the Bears, which had lost a number of marquee players, while the Saints now were bigger and faster than Cal's four-time Pacific Coast Conference champions. Ducky Grant sprinted 79 yards into the end zone on the opening play, but a St. Mary's penalty nullified the score. A subsequent 6-yard punt set up Cal on the Saints' 30-yard line, quickly resulting in a Bears touchdown. St. Mary's rallied with a 65-yard drive, highlighted by Strader's 24-yard run that evened the score. But a Saints' fumble at their 13-yard line resulted in a Cal field goal, then a subsequent Golden Bears touchdown secured a 17-7 win. Cal still had St. Mary's under its thumb.

The Saints then ran the table, defeating U.C. Davis, 42-7, Mare Island, 46-0, Multnomah Club, 14-0, Nevada, 27-0, Olympic Club, 20-7, and Santa Clara, 28-7, before Madigan received the big break he was looking for, a chance to play USC. An eligibility dispute within the Pacific Coast Conference cancelled the 1924 Stanford-USC game in Los Angeles. So St. Mary's graduate manager Louis LeFevre, representing Madigan, approached both schools, suggesting St. Mary's as a substitute opponent. Stanford declined, seeking easier opposition elsewhere, sensing that St. Mary's was on the rise. On the Tuesday before game day, USC accepted St. Mary's offer, the Trojans anticipating a "gift" victory.

St. Mary's viewed it, instead, as a "gift" opportunity, even if travel arrangements needed to be made hastily. Madigan got his team to Los Angeles in time, though with little preparation for USC. The USC marching band asked St. Mary's for permission to play its fight song prior to kickoff. Only St. Mary's didn't have a fight song, or even its own marching band. So the USC band played "The Bells Of St. Mary's." Instantly, St. Mary's had a fight song. But did its football team have enough fight to challenge USC? Trojan halfback Henry LeFevre took a reverse and scurried 73 yards for a touchdown fifteen seconds after the opening kickoff. The Saints looked stunned in the first quarter, but they tied the score in the second period on a plunge by Strader, set up by Rooney's 65-yard punt that pinned the Trojans deep. USC kicked a field goal just before halftime for a 10-7 lead. Madigan wasn't satisfied.

"This generation of Irish has lost its guts," he roared in the locker room. The Saints, sitting with heads down before their lockers, took umbrage at that insult and bolted out for the second half in an enraged mood. They started knocking the Trojans backwards, outhustling them on every play. St. Mary's took its first lead in the third quarter, sparked by the inspired running of Strader. "Gloomy" Gus Henderson, the USC coach, substituted frantically to stem the tide, using an entirely new backfield in the fourth quarter. Conversely, Madigan used only fourteen players, thus fatigue was setting in when the Trojans staged their final march, moving to within a half-yard of the St. Mary's end zone. The exhausted, but valiant, Saints held them off as the clock expired on St. Mary's 14-10 win. St. Mary's had pulled off the decade's biggest upset on the West Coast, and its first win over a Pacific Coast Conference school since 1917. Madigan had achieved the unthinkable in only his fourth season. Now the entire country knew about tiny, tenacious St. Mary's College. Gloomy Gus wished he had found another substitute team to play in an instant, for he was fired after that season.

The *San Francisco Examiner* rhapsodized: "To start in one line of activity in a small way, then to work and develop until first rate excellence is obtained is the American way in sport as in everything else. . . . St. Mary's is on its way of becoming the Notre Dame of the West." The Saints had one more game left, against rival Santa Clara, and Madigan prepared against a letdown after shocking USC. But the Saints took apart the Broncos, 28-7, as Strader rushed for 211 yards, and Underhill and Rooney combined for another 150 yards. History was made that day, but, ironically, by Santa Clara. Len Casanova quick-kicked from his end zone, and the ball sailed over Saints heads and rolled all the way into their end zone—a 97-yard punt from scrimmage, the longest punt in NCAA annals to this day.

In the stands that afternoon was Walter Camp, the originator of the All-America team in 1889. Camp wanted to see the upstart St. Mary's team after its upset of USC. He was so impressed with Strader's play against Santa Clara, not to mention his 1,485 yards rushing that season, that he elevated him to All-America status on Camp's third team.

Madigan had another prominent visitor that season, Knute Rockne himself. Rock had come to see his former player, and they shook hands on a tentative agreement to meet on a home-and-home basis in 1925–26, contingent upon St. Mary's creating enough capital to build a brand-new campus in San Leandro, next to Oakland, complete with a 60,000-seat stadium, with the caveat that it be finished in a year. Rockne wisely saw the impossibility of such a project in giving it his "approval." He wasn't going to play, and possibly lose to, his protégé. Anyway, fund-raising for the project fell through, and with it the proposed St. Mary's-Notre Dame series, just the way Rockne figured. Stadium or no stadium, Madigan had fashioned a 9-1 season, winning the hearts of football followers everywhere. Beating USC tied a ribbon around the entire season. St. Mary's College was the new happening spot in football.

The Twenties, like St. Mary's football, continued to aspire. In 1925, F. Scott Fitzgerald published "The Great Gatsby," the Grand Ole Opry had its first radio broadcast, Nellie Tayloe Ross of Wyoming became the first female governor, and the nation's first motel opened in San Luis Obispo, California. In Dayton, Tennessee, high school biology teacher John Scopes was found guilty of teaching evolution, and fined $100. And, finally, Madigan had enough players to cut down his roster.

But staring him the face, again, was Cal, considered the best team in the West in 1925. The Bears squeaked out a 6-0 victory before a record, non-Cal-Stanford rivalry, crowd of 70,000 inside Berkeley's Memorial Stadium, built in 1923. "The Saints," reported the *Daily Cal*, "launched one of the most stubborn battles ever seen here, never weakening until the fourth quarter. But Al Young, who substituted for Earl Jabs late in the game, proved to be the nemesis of Coach Slip Madigan's squad. Young, making several substantial gains, bore the brunt of the Bruin attack in a thrilling sixty-eight-yard march down the field that resulted in the only score. The California line was too strong for the St. Mary's backs to gain consistently, while their widely chronicled passing attack was completed stopped by the Bruin backfield." The *Daily Cal* referred to its teams, occasionally, as Bruins, not Bears, even though younger "brother" UCLA already had adopted that name. But the Cal albatross had resumed its position around Madigan's neck.

St. Mary's then rolled over U.C. Davis, 32-13, Fresno State, 61-14, Multnomah Club, 41-7, Nevada, 35-0, and Santa Clara, 19-7. Next up was a rematch with USC, now coached by Howard Jones. Bad timing, because the Saints would have to play without Strader, lost for the season with a shoulder separation. Madigan had an adequate replacement in Boyd "Cowboy" Smith, a 155-pound speedster, but the Saints were no competition for USC this time, losing, 12-0, before 40,000 at the Los Angeles Coliseum, thus eliminating the Saints from becoming the West Coast champion. St. Mary's then defeated UCLA, 28-0, the West Coast Army, 52-7, and Whittier, 45-6, to finish a most satisfactory 8-2.

Slip Madigan was among the most talked-about coaches in the country. Colleagues admired how he had reached such towering heights with so small a student body. Plus he was coaching three other sports, teaching three classes, and running the athletic department. Talk about a one-man show! So where, people wondered, did he get his players? Some kids came from San Francisco, but mostly from the farmlands, Visalia up through Stockton. They became easier to recruit with the success, and exposure, St. Mary's was enjoying. Madigan had depth, experience, and talent, and his Gaels were succeeding despite chuckholes on the sloped practice field.

Halfbacks Leo Rooney and versatile Jimmy Underhill were third-year varsity starters in 1926. The ultra-talented center, Larry Bettencourt, was only a junior. Scatback Cowboy Smith and future All-America end Malcolm "Ike" Frankian were sophomores, but already major gridiron contributors. America also was taking shape in 1926, as the first liquid fuel rocket was launched in Auburn, Massachusetts, U.S. Route 66 was established, and trumpeter Miles Davis, academician Alan Greenspan, and author Harper Lee were born.

The 1926 St. Mary's Saints were projected to be Madigan's most powerful team up to that juncture, and that projection proved accurate. Underhill was a major factor in that projection, his coach having compared him with football's immortals. "Underhill is the best backfield man I have seen on the coast," said Madigan. "He is undoubtedly the nearest approach to the late George Gipp I have ever seen. Underhill is not only a triple threat back, but I have never seen a better receiver of forward passes. He is a great interferer (blocker), and his records as a broken field runner speak for themselves. He ran for 135 yards at Gonzaga on that muddy field. I would say that he has every fundamental of football down to perfection. I think he beats any of the 'Four Horsemen.' "

Underhill's coming to St. Mary's, in the first place, was a case of motherly love. He had received an appointment to West Point when his mother interceded. Having lost one son to mustard gas during World War I, she redirected son Jimmy to St. Mary's. "In the north," Madigan pointed out, "they say he is the greatest back in years." Leo Rooney also was headed for West Point, but changed his mind and joined Underhill in the St. Mary's backfield. Another backfield member, Louis "Dutch" Conlan, praised team captain Underhill as "one of the greatest halfbacks I ever saw." And football wasn't Underhill's only athletic contribution at St. Mary's. He was a star basketball player, and captain of that team, too.

"I was told that Slip felt my father was the best player he ever had, pound for pound," son Dick Underhill said in 2016. "I knew a bartender, Tom Brennan, in Santa Rosa. He told me that Bronko Nagurski was the best player he ever saw, and my father was second. The Chicago Bears wanted to sign dad as a blocking back, but there was no money then in pro football. He got married and went into teaching and coaching." Jim Underhill became a high school coaching legend in Santa Rosa, California, as well as a respected National Football League game official. He was a born leader as well as a born athlete.

St. Mary's opened the 1926 season with a 34-6 win over the West Coast Army, exciting its Oakland campus. "The Saints showed remarkable power and reserve strength," said the St. Mary's Collegian newspaper. "The line functioned like a finished product, their tackling was hard and deadly. The boys proved they were well-grounded in the fundamentals, and were well aware of everything they were doing." Cowboy Smith scored three touchdowns, while Underhill averaged five yards a carry and got off a 74-yard punt. The Saints looked like the whole package. They kept it up a week later, throttling St. Ignatius College, the future University of San Francisco, 38-0. "There's a new spirit at St. Mary's," the *Oakland Tribune* commented. "It's been brewing actively for five years. It will reach its climax Saturday. The moss-covered walls seemed saturated with it. The student body is almost stark mad. The walls, floors and classrooms seem to shriek with the spirit—a spirit of victory, victory over California."

But could the Saints, finally, master the Bears? Sixty-seven thousand, including several hundred St. Mary's students, showed up in Strawberry Canyon to see for themselves. The Saints erupted like a volcano before a crowd of 67,000. Ike Frankian recovered Cal fullback Earl Jabs' fumble early in the opening quarter at the Bears' 25. On the next play, Rooney followed his blocking around left end and rambled into the end zone. Later in the same quarter, Underhill found a hole between end and tackle and swerved and darted 53 yards to the Cal 26. Saints fullback Gus O'Gorman cut back against the grain and gained 22 yards. Rooney scored from the 4 on the next play for a 13-0 lead. Cal closed to 13-7 on Jabs' 18-yard pass to Eugene Van Horn. Underhill was injured and had to leave the game, but his backup, Cowboy Smith, then took off. On a reverse play, Smith swept around left end, picked up some key blocks, and raced 80 yards for a touchdown. Cal quarterback Dick Blewett then faked a punt and was dropped for a 10-yard loss at the Saints' 45. On the very next play, Smith shot through a big hole at left tackle and sped 55 yards for his second breakaway touchdown, giving the Saints a convincing 26-7 victory over their former conquerors. Cowboy Smith roped and tied Cal by himself, and Madigan finally shed that monkey off his, and St. Mary's, backs.

The United Press wire service waxed prosaic: "There were those reporters in Memorial Stadium who had seen the great Notre Dame team of 1924 when it defeated Stanford (in the Rose Bowl), and they wondered if the St. Mary's varsity was not the equal of that famous Rockne machine. Today the Saints hold a position on the West Coast akin to that held by Notre Dame in the Midwest." Then *San Francisco Call-Bulletin* sportswriter Pat Frayne led off his story with the phrase "Galloping Gaels," and history was about to be rewritten permanently.

St. Mary's proved unstoppable after Cal, shutting down U.C. Davis, 20-7, Fresno State, 16-0, Nevada, 13-0, Olympic Club, 21-0, College of Pacific, 67-7, and the future USF, 38-0. Only a 0-0 draw with Gonzaga marred a perfect season. Cowboy Smith was a media darling, often pictured in a saddle, though not atop a horse. Wrapping up the season, St. Mary's defeated Santa Clara, 7-0, on Thanksgiving Day at Kezar Stadium to complete a 9-0-1 record. It was Madigan's best season yet after a meteoric rise, and a noteworthy accomplishment that turned heads on the East Coast.

"Stanford, Southern California and the (California) Bears seem to be getting all the attention on the Coast," wrote the *New York Sun*, "but a team that could lick them all with an off-tackle play that would make Gil Dobie of Cornell green with envy is overlooked. I'm referring to St. Mary's, so ably coached by Slip Madigan. Talk about color! They have a lanky halfback, 'Cowboy Smith,' who is as pretty a runner as (Red) Grange was in his Illinois days. Bettencourt is the Coast's premier center, and the passing of Rooney to Underhill is as pretty as when 'Brick' Muller was heaving them for the Bears. This is not atmosphere, but on the up and up. They have licked every tough team that would play them, from the Olympic Club, who could beat any pro team from Grange's down to the (Chicago) Bears; and they didn't pick up soft early season games either, but scheduled every good team they could. Why not give the devil his due, and a small college a chance for the merry ballyhoo?"

Merry ballyhoo? Oh, well, twenty-six skidoo! The United Press ballyhooed further, exulting St. Mary's more conventionally: "Once in awhile, a gridiron eleven from a small school rises to fame with its excellent coaching and unusually powerful material. Years ago, little Beloit College turned back every Big 10 opponent, then there was Centre College of Kentucky. This year Geneva College of New York . . . but perhaps the outstanding little college in the nation will prove to be St. Mary's. . . ."

It was all happening so fast, so very fast. But mighty St. Mary and its magical coach would offer up more proof to support that ringing United Press endorsement with yet another monumental victory in 1927.

6

Soaring Twenties

Following his finest season at St. Mary's, Slip Madigan was determined to raise the bar even higher in 1927, by dominating the local football scene. He had finally defeated Cal and also disposed of Santa Clara and St. Ignatius (USF) during the 1926 season. But he hadn't yet conquered Stanford, against which he was 0-1-1. There was something else about Stanford that he disliked intensely—its uppity arrogance.

For Stanford deigned to play St. Mary's; it had been five years since they last met. Stanford regarded St. Mary's with an air of aristocracy. Stanford was the wealthy private school forty miles away in Palo Alto, while St. Mary's was the financially struggling private school in Oakland. A Stanford graduate, Herbert Hoover, would become the nation's president in two years. St. Mary's most famous alum was a Hall of Fame baseball player, Harry Hooper. But in 1927 there wasn't yet a baseball hall in Cooperstown. Stanford sported a white collar, while feeling St. Mary's wore a blue collar, and never the twain shall mix, except rarely on the gridiron, at Stanford's choosing. In '27, Stanford deigned to throw St. Mary's a bone, yelling, "Fetch!" And Madigan, a sly dog, fetched.

Even the schools' head football coaches were separated by image. Madigan was a coach still on the ascent, a charismatic Irishman with a glint in his eye and a glorious gift of gab. Glenn S. "Pop" Warner of Stanford was stern of visage and tight of tongue, yet he was one of the faces on the football coaches' equivalent of Mt. Rushmore. He began coaching in 1895, before Madigan even was born, at the University of Georgia, which went unbeaten the next year. Warner's legacy took shape at the Carlisle Indian School, coaching one of America's greatest athletes, Jim Thorpe. Warner then moved on to Pittsburgh, where he had three unbeaten seasons. He next relocated to Stanford, where he coached another legend, Ernie Nevers, while producing three Rose Bowl teams, including its 1926 squad (10-0-1), which tied Alabama, 7-7, at Pasadena, earning Stanford its only national football championship. Warner was perceived as inwardly as a coach, but he was expressive as an oil painter. One of his paintings, a lovely depiction of Stanford Stadium from the outside, hangs in that school's Athletic Hall of Fame.

Bay Area fans wondered if Madigan had painted himself in a corner by scheduling Stanford in 1927, as it looked formidable once again. Despite its undefeated run in 1926, St. Mary's still was proving itself in the minds of skeptics, who doubted Madigan's chances against wily old Pop. The two men approached the game differently in strategy. Madigan relied on the offensive shift he learned from Knute Rockne at Notre Dame. Warner utilized single and double wing offenses that he designed himself. Madigan's teams were built on speed and finesse, Warner's on strength and endurance. Youngster versus icon, so who teaches whom?

St. Mary's certainly matched Stanford in bravado, with each school claiming to be the Pacific Coast champion in '26. Warner did worry about St. Mary's line, the finest on the West Coast, he believed, and perhaps the best ever in that region. Pop's concern proved accurate as Stanford disassembled in Palo Alto, fumbling ten times as St. Mary's tacklers dislodged the football with bruising hits. Stanford's first fumble occurred on its opening series; Larry Bettencourt picked it up and ran 15 yards for a touchdown. In the second quarter, Homer Hicks gathered up another Stanford fumble and lumbered 26 yards for a second touchdown. A third St. Mary's lineman, Frank Mulcahy, kicked a 20-yard field goal after a blocked Stanford punt, increasing St. Mary's lead to 16-0, which became the final score, a shocker to everyone but Madigan.

"We used four plays against Stanford," he told reporters. "Only a few more than we used in our (West Coast) Army game." St. Mary's used just one play to beat the Army eleven, 21-0? Whatever the explanation, St. Mary's shut down Stanford, twice stopping the Indians inside the Saints' 4-yard line. The defeat was humiliating for Warner, who lost for the first time in thirty-three years to an opponent he had scouted personally. Wearing his usual knickers and high socks, Warner congratulated Madigan afterward, the old coach smiling through clenched teeth.

Warner, according to insiders, hated Madigan because he was from Notre Dame. That's because he hated Notre Dame. He was overheard before kickoff, saying, "Get those Roman sons-of-bitches." A Stanford player, whom son Ed Madigan identified as "Tricky" Dick Hyland, called St. Mary's end Ike Frankian a "Roman ass, then kicked him in the balls." Frankian retaliated, breaking Hyland's cheekbone, and knocking him out of the game. Roman ass? Frankian wasn't even Catholic. Stanford end Spud Harder was the victim of revenge, suffering a badly injured jaw that sidelined him for three weeks. St. Mary's victory was perceived as a victory of the Catholics over the Protestants, the have-nots over the haves, and pupil over master.

"Seven Stubborn Stalwarts braced themselves against the white-shirted Red Horde of Stanford before 35,000," the *San Francisco Call-Bulletin*'s Pat Frayne wrote of St. Mary's stalwart linemen, "and when the vote was all in, the Seven Stubborn Stalwarts had brought a glowing victory for the Galloping Gaels of St. Mary's. It was a victory of a defensive team over a team that was supposed to have a scintillating offense—a complete outsider over last season's national champs. Coach Ed 'Slip' Madigan of St. Mary's had drilled his team on defense on a 'kick and wait for the breaks' game, and his plan worked to perfection."

Madigan used only fourteen men, while Warner's substituted liberally. Warner vowed never to play St. Mary's again, charging Madigan with "dirty tactics." Dirty tactics? Bettencourt was kicked in the groin while lying on the turf. Teammate Gus O'Gorman had a tooth knocked out and nearly an eye. Pope Ilia received a concussion, Toots Kasper fractured a shoulder bone, and Butch Simas suffered knee damage. Battered but undaunted, St. Mary's buried Stanford, the latest Madigan shocker to reverberate across the nation.

"When St. Mary's beat Stanford, it became a cultural war," analyzed St. Mary's professor Ron Isetti. "The Irish and Italian immigrants, who built the railroad, defeated Leland Stanford, who owned the railroad." Score one for the commoner over the gentry. "(Madigan) had a swagger, and he was Irish and appealed to the ethnic minorities struggling to establish themselves in this country," added Gary Sabatte, a St. Mary's regent. "They couldn't identify with the prestigious public universities. They couldn't identify with the Harvards and the Stanfords. They could only identify with somebody like them, somebody who was poor and struggling."

St. Mary's dismantling of Stanford was a big story in 1927, though not the biggest story, which was Charles Lindbergh's historic solo, non-stop transatlantic flight from New York to Paris. Also in '27, the first talking motion picture, "The Jazz Singer," was released. The Ford Motor Company replaced the Model T with the Model A. The first stage classic, "Show Boat," made its debut. And Babe Ruth swatted his record 60 home runs. Nonetheless, after the bloody war with Stanford, St. Mary's roster was shorthanded for its next opponent, Cal, which won easily, 13-0. Though injured, Bettencourt suited up and played Cal center Roy "Wrong Way" Riegels even, a battle of All-Americans present (Bettencourt) and future (Riegels). St. Mary's ended up 7-2-1 in 1927, its fourth straight season with two or fewer defeats. The Saints shut out seven opponents, while being shut out twice. Besides Stanford, the Gaels blanked Gonzaga, 12-0, Nevada, 38-0, College of Pacific, 20-0, USF, 23-0, Santa Clara, 22-0, and the West Cost Army, 34-0. St. Mary's lost to Cal, 13-0, and the Olympic Club, 12-0, before tying Idaho, 3-3.

The ever-thinking Madigan was conceiving anew that season, deciding to schedule his home games at Kezar Stadium on—Blessed Jesus!—a Sunday. This way, local fans could watch the non-sectarian schools, Cal and Stanford, on Saturday, and the Catholic schools on Sunday. Santa Clara and USF agreed to follow St. Mary's and play in Kezar upon the Sabbath. Two years after Madigan's decision, Kezar expanded from 10,000 to 60,000, becoming, in effect, The House That Slip Built. Nobody was as creative as Slip, and so St. Mary's home attendance soared. To help the crowd count, Madigan let kids into games for a dime. Sunday football had arrived in San Francisco long before the professional football 49ers opened for business in 1946. "It was all Slip Madigan," said Bernie Kish of the College Football Hall of Fame. "Nobody else did that. Notre Dame played on Saturday. He used his head on that. The man was ahead of his time. He was an innovator. If someone else had gone to St. Mary's, I'm not sure it would've happened."

The one St. Mary's player whom the fans flocked to see was Bettencourt, as dominating and exciting a college lineman as ever played on the West Coast, and possibly the entire country. During his storied career, he blocked ten kicks, recovered twenty fumbles, and scored twelve touchdowns. As a center! Plus he blocked punts in six consecutive games. Rockne and Warner dubbed him "the brainiest player on the coast." Red Grange called him the finest center he had ever seen, and encouraged him to join Grange's barnstorming pro team. Bettencourt refused, remaining at St. Mary's to get his degree, then signing a baseball contract with the St. Louis Browns as a catcher. Madigan fared well as his baseball coach. Over a three-year period, St. Mary's was undefeated in baseball against Cal, including 1925 with a three-game sweep of the Bears. Bettencourt played three seasons with the American League Browns, batting .258 for his big-league career. A consensus football All-American in 1927—St. Mary's very first first-team All-American—he entered the College Football Hall of Fame in 1974. He is, arguably, St. Mary's greatest football player.

In 1928, Amelia Earhart became the first woman aviator to fly solo across the Atlantic Ocean, Richard Byrd left New York to explore the Arctic, the iron lung respirator was introduced at Children's Hospital in Boston, and Herbert Hoover defeated Alfred E. Smith for the presidency. And in '28, Slip Madigan was a hot coaching hire despite his 5-4 record that season. His contract at St. Mary's had expired, and the University of Oregon offered him a raise to replace John McEwan as its head coach.

All this happened at the same time St. Mary's moved to a new setting. The Brickpile went up in flames, and the college relocated to the pastoral Moraga Valley, shifting from Alameda County to Contra Costa County, and winding up with four hundred pristine acres. Moraga consisted then of a general store, several ranches, and some cows grazing on the hills surrounding the campus. The campus itself, eventually one of the loveliest small college sites in the nation, remains untouched by commercialization. But as Madigan observed his new campus—built by his own football success—something was missing: A gymnasium. Where would his players dress? So Madigan and his trusted partner, Louis LeFevre, launched a fund-raising drive, and within a year Madigan Gym was built. Well, ghosts need a place to hang out, too.

"Madigan, in the seclusion of Moraga, an obscure place beyond the mighty range of mountains, will be able to work under the best conditions he has ever had at the school," the *Oakland Tribune* wrote in 1928. "The rocky field at the Broadway lot (in Oakland) is replaced by real turf, and the players will be able to get practice that they have not had before." Especially since the new practice field wouldn't be sloped and pockmarked, and Madigan wouldn't have to drag it with his car. For St. Mary's had hired a gardener to lighten his heavy load.

Madigan rejected Oregon and signed a five-year contract in 1928, when it also was rumored that he would leave for the University of Washington. He professed disinterest in Oregon, Washington, and even the National Football League, which also made overtures. "It's a big flop," he said of the NFL. "I'll never take an interest in it." His misread on the 1928 Gaels: "Not any weaker than in the past, and probably stronger." St. Mary's defeated the Young Men's Institute, 25-0 before losing to Cal, 7-0, on a 23-yard pass from Benny Lom to Robert Norton. "California's lack of scoring punch may be laid to St. Mary's line's having held to its advance reputation for durability," the *Daily Cal* commented. The Saints then wore down Gonzaga, 20-7, stomped Nevada, 22-0, fell to the Olympic Club, 6-0, and scored a 20-7 win over Santa Clara in The Little Big Game. "George Barsi of Santa Clara was the best ballplayer, offensively and defensively, on the field yesterday," reported the *San Francisco Chronicle*. Jack Merrick plunged over for one St. Mary's touchdown. Fred Stennett threw a fifteen-yard pass to Brian Driscoll for another. Then Stennett, dangerous with his legs as well as his arm, used an Ike Frankian block to break free on a 45-yard run for a third score. Frankian was carried off the field after a stellar performance.

St. Mary's then silenced USF, 13-0, and the West Coast Army, 12-0, but was vanquished by USC, 19-6. The Trojans struck early on Lloyd Thomas' 31-yard pass to Russ Saunders at the Gaels' 8. Thomas scored on the next play, avoiding Frankian's tackle. Stennett tied it on a 9-yard run, but "Dynamite" Don Williams put USC ahead for good with an 8-yard run in the third quarter. Stennett carried 15 times for 54 yards, while Williams was unstoppable, rushing 35 times for 157 yards. USC had dynamited St. Mary's twice since 1924. Hence payback.

The drop off in St. Mary's from the previous year: An anemic offense. The Gaels failed to score 30 points in a single game, just the second time that had happened in Madigan's first eight seasons. St. Mary's produced its second first-team All-American in as many seasons in Frankian, who proved part hero, part villain. Without facemasks back then, and with helmets optional, Frankian's closed fist kept blockers off him. Besides fracturing that Stanford player's cheekbone, he knocked other players unconscious. Booed by opposing fans when introduced before games, the booing continued with each tackle Frankian made. A magician in cleats, he often stole the football from an opponent's grasp. Foes had the opportunity to gain revenge, for Frankian didn't wear a helmet. But he clearly gave more than he got. On pure talent, he was rated the best West Coast end since Cal's Brick Muller in the early 1920s.

Frustrated by the results of '28, Madigan was re-energized by the time spring practice rolled around in '29. "Watch our smoke this season," he said, confidently. He also had a new gymnasium in his name, complete with an open-air swimming pool, plus ladies and gentlemen lounges, and a reception room—a plush gym in that day and age. At spring practice, he told his players, "Games are not won on the day they are played, but months ahead of time. Therefore, come back prepared (for fall practice)." Without adding what he was really thinking, he envisioned another unbeaten season.

And if Madigan's workload wasn't already loaded down with four sports to coach, plus his wearing an athletic director's hat, St. Mary's added a fifth sport, a boxing team. "I've boxed a little myself," he said, "but I wouldn't want the fellows to go against a team like Cal and get a flock of cauliflowers under my supervision." America found itself in a counter-punching situation in 1929 as the Great Depression hit, punching the nation in the gut, and flooring other news events: the St. Valentine's Day massacre in Chicago, the radio debut of "Amos and Andy," the opening of the first J.C. Penney's store in Milford, Delaware, and Roy Riegels' infamous wrong-way run in the Rose Bowl, giving Georgia Tech an 8-7 victory over California.

Four new rules greeted the 1929 season. Rule No. 1: All fumbles, except the fumbled forward pass, can be recovered by either team; the one difference being the fumbling side can run with the ball, but not the defensive side; the ball is dead upon recovery by the defense. Rule No. 2: The point after touchdown starts from the two-yard line, not the three-yard line. Rule No. 3: A lateral pass is dead once it strikes the ground. Rule No. 4: A fumbled punt is dead at the point of recovery.

Madigan protested the fumbled forward pass rule. "The astute gentlemen of the rules committee," he said, "are taking all the thrill out of football. They will kill the game, condemn it to a long painful death. . . . There is too much legislation today, too much in government, and too much in football. Take prohibition and take the fumble rule." He saw a humorous connection between legal fumbles and illegal hooch. St. Mary's had used the fumbled forward pass to its advantage several times. When the Oakland Raiders scored a game-winning touchdown against the San Diego Chargers on just such a crazy play in 1978, Slip Madigan's name surfaced once again as the play's innovator.

Madigan learned of another change involving the 1929 season, something that would impact the game forever: Football under the lights. St. Mary's intended to play an evening game against UCLA at the Los Angeles Coliseum "if proper lighting equipment is secured by the southern management before the fall," Madigan was told. If there was to be a first in football in anything, it seemed, it must bear Slip Madigan's name. But such a night meeting, if it turned out, was a year away.

So how much smoke would St. Mary's create that fall—big enough for a bonfire? The West Coast Army was first up for the Gaels, who thumped the soldiers, 28-0. Stennett threw two touchdown passes, 28 yards to Dick Boyle and 31 yards to Harry Ebding. Madigan put in a whole new unit in the second period, except for quarterback Barrett, who scored on a 15-yard run. Robert Patterson got the last touchdown, a one-yard plunge, as the Gaels rushed for 352 yards. St. Mary's offense didn't seem so anemic now, though the Army defense was more than accommodating.

A week later, the Gaels came down to Earth in Berkeley, playing Cal to a scoreless tie before 71,106. St. Mary's won everything but the game, throwing for more yards, 85 to 30, rushing for more yards, 135 to 10, and leading in first downs, 11 to 7. The Gaels had a first down at the Bears' 3, but Stennett was stopped all four times, the last time a yard from the end zone. Benny Lom then punted out of danger for Cal. It was a crazy weekend in college football, with seven games ending scoreless. "The game was clean," said Madigan, "just as every California-St. Mary's game is clean. My team did just right; whatever they do is always just right. I never hold postmortems. Cal and St. Mary's now is one of the biggest games on the coast."

But was that '26 victory over Cal a fluke? For St. Mary's hadn't beaten the Bears since. Madigan's dominance of the Bay Area had been fleeting, a shooting star flashing before its eyes. He quickly shifted the conversation to his next opponent, Gonzaga, against which he was 1-1-1. No easy pickin's there either. "We are facing a team that really has me worried," he said. "Some pundits said Gonzaga was the best team in the Northwest." His players disagreed, taking apart Gonzaga, 32-0 before 30,000 at Kezar, piling up 505 offensive yards, 331 on the ground. And, to think, the game was scoreless at halftime before St. Mary's exploded. Stennett threw a 10-yard pass to Boyle to launch the rout. Scheflin delivered a 15-yard touchdown strike to Patterson, before Scheflin scored on a 15-yard scamper. Barrett returned an interception to the Gonzaga 6 and scored on the next play. Cal Pitchford barreled over from the 4-yard line. The only negative: quarterback Butch Simas broke his nose and would be lost for three weeks.

St. Mary's and USF then squared off before a nearly empty stadium, 8,000 at Kezar. The Gray Fog played the Gaels even except for Bob Ackerman, who intercepted a Bob Kleckner pass and returned it 67 yards for the game's only score in a 7-0 St. Mary's victory. "We were going well," Madigan said a few days later, "until last week when we tackled USF. Now the team is down and is faced with battling its way up again. We are probably underdogs this week (against the Olympic Club)." The Gaels had lost two straight to the Olympic Club's older gridders, but had the upper hand this time, winning 17-0 before 35,000, Kezar's biggest crowd of the season. St. Mary's led 3-0 after three quarters on Ackerman's 15-yard field goal, then tallied twice in the final minutes on Barrett's 15-yard run and Stennett's 35-yard pass to Boyle. After five games, St. Mary's and Texas remained the only unbeaten, unscored upon teams in the country.

St. Mary's had played Cal to a scoreless tie, and Cal had beaten Santa Clara, 27-6, so it appeared St. Mary's would have an easy time against Santa Clara on the sixth week of the season. But the Little Big Game isn't predictable, because it's a rivalry game, and the Broncos played the Gaels even until the fourth quarter. Then Stennett threw 26 yards to reserve halfback Bud Toscani, who nearly tripped on a shoestring tackle, but he regained his balance and completed the 61-yard scoring play, thus enabling St. Mary's to escape with a 6-0 victory, while boosting its record to 5-0-1. On a sad note,

Santa Clara lineman Henry "Hank" Louma died after the game of peritonitis, which was related to his appendectomy the week before.

Rumors circulated regarding strained relations between Santa Clara and St. Mary's, and the possibility of their series being cancelled, which both schools denied. Two more rumors: A St. Mary's-Kentucky game on Christmas Day, and a St. Mary's-Vanderbilt game, both on the same day. Huh? Madigan debunked both rumors, believing that his Gaels stood a chance of playing in the Rose Bowl against an Eastern team. A bowl game on New Year's Day sounded more appealing, even though St. Mary's had yet to play in one.

The Gaels then met UCLA, although at 2 p.m., before a paltry crowd of 11,000 in Los Angeles. Madigan, assured of victory, started his second string for the first time, except for All-America tackle George Ackerman. The remaining first stringers played the second quarter and the last seven minutes of the game as St. Mary's coasted to a 24-0 victory. Boyle ran untouched around end for a 10-yard touchdown. Stennett connected with Ebding on a 31-yard scoring strike. Scheflin struck again, finding Patterson all alone in the end zone on a 17-yard pass. Then a blocked UCLA punt resulted in another touchdown. Texas finally surrendered a touchdown that weekend, leaving St. Mary's as the stingiest defense in college football.

St. Mary's picked up the pace against Nevada, routing the visiting Wolf Pack, 54-0, at Kezar. Exciting newcomer Toscani scored three touchdowns, including a 33-yard run. Boyle broke off a 53-yard run and Scheflin a 71-yard run for two more scores as the Gaels improved to 7-0-1. The official All-Coast team was announced afterward, with Ackerman the only Gael selected. Three USC players were picked: quarterback Marshall Duffield, end Francis Tappaan, and guard Nate Barrager, while Cal landed two, halfback Benny Lom and center Roy Riegels. Strangely, St. Mary's had the nation's best defense, and only one Gael was honored. Besides Ackerman, St. Mary's had other defensive stars in Armand Seghetti, Ebding and Hoot Herrin. Madigan felt slighted, but it wouldn't be the last time he felt that way in 1929.

Oregon, co-leader of Pacific Coast Conference, was the last obstacle between St. Mary's and an undefeated, unscored upon season. The Gaels started fast, and then got faster, building a 25-0 halftime lead. Ackerman blocked a punt and pounced on it for a touchdown. Stennett threw a 21-yard scoring pass to Ebding, and then Stennett scored on a 7-yard run. Scheflin completed the first-half's scoring on a 3-yard off-tackle play, before Boyle pushed the score to 31-0 on a 7-yard sweep. Then, finally, in the last quarter of their nine-game season, the Gaels yielded their first defensive touchdown, a 20-yard pass from halfback Bobby Robinson, one of the first African-Americans to play on the coast, to Al Browne.

Oregon reacted afterward as if it had won the game, instead of having lost, 31-6. "It doesn't matter to me what St. Mary's score was," said Ducks coach McEwan. "We scored on them, which is more than anyone else has done this year." A moral victory, if nothing else, but Oregon's players, good sports, voted 25-3 to send St. Mary's to the Rose Bowl. Pop Warner then announced his All-Coast team; Ackerman was the only Gael represented. Pop, it appeared, still was upset by the events of 1927.

Pittsburgh then rejected a Christmas Day game against St. Mary's. Who wanted to face that Gaels defense? Humorist Will Rogers stood up for St. Mary's, declaring, "We have a team out here called St. Mary's. Sounds effeminate, but they haven't lost a game since the gold rush." The New York American newspaper saluted Madigan as "the Miracle Man of football, taking over a program that had just lost a game, 127-0, and in nine seasons produced the nation's No. 1 defense and his second unbeaten season."

Madigan was irate that the Rose Bowl committee, like the All-Coast committee and Pop Warner, still thought of St. Mary's as a little tugboat in ocean waters. So he shut down his season at 9-0-1. And, sure enough, the Rose Bowl committee chose twice-beaten USC, to play on New Year's Day. The Trojans manhandled Pittsburgh, 47-14, but that 1929 St. Mary's team would have handled Pitt just as easily. Given the Gaels' stifling defense, even USC might have fallen to Madigan's mighty men.

Frustrated, Madigan looked eastward for recognition, the cogent advice of Knute Rockne still ringing in his ears. OK, thought Slip, if that's what it takes to get noticed. Get ready, Fordham, here comes St. Mary's.

7

"Sit Down, Slip!"

Slip Madigan seemed a changed person in 1932. His intensity had jacked up over the summer. His players, the fans, and even St. Mary's administration noticed the difference in the fall. An increasingly edgy Madigan paced up and down the sideline in a huff, as if he were mad at the universe. He'd jerk his Borsalino down over his eyes, or squash it, stomp on it, or kick it. He yelled at the game officials, using language he wouldn't dare use in church. The striped shirts regarded him as a moral man, but wondered if he had misplaced his moral compass.

Football coaches in 1932 coached from the bench, dictating their strategy. Fans in that era weren't accustomed to coaches who paced, and so they roared their displeasure at Madigan: "Sit down, Slip!" Their exhortations were unheeded, for he kept stalking the sideline, barking at anyone and everyone, while nervously spitting on his hands. "Sit Down, Slip!" He paid no attention, or he didn't even hear, as he appeared almost manic in driving his Gaels toward some greater destination.

His charged-up intensity didn't escape the press. San Francisco sportswriter Prescott Sullivan wrote: "In every St. Mary's crowd of, say, 50,000, 25,000 are there to see Madigan get licked, 25,000 to see him win." "Sit down, Slip!" Naturally, being Slip Madigan, there was a method to his mania. By firing up the fans, he fired up his players. Yet what that greater destination of his represented remained unclear. He had created a nationally recognized program from scratch in 1921, following that 127-0 debacle the year before. He had coached two undefeated teams, and two one-loss teams, with some of the largest attendance figures in the country. "Sit down, Slip!" The cry had a purpose. Madigan had elevated himself into a celebrity, even meeting the President of the United States at the White House. He was on top. Yet something ate at him, a burning desire that said, "Enough still isn't enough success." There was fire in his belly.

Only that burning desire inside him was an ulcer. Slow down, Slip? It wasn't possible either. His health now was an issue, but he kept driving himself. He scheduled even more ambitiously in 1932.

St. Mary's would play Fordham again in the East, but on the trip home, the Gaels would swing through Los Angeles, meeting UCLA in a night game, of all things. That evening matchup now was confirmed. The Gaels also would meet their first Deep South opponent, Alabama, in a season-ending game at Kezar Stadium. The Crimson Tide had fielded a powerhouse team, plus a bear-wrestling freshman named Paul Bryant, a future all-conference end who was paired with 'Bama All-American, and budding NFL legend, Don Hutson.

Madigan kept lifting St. Mary's higher and higher. And few colleges were as financially dependent on their football coach as St. Mary's was on its coach. Some 400,000 fans watched them play in 1931. The campus chapel in Moraga, a $2 million project, was attributed to Gaels attendance figures. Gate receipts erected additional buildings on campus. Student enrollment jumped from 135 in 1921 to 900 in 1931, largely because of Gaels football. "Sit down, Slip!" was making St. Mary's stand tall, richer. Thus he was rewarded in '31 with four assistant football coaches: Vincent McNally, Red Strader, Ike Frankian and Herc Fletcher. Madigan's coaching of other sports was reduced because of his time-consuming success on the gridiron. Football ruled the Moraga hills.

A high-water mark of eighty-five candidates reported for practice in 1932. Madigan had three key players to replace: Toscani, Fischer, and Fletcher. "Fischer was the greatest guard on the coast last year, and Toscani was a great athlete," said Madigan. "But we have plenty of right halfbacks. Brovelli should fill the bill." Ah, Angelo Brovelli, who won over a nation as a sophomore, and then was an afterthought as a junior while struggling with injuries. "The Dark Angel of the Moragas" was healthy again as a senior, and ready to restore his reputation, but at halfback, not fullback. Bill Beasley was moved from right half to quarterback, or blocking back, where he would switch off with Sid Ahern each mid-quarter. The way that worked, one player got the first eight minutes of the quarter, the other player the last seven minutes. Only Slip Madigan could create such a system. Charley "Rubber Legs" Baird was back at left half, with four fullback candidates—Gord Partee, George Dodson, Santo Garbo, and Al Nichelini, a speedy 200-pound sophomore with the biggest upside. The Gaels backfield averaged 189 pounds per man, which was unusual in the 1930s, when many college lines didn't average that much.

St. Mary's was equally strong up front, especially with its brother bookends, ends Fred and George Canrinus. Guard Mike Steponovich and tackle Carl Jorgensen, the latter born in Denmark, were other All-Coast candidates. But all eyes were on Brovelli, a quadruple threat—runner, passer, kicker, defensive force—if healthy. "Another Gael who might make history is Angel Brovelli, a colorful though brittle player," wrote Gael loyalist Pat Frayne. To meet their head coach's high expectations, the Gaels needed to dominate. That wouldn't be easy, as Madigan noted: "I don't believe there is a state in the union that has such strong teams as USC, California, Stanford, UCLA, Santa Clara and St. Mary's." St. Mary's would play each of those schools, minus Gaels-loathing Stanford, in '32.

New rules were adopted that season: Use of hands on offense was restricted; the flying wedge on kickoffs—a violent tactic—was banned; frequent substitution, instead of substitutions only by quarter, now was permitted; uniform padding had increased; a new fumble interpretation rule stated that if the ball came out once the knee hit the ground, the ball is dead. Madigan protested the dead-ball rule, believing it would make the game dull. Tough-hitting St. Mary's always looked to force a fumble.

Madigan's players feared him, with his booming voice and stern presence. He'd joke with them at times, trying to lessen the tension that had built up, but getting mixed results. He leaned on his educational background to bring a balance to the grueling work on the practice field. And so he read the Gaels poems. He loved poetry himself, including Walt Whitman's "Leaves of Grass." Madigan selected Whitman's "Song of Myself," a segment of "Leaves of Grass," to read to his players.

"I have heard what the talkers are talking, the talk of the beginning and end, but I don't talk of the beginning or the end," he quoted Whitman. "There was never any more inception than there is now, nor any more youth than there is now. And there will never be any more perfection than there is now, nor any more heaven or hell than there is now. Urge and urge and urge, always the procreant urge of the world."

Madigan's message to his players: You're only young once, and if you wish to achieve perfection on the football field, there is only now, and you must urge yourselves forward toward that immediate goal. An undefeated season against a formidable schedule would mean heaven. "There you have it, men. Perfection. So what will it be?" But it felt like hell getting there with a pacing, spitting, and barking head coach.

Would the luck of the Irish be with the Gaels that season? In 1926, unbeaten St. Mary's had Phil Murphy at tackle. In 1929, unbeaten St. Mary's had Frank Murphy at tackle. In 1932, St. Mary's had Joe Murphy at tackle. However, it would take more than four-leaf clovers to make an impression during the Depression. "The St. Mary's-California contest will be the first game of the year that may pack them in, "projected Owen Merrick in the *San Francisco News*, "despite the fact that many of the fans will not have as much loose money as they possessed last year."

St. Mary's opened against the West Coast Army. Both Madigan and Stanford's Pop Warner scouted the Army's 7-6 victory over the Olympic Club, with the two men carefully seated two rows apart. Madigan also scouted Cal's 20-6 victory over U.C. Davis. He was highly impressed with Cal, predicting it would be "very much in the running not only for a conference championship, but also with the high possibilities of competing with the best in our country for national honors."

As for the footballin' soldiers, Madigan said, "The West Coast Army looks like it will be a tough opener for us. No longer is the Army a setup for anyone. I now fear Army." But West Coast Army coach John Stokes wasn't overly confident about his team: "We may not make many touchdowns, but we'll be in there shooting for them sixty minutes of every game." Shooting; perfect military strategy.

Yet with six Army regulars sitting out the St. Mary's game with injuries, it wasn't much of a shooting match. The Gaels won 21-0 before 12,000 at

Kezar. Partee broke off a 10-yard touchdown run in the first quarter. Nichelini added a 7-yard run and Beasley a 12-yard scamper for fourth quarter touchdowns. Brovelli and newcomer Nichelini ran hard for the Gaels. Before his next opponent, Nevada, Madigan received this note from St. Mary's president Brother Leo: "My dear Slip: Merely to say that I'm wishing you and the boys all manner of success on Saturday, and on all the other critical days of the season. Of course, will be pleased with a victory, but whatever the outcome, we're for you and with you. In my own little way, I ask God to fill you with His power and His joy."

Madigan's Gaels wouldn't need divine intervention against Nevada, galloping over the Wolf Pack, 35-0, at Kezar. The state of Nevada had legalized gambling the year before, but the Wolf Pack was a bad bet against St. Mary's that day. The Gaels showed off their depth. Reserve back George Wilson ran for two touchdowns in just the first quarter as the Gaels took a commanding 21-0 lead. Wilson rushed for 63 yards on 9 carries, while the bruising Brovelli piled up 80 yards on 6 carries, scoring on a 1-yard plunge. Local writers called Wilson "a sophomore sensation," likening him to the Brovelli of two seasons past.

Even with two wins, both shutouts, Madigan was cautious about his third opponent, ever-dangerous Cal. "I might say that I always thought we could beat California," he said, "and that we were prepared to beat them, had plays to beat them, but they won the majority of the games. I'll never take a game with the Bears as a cinch until the game is over and we have the long end of the score." A voice from the East Coast seemed to favor the Gaels over the Bears. "From what I've seen of St. Mary's, I would say that Coach Ed 'Slip' Madigan has improved on the Notre Dame system," said Charley Brickley, Harvard's famous All-America back of the early 1900s. Cal would be the judge of that.

The Bears, though, faced St. Mary's without backfield star Hank Schaldach, dealing with a sprained ankle. Only his absence offered the Gaels no advantage as the game ended in a 12-12 deadlock before 50,000 in Berkeley. The tie felt like a loss to Madigan, who made a critical boo-boo in the first quarter with an illegal double substitution that resulted in a 25-yard penalty against his team. The press would show him no mercy for that gaffe. The Gaels scored first on Rubber Legs Baird's 4-yard run, but Cal caught up when Augustus Castro intercepted a Beasley pass and rambled 75 yards for a touchdown. Nichelini put St. Mary's in front again with an 11-yard run, set up by Baird's 53-yard pass to Felix Pennino. St. Mary's needed a goal-line stand to make off with a win, but on fourth-and-goal from the Gaels' 5, Cal's Arleigh Williams cut through tackle and into the end zone. Four touchdowns, four missed PATs. Leon Valianos could have won it for Cal, but his dropkick following Williams' score sailed wide. St. Mary's still had time to pull off a victory, but Brovelli lost a fumble and Wilson was intercepted before time expired. St. Mary's amassed more yards, 131 to 81, and more first downs, 11 to 7, but had more turnovers, 4-2. The end result: Cal still had St. Mary's number.

"California's line played a very important part in this contest, but we were extremely off color in our entire play," assessed Madigan. "We propose to continue the 1932 season undefeated, and we're not gambling on the University of San Francisco situation. I'll start as many of the first squad as are available for next Sunday's game."

USF, the former St. Ignatius, would play St. Mary's tougher in the 1930s, but usually from the short end of the score. The Gaels won, 16-7, in 1932. Dodson scored on a 1-yard run. Then Steponovich and Jorgensen teamed to block a Jack Bradley punt for a safety, also in the second quarter. But it took an 83-yard touchdown pass from Baird to Nichelini in the fourth quarter for the Gaels to ice the victory. USF led in first downs, 9 to 5, and in total yards, 107 to 102, but lost four fumbles, including one at the Gaels' 3-yard line. Brovelli carried once for three yards, and then left the game with a bruised shoulder, the latest injury issue for the Dark Angel.

Death then struck the Gaels. Harry Lawlor, 18, a member of their freshman team, succumbed in an Oakland hospital of injuries—a telescope spine and fractured vertebrae—suffered in an interclass game. Lawlor tackled Harry Masterson by using his head on a grassy field in Moraga. Lawlor had hoped to make the Gaels varsity in 1933.

Next up for St. Mary's was Santa Clara, which had beaten Cal, 12-0, two weeks before the Gaels-Bears tie. Little surprise, but Pop Warner picked Santa Clara to beat St. Mary's. Broncos coach Clipper Smith was optimistic. "They'll have to hit us somewhere else besides the middle of the line," he said. "We're ready for them. I'm confident that we'll handle Brovelli's best shots. We feel we have a good chance to win."

In what would be their best performance of the season, the Gaels turned back the keyed-up Broncos, 14-13, before 59,000 at Kezar. Santa Clara owned the first half. Frank Sobrero threw an 8-yard touchdown pass to Gil Dowd on a fourth-down play. Bill Denser then avoided Steponovich's lunge at guard and rambled 70 yards for a 13-0 Broncos lead at halftime. Madigan read from Walt Whitman in the locker room: "There will never be any more perfection than there is now." The Gaels emerged as a totally different team in the second half. Sobrero was gang-tackled and the ball popped free, Jorgensen recovering at the Broncos 5-yard line. Brovelli, bad shoulder notwithstanding, scored from the 3, and Jorgensen kicked the PAT. Then Jack Baat threw a 43-yard pass to Fred Canrinus down to the Santa Clara 3, from where Nichelini punched it over. Jorgensen's second PAT decided the game in which Santa Clara won the yardage battle, 197-142. Even though, St. Mary's was 4-0-1, it looked vulnerable, a quality Madigan hadn't anticipated before the season. Next up: a revenge match awaiting the Gaels on the opposite coast.

New York City had something new to show the Gaels' traveling show in 1932: the opening of Radio City Music Hall. But '32 also marked the deaths of Broadway follies legend Flo Ziegfield and baby Charles Lindbergh, Jr., who had been kidnapped and murdered. The Dow Jones index reached a record low that year, a farmers' revolt occurred in the Midwest, and Babe Ruth famously pointed to the center field fence and homered in that direction against the Chicago Cubs in the World Series.

But how could Madigan make the trip back to New York City any more inviting than in 1930? Well, he planned an itinerary to outdo even himself. The trip would cost $227 per train passenger, and include, besides railway transportation, lodging and meals (except in New York and Los Angeles), a tour of the Grand Canyon, sightseeing in Chicago and New York, plus tickets to the Fordham and UCLA games. Passengers would board Oct. 30 and return home Nov. 13, a trip that included lively banter, and cocktails, with coach Madigan providing both.

But as the train traveled east, a big block headline appeared: "MADIGAN TO TAKE THE NOTRE DAME JOB?" To the press, it seemed a natural fit, one of Rockne's boys succeeding Rockne as head coach of the Fighting Irish. Madigan quickly denied such speculation: "I built up St. Mary's. I put my coaching life into them. I have no intention of leaving them as my contract with St. Mary's runs until 1933. I am happy there. Conditions are ideal." Besides, in 1932, he moved into a home in the Oakland foothills, the same home that has Madigans living in it to this day. Also in 1932, his first son, and his third child, was born on Feb.12. Three more reasons to stay put, as he was now entrenched.

Fordham had waited two years for this rematch, remembering how its 12-0 halftime lead in '30 turned into a 20-12 loss, making Angelo Brovelli the nation's darling. Fordham wouldn't let this latest opportunity "slip" away. Before 40,000 at the Polo Grounds, the Rams evened the score with a resounding 14-0 victory. St. Mary's caught an early break when team captain Bill Beasley recovered a Fordham fumble at the Rams' 22-yard line. The Rams got the ball right back as Beasley was intercepted by Tony Sarusky, setting up Ed Danowski's 38-yard touchdown pass to James Cowhig. The talented Danowski later hit Frank McDermott with a 38-yard scoring pass. Only two touchdowns were scored, but Fordham had a clear advantage in yardage gained, 223 to 146, the Rams piling up 151 rushing yards.

Brovelli wasn't the hero of New York this time, though he played stalwartly against a dominant defense, carrying 15 times for 46 rugged yards, plus tackling Rams all over the field, recovering a fumble, and picking off a Danowski pass. The Dark Angel tilted the field, win or lose. Madigan said, "Fordham was the hardest-rushing team we faced this season. Brovelli played an inspired game, and never have I witnessed such an ovation to a player on a losing team in a strange city." He added that the Santa Clara game and the 3,000-mile trip "took too much out of the boys." That same cross-county trip didn't seem to fatigue the Gaels in 1930, but the 1932 Gaels weren't quite as tough or determined. On the '32 return trip, the Gaels avoided disaster in Kansas when a train traveling just ahead of their train crashed into five freight cars that had slipped from a siding. The St. Mary's train, with 100 passengers, avoided the accident and proceeded westward toward southern California.

Then in its first night game, and very likely the first evening game played at the Los Angeles Memorial Coliseum, St. Mary's took on UCLA before 63,000 homebodies. The Bruins got on St. Mary's quickly when Mike Frankovich, their quarterback and future Hollywood producer, threw a 50-yard touchdown pass to Bobby Decker. St. Mary's tied the score at 7-7 when Rubber Legs Baird circled left end on a 10-yard run. Beasley settled matters in the fourth quarter with a 13-yard touchdown run for a 14-7 victory. Beasley rushed for 85 yards and Baird for 81. Madigan accomplished a new milestone under the lights. And St. Mary's clickety-clacked home with a road split and a 5-1-1 record.

Only the Gaels didn't return en masse. Brovelli, end Garry Vivaldi, Baird and Steponovich all missed the train. Madigan immediately suspended the four, then rescinded on three of the four suspensions. Steponovich was kicked off permanently; the other three were given a reprieve. "Brovelli told me years later that my father was awfully good to him, maybe when he didn't have to be," said Ed Madigan.

St. Mary's improved to 6-1-1 with a 7-0 victory over a solid Oregon team. The Gaels weren't blowing anyone out, save Nevada, but they weren't being blown out either. Madigan felt the reinstated Brovelli was the star of the game, with 14 carries for 60 yards. "I'm proud of him," Madigan said after Brovelli led an 80-yard drive that resulted in Sid Ahern's 2-yard pass to George Canrinus. Madigan omitted mentioning his benching of the inconsistent Brovelli in the first half. "I thought our boys did mighty well to pull through with one touchdown as Oregon is one of the finest and hardest-playing football teams we have ever met." Oregon coach Prink Callison praised his Ducks, calling it "our best game of the season."

Following the Oregon win, the International News Service selected its All-Cost team, with suspended guard Steponovich the only St. Mary's selection. Brovelli and Jorgensen were second-team choices. Steponovich also was a second-team All-America pick by the *New York Post* newspaper. Brovelli was the only Gael named first team All-Coast by the Associated Press. With Steponovich set to miss the season finale against Alabama, he remained one of the rare college footballers either to be named All-Coast and All-American (second team) after playing only seven games or, take your pick, being suspended for two games.

Alabama became St. Mary's only Deep South opponent during Madigan's nineteen seasons of coaching the Gaels, who later met another southern team—beating Georgia Tech, 41-19, in the 1946 Oil Bowl—before St. Mary's dropped big-time football. Talented Alabama faced the Gaels in

'32 after beating an undefeated Vanderbilt squad, 20-0. The Crimson Tide was led by All-America Johnny "Hurry" Cain, a halfback who was as fast as his name suggested. With 25,000 watching at Kezar Stadium, Cain sprinted 71 yards on the game's tenth play for the only score in a 6-0 Alabama win. Other than that deciding run, it was a bruising defensive battle.

"I've been watching Alabama teams in the Rose Bowl games," said Madigan, recalling when cowboy movie hero Johnny Mack Brown was a standout back for the Tide in the 1920s, "and I think this is the greatest team that has ever represented the South against a western team. Their blocking and tackling were superb." Frank Thomas, the Alabama coach, was equally exuberant about Brovelli: "He's one of the greatest backs I ever saw in my life. I've seen them at Notre Dame, and I've seen them in the Midwest and the East and the South. And I'm telling you this Brovelli is one of the greatest."

Brovelli, playing his final game for the red and blue, rushed 12 times for 65 yards, intercepted a pass, and was a tiger on defense. Thus the sun set on The Dark Angel of the Moragas. He then played two seasons with the Pittsburgh Pirates, the future Steelers, of the National Football League, rushing 97 times for 348 yards, catching six passes for 137 yards, scoring three touchdowns and standing out on defense before leaving the game rather suddenly.

After finishing 6-2-1 in 1932, Madigan wasn't visible on the Moraga campus over the ensuing winter months. Rumors circulated that he was growing too big in stature for the college, or that he wasn't putting in the necessary time because of contract issues, or that he was about to be fired. All that conjecture stirred up his Irish blood to its boiling point.

"It's all a lie," he said. "I don't know where people dig up such rubbish. I don't know of any trouble with a new contract, because we haven't discussed it yet. The reason I haven't been around campus is because my stomach is on the bum. They don't expect someone to go around with a big grin on his pan if he's got a stomach ache, do they?"

An ulcer, not a stomach ache, perhaps explained his sideline demeanor—the pacing, the spitting on his hands, the yelling at game officials, the stomping of his Borsalino, and the fans responding: "Sit down, Slip!" The pressure of winning was eating away at Slip Madigan. That pressure, and his ulcer, weren't about to disappear anytime soon.

8

Catholic Order Disorder

With Christmas approaching in 1933, an envelope arrived on the desk of the Rev. James J. Lyons, S.J., president of Santa Clara University. The contents didn't offer a yuletide greeting, but rather a un-holiday-like letter from an alumnus, San Francisco attorney Norbert Korte, who sounded angry enough to prosecute Slip Madigan.

"I am writing to commend and congratulate you upon the action you took Monday, December 4th, in severing athletic relations with St. Mary's College," Korte wrote. "It took a great deal of courage to do this because of the financial questions and almost certain losses Santa Clara will suffer. However, it is gratifying to see someone at the head of my Alma Mater who places his interest in the young men under his care on a higher plane than material things.

"It must be gratifying to the parents of these young men to see the person in charge of their sons take such drastic action to safeguard the proper forming of their moral characters. Santa Clara is primarily an educational institution and not a football factory, and strives to teach its sons the spirit of true sportsmanship. Continued relations with St. Mary's jeopardized that aim. It is likewise gratifying to see you remove that jeopardy. . . ."

Jeopardy? What jeopardy? Was not Madigan teaching his St. Mary's players the spirit of true sportsmanship as well? Korte was inferring that Madigan preached a rogue brand of football, a below-the-belt accusation that hadn't ever arisen during Madigan's thirteen seasons at St. Mary's, although Pop Warner certainly inferred as much.

In 2016, Madigan's son, Ed, laughed when shown Korte's letter, written eighty-three years earlier. "You know, the Jesuits and Christian Brothers had quite a rivalry," he pointed out. Santa Clara was a Jesuit school, and St. Mary's a Christian Brothers institution, and never the twain shall meet, harmoniously. Nonetheless, cancelling all athletic relations between them seemed a stretch. "My dad's teams played tough, physical football, but they weren't dirty," said Ed Madigan. "But you have to remember that Santa Clara couldn't beat my dad's teams."

Through 1933, Santa Clara had beaten St. Mary's once in twelve tries: A Bronco win in 1923 and a tie in '33. Thus Santa Clara was frustrated in having watched the Gaels achieve national recognition, while the Broncos hadn't yet scaled such lofty heights. It was a blow to Santa Clara, observing the Christian Brothers gloating at their Jesuit neighbor's expense. And so The Little Big Game, the annual St. Mary's-Santa Clara football contest, was cancelled for whatever the explanation.

Slip Madigan had that perplexing situation on his mind as he sailed to Hawaii the day after Christmas in 1933 with his wife and two daughters, leaving 21-month-old Edward home with his maternal grandmother. Aboard ship, Slip thought of some way to save the Little Big Game, while also replaying the previous three months, watching his Gaels lose three games for the first time in five years, churning his stomach even more.

That 1933 season had held such promise, a return cross-county trek to New York to play Fordham, and another trip to Los Angeles to face USC. Plus local nemesis California and a new relationship: College of Pacific, a Stockton, California, school with its new coach, living legend Amos Alonzo Stagg, then 71. For the second time, Madigan scheduled four Pacific Coast Conference schools in the same season: Cal, USC, UCLA and Oregon. He was 3-1 against them in 1931, losing to UCLA.

Madigan received a five-year contract to start the season, without once being asked during the Depression, he noted, "to take a cut." At 37, he was the longest-serving coach on the West Coast, with no interest in going elsewhere, even though he remained in high demand. No coach anywhere could have matched his construction job at St. Mary's, building a castle out of matchsticks. St. Mary's had known two different campuses during his employment, but still without its own campus stadium, unlike Cal and Stanford.

Nevertheless, his annual attendance figures regularly surpassed theirs, not to mention every other school in the country save USC and sometimes Notre Dame. And St. Mary's was winning its football wars with a small army, for its enrollment was miniscule compared to its opponents. Masterfully, Madigan turned negatives into positives. St. Mary's truly was the mouse that roared.

Madigan continued attracting top football recruits. A larger roster, and larger players, showed up in 1933: One hundred candidates, counting the varsity and the freshman teams. Fifty-five players reported for spring practice, with Madigan quickly separating the top fifteen. The other forty drilled on an alternate field; for the first time, he had enough talent to field two solid units. Competition was fierce, as players either were inspired to move ahead or were determined to hold their own. Thus spring scrimmages were as bloody as autumn football games.

Madigan had cornered the market on prime beef. He had the biggest college line in the land, averaging 223 pounds per man, a gathering of size that was unbelievably massive in that day and age. His ends were Fred Canrinus, 206, and Felix Pennino, 205, with George Canrinus, 208, a capable backup. The tackles were Carl Jorgensen, 212, and John Yezerski, 242, while the guards were Matt Basnyo, 257, and Ed Gilbert, 238. The center was Mervin "Hurry Up" Yates at 204. Madigan was high on another guard Hugh Geradin, who weighed 204, but had the strength of a 230-pounder. Speaking of size, most National Football League lines weren't that large. The training table in Moraga required a huge budget.

"Discipline is as essential in football as in life," Madigan lectured his players, "and you young athletes must learn that." He hadn't forgotten the suspensions of Angelo Brovelli, Mike Steponovich and two others from the year before, and he was guarding against further rules violations. And so he introduced his NRA policy—"no running around"—forbidding the players to leave campus during preseason practice.

Pop Warner left Stanford for Temple in 1933, a coaching move he later regretted as paradise lost. Though Warner didn't reschedule St. Mary's after losing to the Gaels in 1927, he predicted, based on inside information, that the two schools would commence, following his departure, a six-year relationship by 1935. Warner needed new sources, because such a renewed relationship had no chance of ever happening.

Madigan's close relationship with sportswriters was something he worked at, even though he enjoyed playing with their minds. He concocted formations that mystified them, to the point of writers opening dictionaries and even scientific manuals to try and uncover their meanings. One such formation was the "Gyroscopic Relevator," with Madigan's guards using "full sense exterior motion." Perhaps, another way of saying "pulling guards?" Sometimes, Madigan even mystified himself with his concoctions. Take his new backfield formation "Italo Balbo," based on, he said, the flight plans of Italian pilots. This concept had the left halfback, quarterback and right halfback lining up side by side by side, from tackle to tackle, with the fullback lined up behind them, and directly back of the center. Well, Italo Balbo barely got off the ground. The topper, though, was Madigan's "Potentochric Energoffense." He was having way too much fun. The press, wisely, changed the subject. "Tell us, Slip, about the deer you shot in the off-season, and the rattlesnake your wife killed with a rake in your backyard." At least, those last two incidents weren't concocted.

Madigan began fall practice brimming with optimism. He projected that Santo Garbo "has the possibility of being St. Mary's greatest fullback since Red Strader." Madigan also praised the heft and toughness of guard Matt Brasnyo. Madigan's optimism shifted toward pessimism when Garbo re-injured the neck that cost him the 1932 season, and Brasnyo came down with pneumonia. Thus their '33 seasons were over before they started. Then on August 29, Madigan learned that the Fordham coach, Frank "Iron Major" Cavanaugh, died after a lingering illness at 57. "I know no more courageous, no finer man than Major Cavanaugh," he told the press. "He was a man to be admired. He was a fighter, fearless. In World War I, he was wounded eleven times. It took courage to continue as he did at Fordham. He was considerably like Knute Rockne—a great coach, a worthy rival." But not until Cavanaugh congratulated him after defeating Fordham in 1930 did Madigan discover that the Iron Major was nearly blind. Fearless, indeed.

Madigan addressed the '33 Gaels: "The first few games will determine our season. We know USC is laying for us. But our big game is with California; that's because it's a question of local supremacy and a long-standing rivalry. The day of the ideal schedule is past. Out here on the Pacific Coast, the competition is so keen. Every one of the games is a big game. Add to this that it's $33^1/_3$ percent harder to play away from home." Madiganmathics at work.

Prior to each season, Madigan customarily treated writers who covered the Gaels to dinner. After the 1933 dinner, the *Oakland Tribune*'s Don Glendon wrote: "Slip is an actor born. He understands people, a ringmaster with color, poise, and a private patented brand of 'hokum.'" Madigan certainly kept notebooks filled. He was quite literary himself, writing for four publications, at a penny a word. A well-rounded man, he read books, he loved the opera, and he loved to garden. He kept up an astonishing pace for a coach, working up to seventeen hours a day with an ulcer during the football season. That why he kept a cot in the back of his office, because he often didn't make it home in the fall.

How serious was USC about playing St. Mary's in 1933? Three USC scouts—plus a USC secretary—scouted the Gaels opener against the University of San Francisco at Kezar Stadium. There wasn't much in the way of excitement to report back to Trojans coach Howard Jones as St. Mary's won, 7-0, before 25,000. The Gaels' Fred Canrinus blocked a Bob Hall punt and Ed Gilbert fell on it at USF's 9-yard line. George Wilson reached the end zone in two runs. Carl Jorgensen kicked the extra point and that took care of the outcome, though the game was more one-sided than the score indicated. St. Mary's held USF without a single first down and minus four yards on offense—the best defense in the country that day. Future college and professional coach, end Eddie Erdelatz, caught two passes for 38 yards in his St. Mary's debut.

What did Howard Jones learn? "Slip Madigan has one of the best lines in the country. We know that," he said. "Our scouts brought back the information that St. Mary's has one of the strongest defenses they have seen." Odds makers must have agreed with Jones as St. Mary's was made a 10-8 favorite over its next opponent, Cal. But because it was St. Mary's playing on Cal's turf, odds made little difference. Strawberry Canyon had become a burial site for St. Mary's aspirations.

The Gaels' reputation under Madigan was starting off games slowly, and then vanquishing opponents in the second half. This reputation was reversed in '33 before 65,000 at Memorial Stadium. St. Mary's built a 13-0 lead early as Gilbert blocked Arleigh Williams' punt and Fred Canrinus pounced on it for a touchdown. Nichelini scored the Gaels second touchdown on a short run, but Jorgensen missed one of his two PAT attempts. Still, the Gaels led 13-7, when Madigan sent in his second unit to hold the lead. That would prove the Gaels' undoing. For with four minutes left to play, and Cal perched on its 26-yard line, Williams began chewing up yardage from his tailback position. The Bears marched 74 yards through St. Mary's staunch defense to score a comeback 14-13 win on Williams' short plunge and Floyd Bowers' second conversion kick. Cal merely had to throw its helmet on the field, it seemed, and St. Mary's was beaten. Madigan now was 2-9-2 against the Golden Bears. "It was a disappointment, but the team that proved better won the game," he said. Then he blamed himself: "I pulled my first unit too early." St. Mary's roster was deep, but not deep enough to conquer Cal.

USC was St. Mary's third opponent, and the Trojans were anxious to reverse their 13-7 loss to the Gaels in 1931, a defeat that cost Troy an undefeated season, though not the national championship. Madigan, fearing USC's penchant for making long gains, started two new guards, Bernard Schaefer and Nebb Elduayan, to plug up the middle. USC was a 10-6 favorite as 80,000 gathered inside the Los Angeles Memorial Coliseum. St. Mary's found itself engulfed by Trojan red and gold.

Once again, St. Mary's struck quickly. Fred Canrinus faked his way into the clear and Wilson hit him with a perfectly led 47-yard touchdown pass. Then St. Mary's dug in against backfield star Cotton Warburton and the explosive USC offense, holding it in check, although Nichelini saved two touchdowns by catching the speedy Warburton twice. Officials' flags proved detrimental to St. Mary's as penalty calls helped the Trojans score two touchdowns and a 14-7 win. An interference ruling against Nichelini occurred ten yards from where the pass was thrown. Then Ed Gilbert said something to an official and received an unsportsmanlike penalty. "I didn't mean to talk," Gilbert told the press afterward in a solemn St. Mary's locker room. "I only said, 'Come on, fellows, hit 'em hard and low.' And for those remarks, I cost the gang the ball game." Then Gilbert cried in front of his locker.

Regardless of his feelings about the questionable officiating, Madigan, as usual, took the high road. "We played our best football," he said. Howard Jones, after achieving his 26th consecutive victory with that revenge win, immediately removed St. Mary's from future schedules. He explained:

"We can't have too many hard games on our schedule. When I schedule a non-conference team, I like to get a rest. St. Mary's is no rest." USC often played the toughest schedule in the country, yet it feared playing St. Mary's, total respect for Slip Madigan.

Unaccustomed to being 1-2 to start a season, Madigan wasn't taking any more chances. He personally scouted the fourth opponent, Nevada. But while rushing to the Oakland Airport to catch a flight to Reno, he was stopped for speeding. Nevada coach Brick Mitchell, needing to motivate his team, called St. Mary's, not USC, "the most powerful team on the coast. No, I mean it, the most powerful and the best, bar none. I saw the St. Mary-USC game. The Gaels didn't get many breaks that day."

The Gaels didn't need breaks against Nevada, walloping the Wolf Pack, 61-0, at Kezar Stadium. Nichelini bulled his way for 103 yards in the first quarter, and Herb Schreiber ran for 107 more in the second quarter as Madigan substituted freely. Even George Canrinus, an end, gained 92 yards on three carries, roughly thirty yards per carry. St. Mary's rolled up 548 yards to the visitor's 39, and 27 first downs to 3 for Nevada, which earned two first downs by penalties.

That year's St. Mary's trip to New York coincided with the 21st Amendment, the repeal of Prohibition. Booze now could be consumed legally, though that didn't seem a factor on St. Mary's previous "streetcar alumni" and working press cocktail-consuming adventures across America. Also occurring in 1933: Calvin Coolidge's death, Mount Rushmore's dedication, the film release of "King Kong," "The Lone Ranger" radio debut, the first drive-in movie (Camden, New Jersey), and Guiseppe Zamora's attempt to assassinate President Roosevelt, but instead resulted in the killing of Chicago Mayor Anton J. Cermak.

St. Mary's had beaten Fordham, 20-12 in 1930, while Fordham prevailed, 14-0, in 1932. So this was the "rubber match." With a new Fordham coach, Jim Crowley of Four Horseman lore, the Rams were undefeated after four games, including a 2-0 victory against a strong Alabama eleven. Gaels assistant Red Strader, after scouting that game, said, "The Rams strength is line play and defense." Right after the Nevada game, the Gaels boarded a train, stopping the first time in Alva, Oklahoma, for a team workout. Then it was off to Chicago for two days of practice and a visit to the Century of

Progress Exposition. The traveling party even stopped by Niagara Falls before reaching New York City. St. Mary's practiced the next two days at the Polo Grounds before taking on the "Big Maroon," as the Fordham Rams often were called.

Despite Fordham's 4-0 record, the 2-2 Gaels were made a 6-5 favorite. Grantland Rice offered his own poetic prediction: "Who says the dinosaurs are dead? Who says the caveman's race is run? Hark! Listen to the tread of mammoth and mastodon! The Ram still guards his spotless den. Here's to the record Fordham's made. And yet today, with shaking pen, I pick St. Mary's by a shade, Slip Madigan's bisonic crew, it seems to me, at last is due." The mammoth-like Gaels hit town once again after sleeping on a train for 3,000 miles and seeing the sights, a pleasure trip. Meanwhile, the Rams slept in their own beds. So who should be favored?

The odds makers were right this time. The Gaels had the upper hand for the second time in three meetings. With 52,000 people watching, George Wilson added to an All-America-like season by smashing through the Rams for one touchdown, followed by Fred Canrinus falling on teammate Gord Partee's fumble in the end zone after the latter coughed up the football following an 8-yard run to the 3. The Rams' Ed Danowski, a single-wing threat who later led the New York Giants to two NFL titles, engineered Fordham's one touchdown drive. Danowski had the Rams moving toward pay dirt again late in the game, but St. Mary's guards Ed Gilbert and Nebb Elduayan led a defensive stand that stopped the Rams short of the goal line. St. Mary's walked out of the Polo Grounds with a 13-7 victory that enhanced its dominant reputation once again. The Gaels had overpowered the Rams on total yardage, 202 to 119, with 192 of those yards coming on the ground as Wilson and Nichelini led the charge. "I love 'em," a smiling Madigan said of his team. "I asked them to go out and win this one if they never win another, and did they give it everything they had? Man, oh man, oh man, but you saw some football today. I knew they had it in them."

There was a new president in the White House from the Gaels previous two trips, but they didn't get to meet Franklin Delano Roosevelt. A message came that he was too occupied with his New Deal plan, focused on reviving a Depression-ridden nation. So FDR's secretary, Mervyn McIntyre, greeted the disappointed Gaels instead. Not even a Secretary of Defense to meet the maestro of defense, Slip Madigan. Then it was back on the train, for there would be another game, against the College of Pacific, awaiting the Gaels in Stockton before they returned to campus. The team stopped briefly in South Bend so Madigan could revisit his alma mater and offer a prayer to Rockne's family. Then it was off to Colorado to fit in another practice, plus seeing the Royal Gorge. After one more stop in Salt Lake for another workout, the team arrived in Stockton, where another face on football's Mount Rushmore of coaches was now employed.

"St. Mary's will be tough," said Amos Alonzo Stagg, the College of Pacific's senior citizen first-year head coach, "but they are not going to push us around easily. Our manpower is not very deep, but we will give them all we got." Stagg was a football pioneer who played at Yale and was named to the very first All-America team in 1889. He turned to coaching the next year at Springfield College before becoming a fixture at the University of Chicago from 1892 to 1932, and recruiting the very first Heisman Trophy recipient, Jay Berwanger. Chicago retired Stagg at age 65, but he unretired himself by coaching at College of Pacific from 1933 to 1946, finally stepping down at 84. He lived to 102.

Stagg was correct in predicting that the Gaels wouldn't romp all over his Tigers. St. Mary's left Stockton with a hard-earned 7-0 victory. The game's one highlight: Nichelini's 44-yard touchdown romp. After that, the Gaels dug in and stopped Pacific seven yards from the end zone to preserve the win. Madigan was so concerned with Stagg's valiant team effort that he opted against going for a second touchdown, instead attempting a field goal, which missed badly.

St. Mary's next faced ultra-rival Santa Clara. Clipper Smith, the Broncos coach, was supremely confident: "We can out-hit St. Mary's, out-pass them, out-defend them on passes, and rise to greater heights. We can beat St. Mary's." Smith was nearly true to his word. The Catholic rivals battled each other in, literally, a slugfest. The two schools disliked each other intensely. After St. Mary's took immediate control on Nichelini's 66-yard touchdown sprint around right end on the game's first scrimmage play, the Broncos punched right back on a 70-yard march, with Frank Sobrero lobbing a fourth-down 9-yard scoring pass to Joe "Salty" Salatino. Jorgensen had missed his PAT attempt for St. Mary's, as did "Diamond" Joe Paglia for Santa Clara, proving pivotal for both sides. For points after touchdowns weren't as guaranteed in the 1930s as later in the century, because the kicking game long ago wasn't a priority and for a specific reason: Kickers then were down-and-dirty two-way players, not today's spotless-uniform specialists. And so the 1933 Little Big Game ended 6-6 before 59,000 at Kezar Stadium.

"We should have won," said Smith, even though his Broncos were outgained, 186 yards to 93. Madigan praised both teams, citing their sportsmanship. But the contrarian, Norbert Korte, sat before his Royal and typed a heated letter to Smith: "My dear Clipper: I am writing you to let you know that I, for one, am behind you one hundred percent, and that if any time you need a shield bearer in your wars with Slip Madigan and his unsportsmanlike conduct, I would deem it an honor and privilege to take up the good fight before any forum that happens to be sitting on the case. You were quoted in a (*San Francisco Chronicle*) article as saying to a reporter: 'What gets me down is that St. Mary's lays for these kids every year and they get away with murder. The officials don't seem to see it.' In the first place, I wish to point out that you do not accuse the St. Mary's players exactly of dirty work; that is the interpretation that has been put on it by St. Mary's themselves, and by some of the sports writers that have become Madigan's puppets because he carts them around the country with him at his or St. Mary's expense. There has been a great deal of effort on the part of these sports writers to praise the clean playing of St. Mary's. Where there is smoke there must be fire."

Korte went on to imply, in a five-page double-spaced letter, that Madigan's players "are coached to infraction of the rules—witness the astounding penalties against them in every game by every official. He likewise, in my opinion, coaches his teams to win by whatever method, and if that method is to remove from the game the players who can and probably will beat them, such method comes within the canon of ethics practiced by him." Korte then cited the injuries sustained by Sobrero and Paglia in the fourth quarter that knocked them out of the game.

"If this thing results in the severance of athletic relations between St. Mary's and Santa Clara, I, for one, will be very happy," Korte continued. "We got along without them very well before; I'm sure we can do it again. They enjoy an unsavory reputation. Madigan has always been difficult to get along with. Adam Walsh had to actually punch him after one Santa Clara-St.

Mary's game, and I'm happy to say that Adam did not come out second best. We want you to know that we are behind you whether you said St. Mary's was laying for you or not, because if you said it, it was the truth. I firmly believe Madigan fears your ability."

Norbert Korte let Clipper Smith know exactly how he felt about Madigan. Korte, a 1919 graduate of Santa Clara, later wrote to the president of his university with the same complaint. Korte was the match that contributed to the brush fire that later turned into the forest fire that threatened to torch the Little Big Game. Football isn't a tea social, and St. Mary's played the game as it's meant to be played—rough, but within the rules. Well, mostly. Things do get out of hand occasionally on a football field, and Santa Clara wasn't exactly a merry bunch of elves themselves, spreading good cheer on the greensward. The Gaels weren't the "Monsters of Moraga" as portrayed by Korte, but failing to beat a team can lead to jaded thinking, and not even an occasional tie can make that thinking go away. Translated: The Broncos' bruised feelings.

Unaware of the rancor transmitting throughout the halls of Santa Clara, Madigan focused on his next opponent, yet another school St. Mary's owned in the same manner of Santa Clara. The Gaels had beaten UCLA four times out of five when they met in '33, once again at the Los Angeles Coliseum. UCLA had lost to Rose Bowl-bound Stanford, 3-0, and held California to a scoreless tie. And so Madigan recognized the Bruins as trouble. Not on this day, though, as St. Mary's played its best first half since the Nevada game by jumping into a 22-0 lead at intermission. George Wilson scored twice on plunges, and reserve Kelly Kellogg on a 5-yard run. UCLA came alive late, but too late, on a 74-yard touchdown pass from Stanley Reel to Sinclair Lott, and Bill Murphy's 45-yard interception return of an Eddie Erdelatz pass for a touchdown, just seconds before the final gun sounded on a 22-14 Gaels victory. This time, the entire Gaels team returned home together from Los Angeles.

During a seven-year stretch, 1929 to 1935, St. Mary's played Oregon seven times and won six of those games, the only loss happening in '33, a dispiriting 13-7 Thanksgiving Day defeat in front of 20,000 at Kezar. That game matched two of the Pacific Coast's best backs, Wilson of the Gaels and Mike Mikulak of the Ducks. Wilson opened the second half with an 8-yard touchdown run, but Oregon responded with two scores, both deceptive. On the first, Gael defenders expected a line buck near their goal, but Mark Temple fooled them by flipping a touchdown pass to Leighton Gee. Then Mikulak, from the Gaels' 6, faked another buck and pitched to Bob Parke, who scooted around right end and into the end zone. The Gaels felt like turkeys on turkey day. Madigan was again complimentary to his conqueror. "We lost to a fine team," he said. "Oregon has a speedy backfield with plenty of power, and their line is one of the best we have encountered this year. You can't win them all."

With three losses and a tie, Madigan was experiencing his worst season since the 5-4 team of 1928, and he still had Southern Methodist University to play. Before SMU came to town, Santa Clara and St. Mary's continued firing salvos at each other, jeopardizing not only the Little Big Game, but every sport between them. Only it was St. Mary's who fired first this time, its Athletic Board of Control recommending dropping the 1934 football game against the Broncos, pending approval by its Board of Trustees. Santa Clara retaliated by going even further. In a letter from Reverend Lyons, the Santa Clara president, to Brother Joseph, the St. Mary's chancellor, Lyons declared that Santa Clara was "dropping all athletic relations with St. Mary's College" indefinitely. Norbert Korte and other accusatory Santa Clara alumni were ecstatic.

But which opponents would each institution choose to fill in the gap? St. Mary's conferred with USC for a game in 1934, while Santa Clara started a conversation with New York University. St. Mary's also spoke with Columbia, and Santa Clara with Temple, though nothing conclusive came out of all those talks. Washington State then contacted Madigan about coming north to coach. But Washington State, unlike St. Mary's, wasn't about to give him ten percent of every ticket sold. Besides, with a lovely home in Oakland, and better weather in Moraga than Pullman, Madigan was perfectly happy where he was. Besides, if he didn't want the Notre Dame job, why would he choose Washington State?

Pass-oriented Southern Methodist University presented a new problem for St. Mary's run-conscious defense. The Mustangs, led by strong-armed Bob Wilson, aired the ball more frequently than was customary in the 1930s. George Canrinus, playing his last game for St. Mary's, just like his brother Fred, scored on a 30-yard end around as the Gaels got on the scoreboard first. SMU's J.R. "Jack Rabbit" Smith then took off on a 66-yard run to the Gaels' 3, caught from behind by Nichelini. Though gassed, Smith scored on the next play. Dutch Schreiber then found Erdelatz wide open on a 43-yard touchdown pass and a 12-6 Gaels lead at halftime. The second half was all St. Mary's. Nichelini picked off a Wilson pass and scampered 38 yards for the touchdown that cemented an 18-6 victory, in a game with no conversions. The Gaels managed to contain Wilson's passing, and both Madigan and SMU coach Ray Morrison praised Nichelini's "All-American" ability. Over an entire season, Nichelini had outplayed his vaunted teammate, George Wilson.

The Gaels' 6-3-1 finish was acceptable, though still disappointing, considering pre-season expectations. Post-season tributes then arrived. Tackle Carl Jorgensen was chosen to play in the East-West Shrine Game in San Francisco. And Jorgensen became the first Danish-born football player to be named an All-American, by the *New York Sun*. Jorgensen also made the United Press' All-Coast team with teammates Wilson and Fred Canrinus.

After exchanging Christmas presents at home, Madigan took most of his family to Hawaii for rest and rehabilitation. "I swam, took long walks, and even got a sun tan," he said after returning home. "Best vacation I ever had, though I've lost most of my tan. Now I got to go back to work." He said his aggravated stomach even felt better, especially after a difficult, lingering problem seemed to soothe in the islands.

While in Hawaii, whom did Madigan bump into but fellow Notre Dame alumni Clipper Smith and Buck Shaw, Santa Clara's head football coach and his top assistant. The three were seen together with leis around their necks and libations in hand, smiling broadly, with no indication whatsoever of strife among them.

Was it Kumbaya, something permanent, or island fever, something temporary? Perhaps, just perhaps, the Little Big Game, a turbulent Catholic rivalry, had made peace.

The Notre Dame football team photo taken in 1919. Knute Rockne is at the far left in the center row. Slip Madigan is the third player to Rockne's left and George Gipp is the third player from the left in the top row.

Slip Madigan (above) in his Notre Dame graduation photo and (right) in his football uniform. Madigan was a star lineman even though he only weighed 156 pounds.

When Madigan arrived at St. Mary's in 1921 he coached all sports including (above) the basketball team.

One of Madigan's many successful players, Jim Underhill, became a coach under Slip. Here Underhill (right) is seen with Felix Pennino (left) and Eddie Erdelatz (center). Erdelatz would also go on to a coaching career.

A year before he was killed in a plane crash, Knute Rockne (right) visited his former player, Madigan, on the St. Mary's campus.

Explosive Al Nichelini (below) was a backfield threat for St. Mary's in the early 1930s.

Slip Madigan's cross-country train trip to play Fordham – "The World's Longest Cocktail Party" – is promoted in the *San Francisco Chronicle.*

Slip Madigan meets the great Babe Ruth on a football, not a baseball, field in New York City prior to a St. Mary's–Fordham game.

Legendary sportswriter Grantland Rice (left) meets Madigan before a St. Mary's–Fordham game in New York City.

In a panoramic photo, Slip Madigan, the St. Mary's football team, and their traveling entourage are shown on the side lawn of the White House in Washington, DC on November 17, 1930. President Hoover is in the middle (space on either side) and Madigan is on Hoover's left side.

Madigan accepts the victor's trophy after his St. Mary's team beat the favorite Texas Tech team in the Cotton Bowl Classic in 1938. It was the Gaels only bowl appearance.

Slip addresses his St. Mary's football team before the start of the season.

Script adviser Slip Madigan (second from the right) with Knute Rockne film portrayer Pat O'Brien (center) on the set of a movie about the iconic Notre Dame coach.

Swashbuckling actor Errol Flynn (center) meets raconteur coach Slip Madigan (right) on Madigan's visit to Hollywood.

National Football Foundation
and
College Hall of Fame

Coach Edward "Slip" Madigan
St. Mary's (CA) 1921-39
Record 116-45-12

has been granted the highest honors of the National Football Hall of Fame in recognition of his outstanding coaching ability as demonstrated in intercollegiate competition, his sportsmanship, integrity, character and contribution to the sport of football. this certificate bears witness that his name shall be forever honored in the
National Football Foundation's College Football Hall of Fame

Elected:
1974

Chairman, Honors Court

Chairman of the Board

Slip was inducted into the College Football Hall of Fame in 1974. His record with St. Mary's was 116-45-12.

Madigan (center) became a successful contractor after his football coaching career. His son, Ed (left), now runs the company. They are shown here at one of the sites.

An aerial view of some of the tract homes built by Slip Madigan. This one is in Contra Costa County in California.

St. Mary's coach Slip Madigan (left) meets with one of the Gaels most famous players, Herman Wedemeyer, on a Madigan family trip to Hawaii, "Squirmin" Herman's homeland.

A dedicated family man, Slip hands off the football to his son Ed.

When his young son was ill, Slip went so far as to cover his newspaper route.

The Madigan family, minus toddler son Ed, enjoy a vacation in Hawaii.

Ed Madigan, Slip's son, and wife Carol celebrate a wedding anniversary.

9
Luck of the Irish

By 1934, St. Mary's College and Slip Madigan had grown up together, a nationally prominent educational institution and a nationally recognized football coach. They made a perfect union, heavily dependent upon each other, and glorified together, written about from sunlit Moraga to the bright lights of Broadway, vanquishers of the country's finest on the gridiron, and invited guests at the White House.

But without knowing it themselves, the school and coach had begun the slow process of separation. Madigan had become enormously popular from coast to coast, while St. Mary's was dealing with its burgeoning fame, yet trying its best to remain that quiet little Catholic college out west. These two conflicting images would lead to an emotional earthquake in those Moraga hills, with jealousy the fault line.

Prior to the 1934 season, Madigan was voted the most popular football coach on the West Coast, a decade before that same coast welcomed pro football. A Portland newspaper polled forty-two sportswriters in '34, and Madigan had 267 points, just ahead of C.E. "Tiny" Thornhill of Stanford with 259. Then followed Orin "Babe" Hollingbery of Washington State, 203, Maurice "Clipper" Smith of Santa Clara, 201, James Phelan of Washington, 195, Bill Spaulding of UCLA, 190, and Howard Jones of USC, 153. Madigan's popularity on the shores of the Pacific was enhanced not only by his stunning record, but his instant availability to the press, and his frequent ability to deliver a good quote. Among football coaches, he was the sportswriter's best friend. He could fill a notebook faster than W.C. Fields could knock down a Scotch.

"This is the fastest team we have ever had at St. Mary's," Madigan informed local scribes in the summer of '34. The fastest, but not the biggest, like the previous year. Twenty of those giants had used up their eligibility, eighteen of whom had graduated, causing sports editor Sid Ziff of the *Los Angeles Evening Herald and Express* to express this accepted line of thinking: "Those 18 graduates are, in itself, a record of some sort. You know what they say of football, that the players go to college for the game, not their educational certificates."

Even though the '34 Gaels had added gallop to their game while, at the same time, were losing weight, they were woefully inexperienced, with just one senior starter in halfback Al Nichelini, and two more starters in juniors John Yezerski, a tackle, and Nebb Elduayan, a guard. Madigan was optimistic, regardless. "Our team will be green—but good," he pointed out. "I have a fine lot of husky boys who are willing to work. Why should I complain?"

Nevertheless, he picked California, Stanford and USC as the cream of the coast, with St. Mary's a notch below. Was Slip lying in the weeds? "Madigan lies low, but points high," Bill Leiser wrote in the *San Francisco Chronicle*'s Sporting Green. "He's one of the best known football coaches in the world." Well, Madigan's popularity might not be international, but from when he and St. Mary's had first joined hands, following that 127-0 defeat, he sat on a throne of his own making, hiding a bottle of anti-acid pills in his robe. Even kings can have ulcers.

Yezerski was the biggest starter at 220 on the slimmed-down, swifter line. Every starter, besides Nichelini, was a junior except for guard Jerry Dennerlein, a sophomore. Erdelatz and Felix Pennino were the ends, Yezerski and Herm Meister the tackles, Dennerlein and Elduayan the guards, Wagner Jorgensen the center, Malcom Friese the quarterback, Harry Mattos or Herb Schreiber at left half, Nichelini at right half, and Kelly Kellogg the fullback. Competition was keen, as it was difficult to distinguish between the first and second units.

Madigan wasn't worried about the Gaels' trimmed waists. "I never put players on the scales to see if they are football players," he pointed out. The only knock against Madigan: His teams didn't score enough. The press emphasized that point, but Madigan noted that his teams had averaged eighteen points a game since he took over in 1921. The Gaels scored in every game in 1933, which couldn't be said of Cal, Stanford, USC, UCLA, Santa Clara, USF, Loyola of Los Angeles, and the College of Pacific. Offensive football wasn't a powerful entity in the 1930s, as the passing game hadn't yet matched the running game, thus teams relied on punting and defense. All those factors generally led to low-scoring games. But Madigan, thinking of more production in '34, fancied reserve quarterback Harry "The Horse" Mattos, a nifty runner and passer with a better throwing arm than Friese, whom Madigan played because "he is the best punter on the coast. Maybe this year, we'll have an offense to match our defense."

George Canrinus and Santo Garbo, his promising career capsized by injuries, joined Madigan's coaching staff. Red Strader, John "Pope" Ilia and freshman team coach Vincent McNally, Madigan's very first hire in the 1920s, filled out the staff. Former standout Bill Fischer left to become a coach and physical education director at nearby Livermore High School. Another famous Gael alum, Angelo Brovelli, was released by Pittsburgh of the NFL because of an "attitude" problem. "I will not consider taking him back," said team owner Art Rooney, though calling Brovelli a "sterling performer." Rooney offered Brovelli to Philadelphia and Boston without success. Rooney wasn't willing to turn his head and look away, as Madigan had done with the talented, but undisciplined, Dark Angel, who left his mark on football as a genuine star of the 1930s.

Catholic peace returned to the Bay Area as St. Mary's and Santa Clara sat down together, an olive branch between them, and agreed on a three-year football contract, with the first game scheduled November 18, 1934. Father Lyons of Santa Clara and Brother Jasper of St. Mary's signed the paper, but it was Madigan and Broncos coach Clipper Smith who made it all happen in Hawaii. "It's the opening of an era of good feeling," Madigan said. Hearing the news, Santa Clara alum Norbert Korte, gagged in disbelief in his law office, especially when Madigan needled, "We never get beaten by Santa Clara." Slip was, indeed, cocky.

Co-eds at St. Mary's? For the first time, women enrolled for classes in Moraga, though summer session only. And for the second consecutive summer, the great white hunter, Madigan, killed a deer locally. That year also produced the unthinkable—a Temple-St. Mary's game. "It's a possibility," hinted Madigan. But against a team coached by Pop Warner, St. Mary's No. 1 meanie? Conventional thinking was that Madigan would kill a deer in the Himalayas before that ever happened. Now it might.

St. Mary's hopes in 1934 rested on the broad shoulders of 203-pound halfback Nichelini, coming off two successful seasons that had elevated him into All-America consideration. Big and fast, he sprinted 100 yards in 9.9 seconds at the West Coast Relays in Fresno, California, the previous spring. Teammate Ed Hallman, a second-string halfback, clocked 9.7 at the same meet. The Gaels were indeed speedy. Asked if there was a better all-around back on the coast than Nichelini, also a stalwart on defense, Madigan replied, "No, nor in the nation." Nichelini, the tenth of twelve children from a Napa Valley winery family, was inspired by what he saw in fall practice. "I'm surprised at the hustle and fight on the ball club," he said. "In fact, I've never seen such spirit before. Those big guys last year were all right, but they tired easily, and we were a hard-luck club besides. With the backfield as improved as advertised, we should win every one of our games." The gauntlet was thrown down, but Madigan offered a cautionary tone. "Very poor," he said of St. Mary's chances against Cal, its chief adversary. "Our only hope is by playing superhuman football."

Madigan was depending on a big season from Erdelatz, an able pass catcher, not to mention a cartoonist and singer. After the '33 win over Fordham, Erdelatz, showing a smooth baritone voice, sang a solo at New York City's Cotton Club in front of the club's celebrity singer Cab Calloway of "Minnie the Moocher" fame. A smiling Calloway applauded. Madigan envisioned the passing combination of Mattos to Erdelatz making beautiful music for the Gaels, with the running of Nichelini adding another key instrument to the '34 season.

Madigan handpicked a special opponent to open the nine-game season. He coached at Columbia Preparatory School in Portland, Oregon, for one year, 1920, before moving on to St. Mary's. Columbia Prep then evolved into a separate institution, Columbia University, which had its first graduating class in 1929. In 1935, Columbia became the University of Portland. Against Columbia U. in 1934, St. Mary's coasted to a 61-0 victory before 10,000 at Kezar Stadium. Nichelini scored on 16- and 25-yard runs, and Mattos uncorked a 59-yard touchdown pass to reserve end Bob Timm. Nichelini, though, fumbled the ball away twice, causing Madigan to complain about his team's "ragged" play. Columbia coach Gene Murphy praised the Gaels, saying, "We have never faced a stronger team." The press, after noting that the Gaels dominated in yards gained, 429 to 78, and in first downs, 17 to 2, mentioned their fumbling tendencies and their 10 penalties to the visitors' none. Cal, their next opponent, began focusing on those two negatives.

Cal was made a 5-to-4 favorite over St. Mary's after opening the season with a 54-0 trouncing of U.C. Davis and a 33-0 whipping of Nevada. Regardless, Cal coach William "Navy Bill" Ingram, sensing his job was in jeopardy in spite of a 23-8-4 record in three-plus years in Berkeley, had a sinking feeling before taking on the Gaels. "This is the week we have to get over the hump," he said. "If we beat St. Mary's, we can go along nicely. We're better than we were last year." Why the apprehension, Navy Bill? After all, Madigan had beaten Cal twice in twelve games. Then Ingram got word that Madigan had "accused" him or his assistants of spying on St. Mary's practices. Upset by that charge, Ingram fired back at Madigan, who denied saying any such thing.

Under blue skies in Berkeley, the Gaels upset the odds makers and the Bears, 7-0, before 70,000 mostly disappointed Cal loyalists. Two plays decided the outcome. Meister broke through the Bears line and blocked Arleigh Williams' punt, Yezerski recovering at the Cal 16. Then Kellogg blasted through a big hole and headed for the end zone, but Cal's Bill Archer hit him at the 2, dislodging the football. The ball rolled into the end zone where Herb Schreiber fell on it for a Gaels touchdown. A win is a win, but Madigan said, "The luck of the Irish was with us today." Nichelini was held to 29 yards in 10 carries, while Archer was the day's rushing star with 51 yards in 7 carries. Jimmy Hatlo of the *San Francisco Examiner*, a famous sports cartoonist during a bygone age of newspaper cartooning, depicted "Senor Moraga" giving the Cal Bear a big boot. Navy Slip began thinking higher, while Navy Bill sank further.

Madigan's confidence was skewed by the lucky win over Cal. He decided to start his second unit against Nevada, which Cal had shut out. Perhaps Madigan was thinking one week ahead to the next cross-country trip to play Fordham. But St. Mary's was over-confident against Nevada, which registered a shocking 9-7 upset of the Gaels before 25,000 at Kezar. Schreiber connected with Erdelatz on a 24-yard touchdown toss before Nevada's George Tharp squeezed over on a one-yard run. The Gaels led 7-6 until the game's final minutes when Wolf Pack center Tom Cashill dropkicked a 40-yard field through the posts. St. Mary's had one last chance, but Mattos' pass to Erdelatz was caught just beyond the end zone. Nevada had pulled off its biggest upset since holding Cal's Wonder Team to a scoreless tie in 1923. Madigan credited punter Dick Haman with pinning the Gaels deep much of the game. Nichelini was held in check once again. An embarrassed Madigan analyzed the upset as "beyond the comprehension of a humble coach." But he, diplomatically, acknowledged Nevada as the better team.

There went Madigan's dream of an unbeaten season. The gored Gaels immediately boarded a train and carried their disappointment east. "Every time the train would stop, the players got off, ran around to get the kinks out, then got back on the train, and off they'd go again," said Allen Nichelini, Jr., son of the team's star running back, in 2016. The St. Mary's traveling party, numbering 150, stopped in Chicago to catch the World's Fair before traveling to Washington, D.C.—no White House visit was scheduled that year—and then arriving in New York City, but not in one piece. Backup quarterback Hugh Sill damaged knee cartilage while practicing in Alva, Oklahoma, and was lost for the year. Madigan would need more of Mattos than he planned against formidable Fordham.

Assistant Red Strader scouted the Rams and told the accompanying press, "It will take a great team to beat Fordham. But I saw a couple of weaknesses in their defense. Boston College completed 10 passes against them, and we ought to be able to click on a few." But Strader cautioned, "Fordham is better than it was in '33," when the Gaels beat the Rams, 13-6. How much better, St. Mary's would soon find out.

Fordham opened their fourth intersectional with St. Mary's with Joe Maniaci intercepting Schreiber's pass and covering 82 yards of green turf for the game's first touchdown. Mattos entered the fray at that point and began opening up the Rams defense, which had a 5-foot-8, 180-pound sophomore tackle named Vince Lombardi. Behind Mattos' passing and running, the Gaels reached the Rams 1-yard line. Mattos then dove into the end zone for a 7-7 tie. Then in the fourth quarter, Mattos threw a 10-yard scoring strike to Erdelatz, and St. Mary's had the lead for good, although a blocked Gael punt for a Rams safety narrowed their convincing win to 14-9 before 55,000 at the Polo Grounds.

Madigan analyzed that victory by quoting the classics: "I cannot help but repeat the words of the mortally wounded Montcalm when he was told that he had successfully defended his remarkable city: 'I can die happy.'" Madigan added that over his fourteen seasons at St. Mary's, "I cannot recall when a victory brought greater elation to a coach, team and rooters alike than this triumph did." He had said basically the same thing, without quoting Montcalm, after vanquishing Fordham in 1930 and USC in 1931. But who's quibbling or quoting? Certainly not St. Mary's, now 3-1 against Fordham.

Erdelatz played a huge role in that victory. Besides his game-winning catch, he played an equally significant role on defense, containing Maniaci on running plays. Erdelatz defeated the blocking efforts of Fordham linemen Joe Ludinowicz and Ralph Woldendale to stop Maniaci in his tracks. One New York sports writer called steady Eddie "one of the best ends who ever played in New York."

But it was Mattos, "The Horse," who became an instant hero in the national press after beating Fordham, just like Angelo Brovelli four years earlier. Mattos completed only 5 of 18 passes, but his key completions turned the tide. He ran effectively, too, as St. Mary's also won the statistical battle: Yards gained, 388 to 134, and first downs, 21 to 4. Renowned New York columnist Damon Runyon wrote: "Harry 'The Horse' Mattos heaved forward passes like a Babe Ruth hitting fungoes." Runyon was a St. Mary's convert, but how could St. Mary's be so effective against Fordham, and so ineffective against Nevada? Madigan berated himself all the way home, knowing he had blown the opportunity for an unblemished season. The "World's Longest Cocktail Party" arrived in Montreal. The Gaels visited there from 12 until 10 p.m., and then continued through the Canadian Rockies and Vancouver, B.C., all the while with Madigan inhaling pills to quiet his stormy stomach.

Madigan added a new foe in 1934: the Cougars of Washington State College. Remembering the Nevada letdown, he anointed Washington State as "The best team on the coast." The Cougars were anything but, though Madigan couldn't chance another collapse after beating Fordham. He hoped that Nichelini, less of a factor in '34, would regain his previous form. But Mattos remained the catalyst, coming through in the clutch again as 25,000 watched at Kezar. The Cougars fired the first salvo, a 38-yard touchdown pass from Ed Goddard to Ed Brett, but the PAT placement was errant. After Meister kicked a 23-yard field goal, the score remained 6-3 until the fourth quarter. Then Mattos heaved a 43-yarder that reserve end Vic Strub grabbed deep in the end zone for a 9-6 victory, a clutch-throw-and-catch finish.

Strub was forced to play after Erdelatz suffered a knee injury that required surgery and terminated his season. "I thought I had a chance of getting it," Strub said of the winning touchdown. "But, then, I remembered that this was Eddie Erdelatz's bad luck corner against Nevada when he stepped outside (the end zone making a catch)." St. Mary's dominated Washington State in total yards, 297 to 80, and in first downs, 13 to 2. Madigan was asked again why the Gaels didn't score as often as their statistics would indicate. He shrugged and pointed to the team's 4-1 record. But the loss of Erdelatz, he said, could have long-range consequences.

Or possibly even short-range consequences. For the unpredictable Gaels traveled south and suffered a 6-0 defeat against UCLA, a stunner observed by 25,000 at the Los Angeles Coliseum. This time, Mattos was anything but a hero. He fumbled a punt while backed up against his goal line, with the Bruins' Wendell Womble recovering at the 4-yard line. Sully Funk pushed his way into the end zone from the 2, and Mattos and the Gaels offered little resistance afterward, having their one scoring bid shut down three yards from the end zone. Besides his dropped punt, Mattos was intercepted twice. He then read his name in the next day's newspapers as "the goat" of the game. But St. Mary's fumbled seven times as a team. "We could not hold onto the ball," said Madigan. "And passes that meant touchdowns slipped out of our hands." Nichelini was guilty in both instances. UCLA even led St. Mary's in total yards, 186 to 106. The Gaels didn't rack up enough statistics or points this time. Madigan's midsection felt more tremors.

Up next was Santa Clara. "The Big Spat" was over, and The Little Big Game resumed, albeit with new controversy: A dummy of "Senor Moraga" was strung up on the Santa Clara campus, which didn't play well in Moraga.

The Broncos sophomore backfield of Henry Thomas, William Hall, Don DeRosa and blossoming legend Nello Falaschi also vowed never to lose to St. Mary's. This bravado made the Bay Area's sports pages, in which the undefeated Broncos were reported a 2-to-1 favorite over the "Menacing Marauders of Moraga," who were no longer quite so menacing.

Before kickoff at Kezar Stadium in San Francisco's Golden Gate Park, the skies opened up and a downpour occurred, turning the turf into a quagmire. Rushing yardage would be limited in the muck, and the ball would be too slippery to throw accurately. The game came down to the unexpected—or the luck of the Irish. Santa Clara's Frank Sobrero, in a rush to punt from his end zone with Jim Austin closing in on him, saw the ball slip from his hands and roll into the end zone where St. Mary's Felix Pennino fell on it for six points. There was a double dose of Irish luck for the Gaels that day. Santa Clara thought it had scored a tying touchdown on Bill Dutton's plodding 25-yard run across the goal line. But field judge Bruce Kilpatrick called holding on Bronco lineman Bruce Finney, nullifying the score. The ruling was controversial, to say the least. Santa Clara was incensed to the point of protesting the game. Game film couldn't determine if Finney actually was holding. "Nothing could be seen," said Madigan, perhaps with tongue in cheek. And St. Mary's was fortunate to steal off with a 7-0 squishy squeaker.

Clipper Smith accepted defeat graciously. "We have no alibis. Every man played well and fought well," he said. He added, with a jab at St. Mary's, "Anyhow, it cleared up the question of which is the best team on the coast today. It leaves Stanford away out there in front." Madigan couldn't argue with Smith, and possibly even agreed with him. After this questionable win over Santa Clara, plus the lucky bounce of the ball against Cal, he had four-leaf clovers stuck in both coat pockets. For how could he explain his 5-2 record in any other way that made sense?

The Gaels had a revenge game coming up against an Oregon team that dumped them, 13-7, the previous year. The Ducks sought to make it two in a row, meaning the Moragans would need something extra to avoid another setback. That added element, in the eighth game of St. Mary's season, was the return of Nichelini as a dominant force. He had the best game of his senior year, rushing 13 times for 88 yards, highlighted by a 41-yard touchdown burst, his longest run of the season. Oregon scored early on Maurice Van Vliet's 15-yard pass to Stanley Riordan. The Ducks still led, 7-0, when Nichelini shot through a hole and used his blazing speed to run away from defenders for six points. St. Mary's then sealed the victory when Wagner Jorgensen blocked Riordan's punt from the Oregon 10. The ball bounced back into the end zone where Everett Pendleton recovered it for a Gaels touchdown and a 13-7 victory before 14,000 at Kezar. Fumbles identified the Gaels' 1934 season; those they gave away, and those they recovered in the end zone. Nichelini capped the Oregon weekend by being named team captain.

After that win, Madigan was stricken with a cold that sacked him before the season finale against the University of San Francisco. He pulled himself out of bed and drove over the mountain from his Oakland home to Moraga—the Caldecott Tunnel wasn't yet built—to hold practice, but had to leave early and return to bed. Still not 100 percent, he joined his team at Kezar Stadium, where the Gaels faced USF before 45,000 fans, who shouted the familiar "Sit Down, Slip!" If only he could sit down; he was that sick. But this was a different USF team from its former St. Ignatius days in the 1920s. Now known as the Dons, and not the Gray Fog, they were a more worthy opponent in the 1930s under coach Spud Lewis. The *San Francisco Examiner*'s Jimmy Hatlo positioned "Senor Moraga" and "Don Frisco" in a shootout at the "Hill Top Mine" in a pre-game cartoon. The USF campus was on a hilltop, and its athletic teams picked up an additional nickname, "Hilltoppers." Now the Hilltoppers would try to take down the mountain men of Moraga.

USF tackle Pop Blewett kicked a 43-yard field goal in the first quarter, but there was no more scoring until the fourth period. Then, once again, fate smiled on Madigan and his Gaels. Hugh "Bucky" O'Connor, a third-string St. Mary's guard, grabbed the football as it inexplicably popped out of the grasp of USF halfback Carl McInnis, and ran uncontested 61 yards into the end zone for a 7-3 victory—a third four-leaf clover for Madigan. "We were lucky to win," he acknowledged, even though twelve Gaels missed the game with injuries. And St. Mary's did bow its necks defensively to stop USF's only serious touchdown threat after the Dons reached the Gaels 1-yard line. There, on fourth down, Schreiber crashed through and dropped fullback Ray Peterson for a two-yard loss.

And so St. Mary's finished the season at a blessed 7-2. Nichelini didn't achieve All-America recognition, but he and Pennino were selected to the West team for the annual East-West Shrine Football Game For Crippled Children, played at Kezar. Nichelini, in addition, was chosen to play in the College Football All-Star Game in August 1935, where one of his coaches would be Slip Madigan. Nichelini had become friendly with Cotton Warburton, USC's All-American quarterback, in 1933. They drove to Chicago together for the All-Star Game with Warburton's new bride, as Warburton was the NFL property of the Chicago Bears. To save money, the three agreed to room together on the trip. "Only dad could pull that off," said Allen Nichelini, Jr. The Bears won the game, 5-0. Nichelini started at right half, had a few short runs, completed a pass, and was dominant on defense. An All-Star teammate was a future President, Michigan alumnus Gerald Ford. Warburton rejected the Chicago Bears offer and became a successful Hollywood producer.

Nichelini remained in Chicago after the game to begin his rookie NFL season with the Chicago Cardinals. He was a Cardinal in 1935 and 1936, rushing for a combined 423 yards and catching passes for another 133 yards. He scored four rushing touchdowns in '35, tying him for second in the league, and played his usual dependable defense.

"Then my dad played for the Los Angeles Bulldogs of a California professional league, making $100 a game," his son said. Nichelini, Sr., earned his master's degree and teaching credential at USC while marrying "Helen of Troy," a USC campus queen named Patricia McClure. He then taught and coached, mainly at Selma (CA) High School, before entering the insurance business. "Everybody knew and liked my dad. He and Slip had a close relationship, though it was football-related. He said that Slip had a 'Notre Dame attitude, very competitive.' A lot of Slip's players worked for the Union 76 oil company during the summer months. So Slip had my dad wear number 76. You'd get in trouble with the NCAA for doing that today."

That same year, football took a back seat to organized crime in terms of headlines. Clyde Barrow and Bonnie Parker killed two highway patrolmen near Grapevine, Texas, while fellow gangsters John Dillinger, Pretty Boy Floyd and Baby Face Nelson were gunned down by FBI agents. On a much less violent note, the first Soap Box Derby was held in Dayton, Ohio. And St. Mary's and Santa Clara seemed at peace.

As a footnote to St. Mary's 1934 season, both Slip Madigan and Spud Lewis, USF's coach, were scheduled to fly to a coaches meeting in Palm Springs. Lewis' wife was nervous about her husband getting on a plane until she heard Madigan was taking the same flight. "Oh, you're flying with Madigan," she said to her husband. "Well, go ahead. Nothing can happen to you when you're in the company of a man as lucky as Slip."

10

Mrs. Slip Madigan

Ed Madigan was born into the home of a famous coach, but a home run by a woman, not a man. Charlotte Madigan, wife of Slip Madigan, was ruler of the manor while her husband spent countless hours away, elevating St. Mary's College into the upper echelon of college football. The Madigans, husband and wife, were no doubt a team, but someone had to stay home and tend to the daily needs of their three children.

"My mom was a very warm, kind woman, with a strong personality that was different from my dad's," said the son. "Her personality was more family-oriented. She was the homemaker, and he was the breadwinner. She helped him in his work by holding parties at the house. She helped him entertain, but she didn't need the limelight."

Slip and Charlotte were devoted parents, but she had to be both mother and father to the children because of her husband's grueling work schedule. He rarely made it home to Oakland during the football season, sleeping on a cot in his Moraga office. Fame had its upsides, but also its downsides.

"I don't believe that the separation wore on them," said the son. "They were, indeed, a team." And when the football season ended, Slip Madigan, during the 1920s, moved right into basketball, then baseball, and track and field, before boxing was added to his already unimaginable coaching responsibilities. And, oh, yes, he also was St. Mary's athletic director. Although his coaching load lessened in the 1930s, it's hardly surprising that his health was failing.

"My mother had my two older sisters and me to take care of, so she had all the responsibilities of being a mother," said Ed Madigan. "But she went with my dad on most of the Fordham trips, and you can see her in the picture with my dad, President Hoover, and the St. Mary's football team at the White House. On one of those trips, I got a bad case of pneumonia, and she got on a train in New York and came back home all by herself. But, normally, on those trips back east, while my dad was busy with the team, she would go with Uncle John, my dad's brother, to the speakeasies in New York. She enjoyed that, even though, as I said earlier, she wasn't as outgoing as my dad. Nobody else was close to my dad in that outgoing way either.

"However, my mom could speak her mind. When my dad took his (financial) take after the Fordham game in the 1930s, he was criticized by a lot of people, who felt he was taking the money for no good reason. But it was money owed to him from the past. Here's how that happened. My mom was sitting next to Brother Albert at the Polo Grounds, and she begged him to pay my dad the money that was promised him. Mom made that happen. She could be tough, and she was a fighter. She even taught herself how to drive a car. My dad didn't want to teach her, so she got in the car, backed it out of the driveway, and taught herself to drive."

Ed Madigan was proud of Slip Madigan, the successful coach and celebrity, but equally proud of him as a father. "There wasn't much difference," he said. "He stressed that my sisters and I do well academically, and he told my oldest sister after she graduated from Cal to get a teaching credential. And she did become a teacher. Both my mom and dad emphasized academics. My dad wanted his players to get their teaching credentials as well. Remember, this was the Depression, when jobs were hard to come by. I read it somewhere: My dad put more of his players into the teaching profession than any other football coach.

"Mom and dad were Catholics, good Catholics, so she never had to worry about him morally. They were both straight and true, and they were disciplinarians. My dad just had to look at us to make his point, but my mom was around us more, and she was very strict. My dad had a big temper, but he would blow it off in two seconds. My mom had a temper, too, though nothing like my dad's. He was the extrovert, and she was somewhere between an extrovert and introvert, a happy medium."

Ed Madigan remembered his father's health problems as a coach, and how Mrs. Slip took care of him. "For breakfast, he would have milk toast—three or four pieces of toast in a bowl with milk over it," said the son. "That would settle his stomach, but I thought, 'He's eating baby food.' His stomach problems continued through the 1930s—ulcers and a bad gall bladder. My mom worried about him constantly. She had good health, but I remember her being in a Wisconsin hospital while my dad was off at the 1936 Olympics in Berlin; he got a journalist's credential. I don't remember what mom had, but dad was going to rush home early on the Hindenburg blimp. But she got better and so he stayed in Berlin.

"Mom got phlebitis in her legs later on, and was in bed for a couple of weeks. So dad had to do the chores, like cooking. And he was a good cook. He could bake, too. He'd be doing the batter on one of my grandmother's recipes, and his cigarette ashes fell into the batter. He smoked a lot while coaching football, then gave it up after he retired. My mom didn't smoke, but she was a good cook. She made sure that we had our lunches for school, and then she'd cook dinner for us. Her meatloaf was wonderful, and we always had roast on Sundays or leg of lamb. One of my dad's favorites was leg of lamb with mint jelly. He loved that."

Charlotte Kopp Madigan grew up in South Bend, Indiana, the daughter of early pioneers from Pennsylvania and Indiana. Her mother was born in a log cabin, and her father was a wagon maker for Studebaker, before that company made cars. "They had a nice home, and my mom even had a pony while growing up," said her son. "She didn't go beyond the eighth or ninth grade, but she was well-educated and well-spoken. She was a beautiful writer, either with grammar or penmanship, and she was always reading. She loved books.

"As for their courtship, I have a picture of them taking a canoe ride in the St. Joseph's River in South Bend. While he was selling tickets at a Notre Dame event, she approached him by surprise, and he swallowed some chewing tobacco. He would have been embarrassed if she caught him with that lump in his mouth. She was seeing another Notre Dame student, but my dad won out, and they dated for a year. Then they got married in 1917 while my dad served in the Navy during World War I."

Ed Madigan recalled that it wasn't always lilacs and clover inside the Madigan household. "My mom and dad had their ups and downs, and they would fight and argue. She would get upset if he stayed out too late. She always told this one story about his coming home early in the morning. She got on his case, and he said, 'Oh, I ran into some relatives in San Francisco.' She said, 'Slip, all you Irish are related after midnight.' She eventually forgave him. Their fights and arguments weren't excessive.

"I'm not sure if she encouraged him to quit coaching. All I know is that she was really worried about his health toward the end of his time at St. Mary's. Things were going bad, and people at St. Mary's were plotting against him. But she'd take us to St. Mary's games at Kezar Stadium, and the policeman there would wave us in to the parking lot. While my dad was coaching basketball, a woman came down from the stands at Kezar Pavilion and hit him over the head with an umbrella. She said to him, 'Why aren't you coaching football, where you belong?'"

Born in 1932, Ed Madigan was 7 when his father coached his last football game at St. Mary's in 1939. "My mom would bring us out to St. Mary's a lot, to watch dad coach football," he said. "It was a routine. We'd go over the hill at Fish Ranch Road to see practice." So why didn't the parents move from Oakland to Moraga, shortening the drive to campus? "My dad was offered a home in Moraga," the son said, "but my mom didn't want to go out there. She'd say, 'Moraga is where the foxes and rats say good night.' And there was nothing out there. No high schools for the girls. Not much of anything."

The son didn't remember his mother encouraging his father, a coach with a troubled stomach, to walk away from football. But he recalled the immense pride she took in his accomplishments, a pride she never got over. "Long after my dad had died, we were over in Mauna Kea in Hawaii. At a cocktail party, my mom was asked to join this prominent hotel owner at his table, merely as a friend. Afterwards, I asked how she liked the man. She said, 'He'll never be anything like your dad.'

"My dad always called her Toots. She just called him Slip; everyone called him Slip. He doted on his children. We never saw him as an absentee father. I'd sit on his lap and he'd read me stories or the Sunday funnies. That was a Sunday morning routine. He was very concerned about where my oldest sister was going in life, because she was the oldest child. But he was very concerned about all of us. We went to church every Sunday morning. Or he'd take the team to church early on Sundays before their games at Kezar Stadium. The Catholic schools played their games on Sunday, except when they played the state schools on Saturday."

Charlotte Madigan wasn't as social as her husband. Her activities revolved around family, though she had lady friends she met with occasionally. During summer, the Madigans rented a house in Ben Lomond in the Santa Cruz Mountains. They spent the entire summer there, dad joining them when he could. The Madigan family also enjoyed road trips. Slip, a history buff, took his family to visit the battlegrounds of the Revolutionary War, the French-Indian War, and the Civil War.

"Dad would close the windows of the car, and we'd have to smell the oil and wintergreen he spread on his neck, from his broken vertebrae playing football," said his son. "The rest of us would be killing ourselves with the heat, and he'd say, 'Never felt so good in my life.' There was no air conditioning in those days. It was summertime, and that oil and wintergreen would smell up the car. Dad would have to lift his right leg with his hands in order to drive, because of another old football injury."

When football season rolled around, Slip would be ensconced in Moraga, while his wife drove the kids to school, then picked them up afterward, and got them to their music lessons. St. Mary's College should have awarded Charlotte Madigan a varsity letter for making her husband's coaching life possible.

"They had a very happy marriage," said the son, "and they became very close when dad got out of football and into the contracting business. I graduated from Notre Dame and went to work for my dad. We'd be in Pittsburg (CA) or someplace, and we'd call and tell my mom when we'd be home, and she'd have a nice dinner for us. Or on Sundays, we'd meet at some restaurant, and my dad would want to know how many houses I sold. The three of us got very, very close. I don't remember my parents being overly affectionate in front of their children. Kind of normal, I guess. I probably saw them hug and kiss, though I can't say when. But theirs was a great love."

Slip Madigan died in 1966 just shy of his 70th birthday. Charlotte Madigan passed away at 86 in 1983, living the last seventeen years of her life without her husband of nearly fifty years. "She really missed him," said her son. "Then she became really dependent on me; she transferred that from my dad to me. She never considered remarrying, or even dating. He was the one man in her life, and there would never be another. She died in the home that she and my father moved into in 1932, the home where my wife and I raised our own family, and the home in which we're now doing this book interview.

"My mother wanted me to be a strong person, a moral person, a good person, a hard worker, and a lover of my own family. I was a bachelor for a long time; I didn't get married until I was 51; Carol and I dated three years. My parents didn't chastise me about my long bachelorhood, and wondering if I would ever give them grandchildren. They knew my girl friends. My mother and dad liked some of them, and they didn't like some of them. It's life."

Ed Madigan married after his father died, thus couldn't give him grandchildren. Ed thinks about his parents often—the outgoing, flamboyant father, and the more reserved, behind-the-scenes mother. "She was just a good kind woman who loved her family," he said. "I said that before, but that's just who she was, and it's worth repeating. My dad's legacy is pretty well known, but my mom's legacy was that she took care of her family. She was devoted to us, so, in that way, she helped my dad focus on his career. That wasn't always easy for her, even from the beginning of their marriage. During World War I, he was stationed in New York, living on a ship, and she was living by herself in New Jersey. She said it was the loneliest period of her life.

"But I would say that her life turned out perfectly, the way that she wanted it."

11

Slip-Sliding Away

Some exceptional football players attended St. Mary's in the 1920s and early 1930s: Three first-team All-Americans in linemen Larry Bettencourt, Ike Frankian and George Ackerman; a plethora of backfield stars in Cowboy Smith, Red Strader, Fred Stennett, Jimmy Underhill, Bud Toscani, Angelo Brovelli and Al Nichelini, and standout receivers in George and Fred Canrinus and Eddie Erdelatz. But by the mid-1930s, Slip Madigan's high-powered program had short-circuited.

From that point forward to 1939, by which time Madigan's long run at St. Mary's was no longer valued, he wouldn't coach another All-American or nearly the same number of All-Coast players he had mentored beforehand. And the players who did show up at St. Mary's—recruiting was a matter of good fortune back then compared to the calculated obsession it is nowadays—had difficulty holding onto the football. The Gaels had butterfingers during the Great Depression, fumbling far too often, thereby damaging a promising season in 1935.

St. Mary's justly earned its reputation as the most fumbling team on the West Coast. Combine that with diminished talent, and the prospect of undefeated seasons, as in 1926 and 1929, became wishful thinking for the Gaels. Unknowingly, in 1935, Madigan had taken the first step towards his eventual ouster from the college that he, and he alone, had raised from obscurity to eminence.

As proof of Madigan's popularity, a nationwide poll of football fans selected him to coach in the 1935 College All-Star Game, matching the best college graduates against the NFL champion Chicago Bears at Chicago's Soldier Field. Yet as Madigan's fame reached its peak, his status at St. Mary's was plummeting. He was making $12,000 annually in salary, plus receiving ten per cent of gate receipts, with two years left on his contract. But the Gaels, once an attendance magnet, played to much smaller crowds in 1935, while at the same time fumbling away games. Because of the nation's financial crisis, St. Mary's enrollment was reduced drastically in '35, from 770 students down to 500, as families couldn't afford a private education. The end result: Money emanating from tuitions took a hit, Madigan's teams weren't bringing in the same revenue that led to the college's growth, and St. Mary's began to regard Madigan differently, lowering his status from sainthood to commoner.

He quickly transformed from Holy Slip to holy cow. "There was always money in the till when I was coaching," Madigan said in defending himself. Another college football legend from that era, coach Bo McMillin, understood the quandary occurring out west. "It's wrong to say that little St. Mary's College cut Slip Madigan in on the receipts," he said. "The truth of the matter is that Slip actually cut St. Mary's in for a share." Either way, that unsettling feeling wouldn't subside.

The Great Depression was the culprit more so than Madigan. But St. Mary's only saw red instead of black on its financial ledger. St. Mary's defaulted on $1,370,500 of a $1,500,000 bond issue that was to finance new buildings on campus. The bond muddle wasn't Madigan's doing, but the United Press projected that St. Mary's might give up football in a year because of its "precarious financial situation." Madigan laughed off the report as "absolutely silly." He had another issue in mind, namely—who else?—Santa Clara, driving yet another spike into the rivalry.

Madigan contended that Santa Clara broke a "gentleman's agreement" by not scheduling a game before playing St. Mary's on Nov. 16, thus giving the Broncos a bye week at the same time the Gaels were traveling to and from New York for the Fordham game. Santa Clara's reaction: "What gentleman's agreement?" Thus peace between the two schools was short-lived, and the Little Big Game was up in the air again.

If that wasn't enough of a headache, Madigan was accused by the University of California's student newspaper of holding illegal practices in the off-season. *Daily Cal* sports editor John Trager wrote, "Why was the gym closed to visitors? Why is the team running plays inside the gym?" Madigan's response: "If players kicking soccer balls and rugby balls is a violation of conference rules, St. Mary's isn't stepping on the rules any more than the other schools." As for his insinuated culpability, he said, "I have not been at the St. Mary's campus for the last four days." His comment deflated the situation, but with St. Mary's playing Cal the second week of the season, it was something else to distract Madigan.

One positive to the summer months was Madigan's selection to coach in the second College All-Star Game. A poll of 7.3-million football fans picked Madigan as the fourth most popular college coach in the country following, in order, Frank Thomas of Alabama, Charlie Bachman of Michigan State, and Clarence Spears of Wisconsin. All four men would coach in the game, Thomas serving as the head coach. Though the All-Stars lost 5-0 to the homebody Chicago Bears before 77,450 at Soldier Field, Madigan lauded Gael alum Al Nichelini's effort: "He was a tower of strength on defense, and were it not for his many tackles in the first quarter, the Bears might have rolled up several points. His blocking enabled Bill Shepherd to get away on many long gains."

Nonetheless, just kicking off the 1935 season required considerable effort from Madigan. For three St. Mary's starters from 1934—tackle John Yezerski, guard Nebb Elduayan, and quarterback Harry "The Horse" Mattos—flunked out of school. During the 1930s, college athletes, especially at private institutions, weren't coddled. They attended class and achieved the same grades as non-athletes in order to stay eligible. Madigan, a true student-athlete himself, expected the same effort from his players. For the most part, he achieved that goal, although during the Depression, his players also left school for financial reasons. Anyway, his star power had decreased even before the 1935 Gaels showed up for fall practice.

Madigan truly saw the value of football from an academic perspective, believing the two went hand-in-hand. Speaking to a Kiwanis Club in neighboring Benicia, he said, "Football teaches the player initiative, resourcefulness, and the ability to think for himself. It takes brains to play football. Academic work must be kept up because it is the most important part of college life. I teach the boys to play to win. If they're defeated, take it gracefully, and tell the opponent that we will return to play them. To play football, young men must have a clear mind, a sound soul, and a healthy body." His speech was applauded resoundingly, and he was presented with a bouquet of flowers to give to Mrs. Madigan, the green thumb in the family.

Speaking specifically of his team's prospects to Pat Frayne of the *San Francisco Call-Bulletin,* Madigan said, "Despite the loss of such a fast man as Nichelini and the triple threat of Mattos, we will still have the necessary speed in the backfield with Eddie Hallman and Mal Friese, a couple of real sprinters. Les Groux can throw the ball just as well and as far as Mattos did. We are going in for a lighter, faster backfield." Fall practice commenced September 14 with forty-five of the forty-seven players signing a pledge to give up smoking until Dec. 14, when St. Mary's played UCLA in the ninth, and final, game of the season. The '35 Gaels averaged 203 pounds a man. "I'm as confident of the prospects of my present squad as I have ever been at the opening of a season," Madigan said before getting specific. "As our ends go, so goes our season." Madigan praised Erdelatz in that regard: "He's as good as any end in the country. Wagner Jorgensen is the best center on the Pacific Coast, while Herm Meister is as good as any tackle on the Pacific Coast."

Madigan's optimism wasn't a new character trait; he presented a lofty view prior to every season. And, in '34, his lofty grew loftier because he announced his intention to coach games from the press box. "The bench is the worst spot in the stadium from which to watch a game," he explained, adding that assistant Red Strader would take his telephoned instructions from upstairs down at the bench. Prescott Sullivan of the *San Francisco Chronicle* found humor in that arrangement: "If the press box sandwiches are satisfactory, Slip will remain there all season." The move never happened; Madigan was more suited for the sideline. How could fans shout, "Sit down, Slip!" if he were seated in the press box?

Sullivan then left himself open for criticism by boldly predicting that the Gaels would go undefeated. Madigan tended to agree with this heady prognostication: "We've got everything—the greatest collection of running backs I've ever had. We've got punters, passers, and our linemen are, at least, three deep at every position. Every other team shows some form of weakness. St. Mary's shows none." Add those speedy backs, and the Gaels did look formidable—certainly in their own minds. But the bigger picture: Could these stars hold onto the football?

That risky proposition might have made a grown man drink, though Madigan knew his limits with liquor. Therefore, the founding of Alcoholic Anonymous in 1935 went unnoticed by him. Other publicized happenings that year: FDR signed the Social Security Act; "Fibber McGee and Molly" debuted on radio; humorist Will Rogers and aviator Wiley Post were killed in a plane crash; Richard Hauptman was sentenced to death for the killing of the Lindbergh baby, and Huey Long of Louisiana made the longest speech in U.S. Senate history, fifteen and a half hours. Even the loquacious Madigan couldn't filibuster that long.

The Gaels first opponent was Nevada, which stunned them the year before, 9-7. Red Strader was kicked in the leg during a spirited practice before the opener and was hospitalized briefly. Madigan gave up his press box idea right then. Only 15,000 fans showed up at Kezar for the new season, and the Gaels rolled to a 20-0 victory behind their speedy backs, rushing for 185 yards to the Wolf Pack's 30. Herb Schreiber scored from the 3, Floyd Maxham intercepted a Nevada pass and raced 56 yards for a second touchdown, and 200-pound Les Groux broke through right guard and sprinted 46 yards into the end zone. Madigan remained unimpressed afterward. "They looked pretty ragged," he said of his Gaels. "I hoped they'd look a lot better. They will have to improve if they are going to beat Cal next week."

Cal had a new head coach, Leonard "Stub" Allison, who replaced "Navy" Bill Ingram after a 6-6 season. While the Gaels shut out Nevada, Cal barely beat Whittier, 6-0. "I think St. Mary's will beat us," said Allison. "They are too much for us now." Both Madigan and Allison utilized "poor me" strategy that week as St. Mary's was established as a 2-to-1 pick. Little did Madigan know that Allison was playing possum, as Cal would build a 9-1 record and become Pacific Coast Conference co-champions that season. On a sunny autumnal afternoon before 55,000 at Cal's Memorial Stadium, a St. Mary's team that had no weaknesses in Madigan's mind, showed no offense in losing, 10-0. Ken Cotton scored on a short plunge, Henry Sparks kicked a 23-yard field goal, and Cal's defense did the rest. "I don't remember when California ever looked better against us," said Madigan. Allison was equally impressed, saying, "California dominated the game, and had it under control at all times. But St. Mary's wasn't as bad as the score indicates. It has plenty of stuff, and will be up there before the year is out." Once again, Cal had the upper hand, and Madigan questioned his own pre-season optimism. He now wondered: Does his team have enough fighting heart to win?

College of Pacific represented St. Mary's third foe and Madigan's second matchup with Amos Alonzo Stagg. "I fear Stagg," Madigan told the press, mentioning the COP-USC game the previous week. Stagg's Tigers led, 7-6, in the fourth quarter before the Trojans pulled away for a 19-7 victory. Would the old man pose the same threat to St. Mary's? The odds makers believed not, installing the Gaels as a 2-to-1 favorite, the same odds that blew up in Berkeley the previous Saturday. Stung by that loss, the Gaels roared onto the turf at Kezar and laid into COP, 33-0, before a small turnout of 12,000. Schreiber was the game's star, rushing for 106 yards and throwing a pair of scoring passes to end Bob Timm. Maxham rushed for 67 yards and two touchdowns, while Hugh Sill intercepted two passes and scored, offensively, on a pass-lateral play. St. Mary's amassed 434 yards to 55 for COP, but the Gaels fumbled five more times, though recovering four. Madigan saw only the positives. He talked up his new backfield starter, Les Groux: "He is better than Nichelini, not only because he can kick and pass, but because he matches big Nick's power as a runner, and tops him in the matter of finesse." Strong words, but Groux lacked Nichelini's sprinter speed.

The Gaels exuded confidence as they prepared for the University of San Francisco. That same week, gale winds of 55 miles per hour in Oakland felled a tree in Madigan's backyard, landing by the porch where his daughters Mary, 12, and Patsy, 8, slept. Fortunately, Madigan and his wife had moved them inside in the nick of time. Madigan hoped USF was less threatening. "My dad always scheduled USF and Santa Clara to pick them up, and to keep their programs going with big attendance," said Ed Madigan. "It was a Catholic thing, but those two schools improved in football and gave my dad close games. I think he regretted being so generous."

At least, USF wasn't as devious as Santa Clara when playing St. Mary's. There wasn't the same rancor either. But football is football, USF is USF, and the Gaels scored a 13-0 victory in damp conditions before 18,000 at Kezar. After a scoreless first half, Wagner Jorgensen blocked a Ray Peterson punt to set up Meister's 23-yard field goal. USF's "Madcap" Mike Bacciarini then fumbled, and 6-foot-7 Wilbur "Wee Willie" Wilkin draped himself over the ball at the Dons 27. Schreiber's 9-yard pass to Arvin Shock at the 1-foot line set up Mal Fiese's scoring plunge. Then another USF turnover—Prentiss Wells' pass that was intercepted by Schreiber—led to Kelly Kellogg's 33-yard field goal. USF actually gained more yardage, 163 to 149, but St. Mary's feasted on USF's mistakes, chiefly recovering a Dons fumble at the Gaels 5 to preserve the shutout.

Then it was time, once again, for "Slip Madigan's Fordham Football Tour Around America," as the Gaels' fifth junket to New York City was advertised. Only it would be a different tour, directed southerly with stops in New Orleans, Miami, and St. Augustine, Florida. After those stops, the traveling party headed toward Baltimore and Richmond, Virginia, en route to the Big Apple. Thirty-four players and 150 followers, including the press, boarded the train, this time with a stronger female presence. Besides Charlotte Madigan, who normally made the Fordham journey, the beauteous Dodie O'Doe, heiress to her family's catsup fortune, was aboard. She looked forward to seeing New Orleans, as she was fluent in French, and to being seen in New York. Miss O'Doe brought along numerous suitcases and a personal maid.

The train stopped first in Arizona, where the Gaels scrimmaged the Tempe Teachers, the future Arizona State University. Then it was on to Lubbock, Texas, to practice against Texas Tech. Next stop: New Orleans, to work out against Loyola University. Then Virginia Governor George Peery greeted the Gaels in Richmond. The train served as an elongated classroom. A dozen students were taking Louis LeFevre's History 105 class, a course in historical method and research. The students' assignment: Describe every historic sight on the trip, starting in New Orleans, and then write an essay on their findings, including an overview of the New York newspapers' reportage of the Fordham game. Other Gaels were in Brother Leo's class on Dante, and they needed to keep up their reading because a test awaited them their first day back in school. Lineman Jerry Dennerlein, an honor student, already was receiving an A in that class.

Traveling Bay Area newspapermen scrambled for quotes on two stories unrelated to Fordham. The first dealt with budding friction between Madigan and Stub Allison. Madigan let it be known that he disapproved of Allison's teaching his offensive line to "feint" in order to draw the defense offside. "That's dirty football, unsportsmanlike football, and it should be abolished the same as slugging or clipping," Madigan charged. After his accusation reached Berkeley, Allison contended that he had utilized the feinting technique for years, and Madigan was the first to complain. If Madigan had a problem with it, Allison added, he could cancel the Cal-St. Mary's series. Suddenly, the press had a big story on its hands. It couldn't just drink its way across America, even with free drinks. Then another, sadder, story emerged: Brother Gregory, the former St. Mary's College president who hired Madigan in 1921, died on campus at 58. Madigan was crushed when he heard the news, remembering how Brother Gregory took a chance on a basically untested young coach. A memorial was held on the train.

Meanwhile, Fordham sought revenge after two straight defeats to the touring Gaels. The Rams were led again by backfield star Joe "The Maniac" Maniaci, plus the formidable "Seven Blocks of Granite" line of Vince Lombardi, moved from tackle to guard, and another future Pro Football Hall of Famer, center Alex Wojciechowicz. The Bay Area press had to ask numerous times, "How do you spell Wojciechowicz?" The Polo Grounds was welcomed relief to the Gaels after an emotional trip, that is until kickoff. Then St. Mary's received a gift touchdown before a partisan crowd of 50,060. Floyd Maxham boomed a punt deep into Fordham territory, the ball taking a crazy hop off Maniaci's hip and bouncing into the end zone, where Meister covered it for six easy points. He booted the PAT and the Gaels led, 7-0. But with halftime looming, Fordham scored on Andy Palau's 41-yard pass to Frank Mauette. Palau's conversion placement evened matters at 7-7. The game was, in effect, over because neither team scored in the second half.

The Gaels had traveled all that distance for a tie. There was no overtime back then, but the visitors let victory elude them with yet another demonstration of butterfingers. St. Mary's had marched to the Rams' 1-yard line, from where Mal Fiese found a small crease in the Seven Rocks of Granite and ducked through toward pay dirt. Only the ball was jarred loose before he crossed the goal line, and the Rams recovered for a touchback. The Gaels, in fact, lost all four of their fumbles that day. They outgained the Rams, 185 yards to 144, then replayed a missed opportunity in their minds all the way back to California. This time, they took a northerly route, getting off the train to practice in such places as Dodge City, Kansas. Unfortunately, the Polo Grounds wouldn't be the last place they stumbled and fumbled in 1935.

And who awaited the fatigued Gaels when they got home, but the fresh and frisky Broncos of Santa Clara, who had two weeks to prepare for the latest Little Big Game. Cartoonist Jimmy Hatlo of the *San Francisco Examiner* drew the Bronco chomping down on Senor Moraga's mustache, implying the end of Madigan's dominance of Santa Clara—an 11-1-1 record. Madigan was confident the dominance would continue. "I think we'll beat Santa Clara," he predicted. "I don't think the margin will be large, but I think we can turn the trick." Reading that, Clipper Smith, Broncos coach and fellow Notre Dame alum, worried that his breaking a "gentleman's agreement" had infuriated the Gaels.

Before St. Mary's and Santa Clara's largest attendance of the season, a Kezar capacity crowd of 59,967 that included homegrown hero Joe DiMaggio, the rivals squared off once more. St. Mary's-loathing Norbert Korte was there, fingers crossed. But lady luck, once again, was on the side of the blue-and-red-clad Gaels, who led 3-0 at halftime on Meister's 34-yard field goal. Then a wide-open Everett Pendleton dropped Herb Schreiber's perfectly thrown 27-yard pass on the goal line. But it didn't matter as the Gaels ran roughshod over the Broncos, outdistancing them, 197 yards to 18, and dominating in first downs, 11-3. Schreiber scored the game's lone touchdown in the fourth quarter, a two-yard run for a St. Mary's 10-0 victory. It was a major whipping, regardless of the score, for the Gaels, who stuck that broken gentleman's agreement in Clipper Smith's eye. And Norbert Korte left the stadium a crushed man.

St. Mary's had re-righted itself after the Fordham giveaway, standing at 4-1-1 with an opportunity for a big season by closing well. Washington State, which lost, 9-6, to the Gaels the previous year, was returning to Kezar to uphold the prestige of the Pacific Coast Conference. Madigan hailed the Cougars as the best team in the PCC's northern half, attempting to pump up the gate. But only 10,000 showed up for the game, another telltale turnout for financially suffering St. Mary's, and for Madigan's future in Moraga. Schreiber, now the Gaels most dependable back, threw a 42-yard touchdown pass to Erdelatz in the second quarter. Washington State came right back on a 48-yard scoring drive. Ed Goddard threw a 35-yard pass to Levi McCormack, a Nez Perce tribe member, before Goddard covered the final 13 yards on four runs. Mel Johansen matched Meister's PAT kick, and the game ended in a 7-7 tie. St. Mary's covered more ground, 225 yards to Washington State's 166, but had nothing to show for it except its second tie of the season, a new experience for Madigan. Once again, he reflected on his preseason high hopes, and how he had been so wrong.

The following week, Madigan became, so familiarly, the most rumored coach in the country to leave for another position. This time, it was to, of all places, Fordham, which reportedly was severing relations with the embattled Jim Crowley. Despite shaky times in Moraga, Madigan denied his leaving for the umpteenth time. Crowley then signed a three-year contract to remain at Fordham. But Madigan wanted St. Mary's, it was becoming clearer, more than St. Mary's wanted him.

St. Mary's faced a second straight PCC opponent in Oregon, against which it was 5-1. "This is Oregon's best team in many years," said Madigan, who would miss three regulars for the game: Erdelatz (shoulder), Jorgensen (groin) and end John Giannoni (appendicitis). Thus Madigan started eight sophomores against the Ducks, a chancy situation. But the valiant Gaels scored a resounding 18-0 victory, achieved before another paltry turnout of 15,000 at foggy Kezar. The Gaels had lost their fan appeal for "home" games, other than against Santa Clara. Those who weren't there missed a one-sided show. Hugh Sill found a huge hole in the left side of the Oregon line, cut back toward the middle, and dashed 67 yards for a touchdown. Schreiber later scored on a 6-yard run before Ned O'Laughlin, on the game's final play, tossed a 12-yard pass to Ed Hallman in the end zone.

The press wondered afterward: "Were you piling on the score, Slip?" He replied: "I just wanted to give O'Laughlin, a good kid who doesn't play much, a chance to show what he can do." Oregon couldn't complain, though. The Ducks were manhandled throughout, yielding 422 yards and 14 first downs, while totaling only 59 yards and 3 first downs themselves. The Gaels ran for 363 of those yards, led by Fiese's 86 yards on 12 carries, averaging six yards per carry as a team. When the 1935 Gaels were at their best, they were magnificent. But they could be just the opposite a week later, with butterfingers usually the culprit.

UCLA was St. Mary's final opponent. A 6-1-2 record was possible for the Gaels if they could only hold onto the football. Madigan lifted his team's smoking ban, but the Gaels looked winded anyway against the Bruins. Before another skimpy crowd of 10,000 at Kezar, UCLA opened the scoring on Bill Murphy's 28-yard pass to Bob Schroeder. Lou Ferry blocked Chuck Cheshire's PAT try, leaving the Bruins with a 6-0 lead at halftime. St. Mary's pulled ahead, 7-6, in the third quarter after an 80-yard drive, ending on a short scoring burst by Maxham and Ferry's perfect placement. Billy Bob Williams put UCLA back in front, 13-7, on a 12-yard scamper and Cheshire's successful PAT kick. St. Mary's marched down the field again and was in perfect position for a win, or certainly a tie. Maxham squeezed through a hole at the 1-yard line and was about to cross the goal line when the ball was jarred loose, rolling into the end zone where three Bruins pounced on it for a touchback. More fumbling blues for St. Mary's, or what was it? Madigan wanted to know.

The question he wanted answered: Did Maxham lose possession in the end zone, which meant a touchdown and a tie score? The head official said "no," emphatically. That official was Clarence "Nibs" Price, basketball coach at the University of California, who was moonlighting as a football official. The fumble, he insisted, occurred before the goal line, therefore a touchback. Was there bias afoot, considering what Madigan had said about Cal football coach Stub Allison's feinting tactics? Price also had been Cal's football coach in the late-1920s, so perhaps he was offended by what Madigan had said? No way.

"My dad loved Nibs," said Ed Madigan. "He thought he was a great guy." Whatever the ruling, Price paid for it as he walked off the field. An inebriated St. Mary's fan blind-sided him with a punch in the nose. The fan was apprehended and brought to the locker room where Price and the other officials dressed. Price asked him if he wanted to continue the "conversation," and the tipsy rooter said "yes." Calmer minds intervened, and the fan was allowed to go without being arrested, or being punched by Price, who left with a scarred nose. The Gaels, even though outgaining the Bruins, 204 yards to 131, wound up with a 13-7 defeat and a 5-2-2 record. Except for two costly fumbles, at Fordham and UCLA, they might have been 7-1-1, Madigan's best record since 8-1 in 1930. Alas, he wouldn't put together another undefeated, or single-defeat, season in his remaining time in Moraga.

Madigan ruminated on the season that could have been when it became official that Temple and St. Mary's would play each other in 1936. This is the same Temple team that was coached by Pop Warner, Madigan's adversary, who once vowed never to play St. Mary's again. But Warner made that statement at Stanford. Seeing the success of the intersectional rivalry between St. Mary's and Fordham, old Pop wanted to create the same environment, or at least give it one good try.

Madigan, naturally, wanted to match himself against Warner, a gridiron giant, anytime he got the opportunity. But, first, there was the nagging issue of fumbling. No team on the coast was looser with the football than St. Mary's, which fumbled 32 times to 13 for its opposition. What a shame, because the 1935 Gaels scored more points than their opponents, 115-37, including five shutout wins. They piled up more yards, 1,612 to 542, and amassed more first downs, 88 to 46.

Oh, what a year it might have been except for those butterfingers. This problem needed to be corrected before the ensuing season, because Slip's teams had become too slippery for their own good.

12

Gridder and the Sex Symbol

When Slip Madigan donned his blue blazer and offset it with bow tie, white slacks and two-toned shoes, he drew comparisons to "The Great Gatsby." That Hollywood connection wasn't too far off as Madigan had many friends on the film set, namely Errol Flynn, Pat O'Brien, Robert Taylor, Bob Hope and Bing Crosby. Slip mingled with entertainers, and perhaps that's why he permitted a film land story involving one of his Gaels to become gossip material. Because as any studio press agent will attest, it doesn't have to be true, necessarily, to be believed.

Jim Austin, who played end for St. Mary's, was eye candy for the female set. Co-eds at Mills College voted him "America's handsomest football player." He stood 6-foot-1, had blond, wavy hair, and possessed a he-man's build. A Hollywood native, he spent his summers working as a handyman at Metro Goldwyn Mayer. Ever on the prowl for a good story, St. Mary's publicist Tom "Tom-Tom" Foudy asked Austin if he had met any stars at MGM. Austin replied that actress Jean Harlow waved to him once. Or he thought it was a wave, but wasn't sure.

Didn't matter. A wave, perhaps fictitious, was all Foudy needed to turn the mere hint of something into an actual event. The next day's *Oakland Tribune* reported that Austin was giving up football for Jean Harlow, known as Hollywood's "Blonde Bombshell" and "Sex Symbol of the Thirties." Newspapers across the country picked up the story and bombarded MGM and St. Mary's College, seeking confirmation of the romance. MGM put out a press release, saying Harlow and Austin "were just good friends." The playful Madigan wouldn't let any story, real or imagined, die if it meant publicity. So Foudy let it be known that Harlow had made a mysterious trip to San Francisco before the 1936 St. Mary's-Gonzaga season opener, making Austin late for practice. "You can play with Jean Harlow or you can play for St. Mary's," an irate Madigan told Austin, according to publicist Foudy. "I won't have any glamour boy on my ball club."

The press went hunting for Austin, who was hiding out in the homes of relatives. Foudy gave the story more legs by indicating that Austin had been kidnapped. Finally, Austin showed up for football practice, followed by Foudy's announcement that Austin had renounced Harlow for the gridiron. Madigan wouldn't allow the press to interview Austin, saying he needed to concentrate on football and his studies. But Foudy concocted more fiction, saying Austin had five or six girls he was more interested in than Harlow. The press ate it up, as mythical as it all sounded. Madigan had built a publicity machine in Moraga, with clever men like Will Stevens and Tom-Tom Foudy assisting him in turning a tiny regional college in California into a major national story. Eventually, the Harlow-Austin romance died, for a larger story emerged from St. Mary's, namely its financial future and the job security of its famous coach, a strained relationship that even Hollywood couldn't make up.

To outsiders, everything was positive between coach and administration. Billboards appeared around the Bay Area, showing a smiling Madigan handing a football to his helmet-wearing 4-year-old son Ed, with a script that read: ". . . and drink Milk, a quart a day—Slip Madigan." It was an advertisement for the Lucerne dairy company. Further positive publicity was directed toward Madigan. One magazine article said: "Slip is to St. Mary's what Rockne was to Notre Dame." Another article contended that St. Mary's was the "David of the football world, for her opponents have been chiefly Pacific Coast Conference teams and such intersectional colossi as Southern Methodist, Alabama and Fordham." Madigan wasn't afraid of the Goliaths of the world; his own administration scared him more.

Hollywood might have invented Slip Madigan if he wasn't already real, but the film capital already had its sights on another story: "Gone With the Wind," published as a book in 1936. Other, non-fictional, stories surfaced that year: The construction of Hoover Dam, FDR's landslide presidential win over Alf Landon, Max Schmeling's knockout of Joe Louis, LIFE Magazine's first publication, and the St. Patrick Day's flood in Pittsburgh, the worst flood in history up to that point.

Madigan began his sixteenth season at St. Mary's in 1936 as the dean of West Coast coaches. Though rumors of his leaving continued to surface, he still received 10 percent of gate receipts during the Depression, making him the envy of other coaches. Largely because of him, St. Mary's had grown up, both academically and architecturally, advertising itself as "The most cosmopolitan college in the land. Students registered from twenty-two states and seven foreign countries." Madigan had taken St. Mary's on an unprecedented journey, from The Brickpile in Oakland to the Moraga Valley, and then throwing in cross-country train trips to fuel its national prominence. It had been quite a ride for Madigan and St. Mary's, and it wasn't over.

Speaking of destinations, Slip took off for Berlin, Germany, in the summer of '36 to attend the Olympic Games. He set sail on the U.S.S. Washington from the nation's capital on June 30, traveling through Ireland, England, France, Italy, and finally back up to Germany. Supposedly, he was conducting an educational tour for tourists, but he also received a press credential, thus gaining access to many of the Olympic competitions. Madigan spent most of his time filming track and field events, including Jesse Owens's exploits. He also had the opportunity to meet Hermann Goring, the Nazi Party leader. "My dad said that Goring was a big affable guy," recalled Ed Madigan. "But dad could see that Germany was preparing for war, because of its youth movement." Slip Madigan decided to cut the European trip short after his wife took ill back home. But when she was reported out of danger, he returned to California as originally planned in early September.

He brought home an Olympic program with a male and female German athlete, both blond, sketched on the cover, a javelin positioned between them. This was Hitler's Aryan race for the universe to see, and for the United States to confront in the decade to come. Madigan arrived in Oakland, fending off a political rumor that he would run as a Democrat for the Congressional seat in the Sixth District. His response: "I've had quite a bit of practice kicking the football around, and they tell me that political football is about the same." He didn't need a political speechwriter to come up with that gem, and he didn't run regardless.

Prescott Sullivan, the Bay Area's most popular sportswriter, left the *San Francisco Chronicle* to join the rival *Examiner*. He asked Madigan to name the best team on the coast. "It looks like California to me," he said. "I'll be happy if St. Mary's loses no more than two." St. Mary's hadn't lost more than two games since 1928, and hadn't been beaten by more than 14 points since 1924. Professional wrestler Gus "The Goat" Sonnenberg accompanied Sullivan to a Gaels practice. The Goat wasn't impressed, noting in Sullivan's column that, "If St. Mary's loses any ball games this year, it will be because of slowness in the line. They're too big. I don't think they can get out of their own way." Countering The Goat, Madigan said, "That's the way I like them, big and tough. I'm going to keep them."

Madigan was high, naturally, on his Gaels. Fullback Jerry Dowd "has possibilities of developing into one of the greatest fullbacks in Pacific Coast history. He can do everything well. It all depends on whether he wants to work hard." To recruit Dowd, the younger brother of Santa Clara star Gil Dowd, Madigan brought along a St. Mary's professor on a home visit. When the professor addressed Dowd's father in Gaelic, he told his son, "You're going to St. Mary's."

Madigan knew how to sell his product. He told the press that halfback Ned O'Laughlin was so fast, "he can run where other so-called fast ones can only dog trot." When the press mentioned that starting guard Marty Kordick had been dropped off the freshman team for poor practice habits, Slip said, "He might be the worst practice player I've ever coached, but once the lights come on, he's one of my best players." Kordick, later a varsity star, was registered in St. Mary's School of Foreign Service, and planned to join the United States diplomatic corps following graduation.

Madigan missed the start of fall practice for the first time in sixteen years, while arranging final details in Los Angeles for the St. Mary's-Loyola game on Oct. 11. Upon returning, he talked up his new "Flying A" formation, which evolved out of a double shift, yet was more adapted to passing than running. The "Flying A," in actuality, was a petrol station chain, and the skeptical press waited to see if Madigan's latest innovation had any gas. The Gaels hadn't enjoyed consistent passing success since Fred "Mack" Stennett in the 1920s, so the press was skeptical, by now aware of Madigan's playing games, on and off the field.

First up for St. Mary's was visiting Gonzaga on September 27. As the Bulldogs, or Zags, began fall drills, coach Mike Pecarovich offered this dismal forecast: "Only seventeen days to prepare for the slaughter. I could coach this squad for a year, and it wouldn't be ready for the Gaels. We can't out-power them, but we might out-speed them or out-trick them." Gonzaga beat Washington State in 1935, the same year St. Mary's tied the Cougars. Gonzaga, it turned out, was miffed at St. Mary's for dropping it off the schedule in 1931, just so the Gaels could play Oregon. "The St. Mary's game had been important to us as a money-maker," said Gonzaga publicist Buck Weaver. "We have waited a number of years for this chance." But by fanning the flames, the Zags might be burned.

Madigan's stomach problems flared up again just before the Gonzaga opener. He stayed in bed for two days with a temperature of 101. He hadn't missed two consecutive practices prior to 1936. Assistant Red Strader conducted workouts in his absence, though Slip returned before the week was out. Pecarovich hardly prepared for a slaughter, unless it was the Gaels who would be slaughtered, as Gonzaga held a 13-12 halftime lead before 30,000 at Kezar. The Zags produced two long-range touchdowns—Pete Higgins' 82-yard interception return and Mike Karamatic's 91-yard kickoff return, with Karamatic making one of two PAT kicks. The Gaels' first touchdown came on a 50-yard pass from Lou Rimassa to Hugh Sill. Maybe Madigan wasn't joking about the "Flying A" formation. Groux scored on runs of 5 and 1 yards to give the Gaels a 19-13 lead, then followed up with a third score, a 2-yard smash set up by Wally Garard's interception. The Gaels won, 26-13. Statistically, it was a slaughter. St. Mary's dominated in yards gained, 314 to 45, and in first downs, 15 to 0—a shutout—in one of the most dominating defensive efforts of the Madigan era.

Still, Madigan wasn't moved. "We played a ragged game," he said. "To do the same against California next week would be fatal." Cal coach Stub Allison sounded equally cautious. "St. Mary's has everything it takes," he said. "I don't know how we're going to beat them, for they're out to avenge their defeat of last year. Our morale is good, but we haven't got old-man experience on our side this season, and that may cost us three or four games." Just two calculating coaches, playing off each other. The respective student bodies turned prankster the week of the game. Some St. Mary's males splashed red paint at the Sather Gate entrance to the Cal campus, and got away with it. Then six Cal students were caught painting the St. Mary's water tower blue, and had their heads shaved and their faces painted with Mercurochrome.

More calculating? "Stub Allison is the best coach on the Pacific Coast," Madigan said. "He has a good man that fits every position. I will admit that we have better tackles than California. That is all." Madigan singled out Gael tackles "Wee Willie" Wilkin and Jerry Dennerlein. But Allison, when asked to name the best coaches on the coast, mentioned Tiny Thornhill of Stanford, Howard Jones of USC, Bill Spaulding of UCLA, and Jimmy Phelan of Washington, dismissing the man in Moraga. Madigan responded, sarcastically: "Well, Stub won nine straight games in his first year as California head coach in 1935. Of course, he lost the one that mattered most, but he's still No. 1 in my opinion." Allison got in the last word: "I accept the nomination, but not the prevarication." Madigan wasn't lying. The Bears did win nine straight before bowing to Stanford, 13-0, which earned the Rose Bowl bid.

Allison beat Madigan, 10-0, in 1935, but Madigan then returned the favor, 10-0, in 1936 before 60,000 in Berkeley. In the second quarter, the Gaels marched to the Bears' 1-yard line before Lou Ferry kicked a 15-yard field goal. The only other score came in the third quarter, the Gaels marching once again to the 1, with Groux gaining the final yard. Make no mistake, it was St. Mary's day, amassing 296 yards to Cal's 140, with more first downs, 16 to 5. And for the second straight week, the Gaels didn't give up a defensive touchdown. "It was a great team victory," said Slip. "We played conservative football to insure victory. Even a 3-0 score at the finish would have made me feel satisfied, that our victory was decisive." And that was no prevarication.

The Gaels then turned their attention to third opponent Loyola at the same time that Brother Albert, the St. Mary's president, turned his attention to Jean Harlow. Embarrassed by the fabricated romance with Jim Austin, and the threat of a suit by MGM, Brother Albert wrote a letter of apology to Harlow. Surprisingly, she wrote a letter back, inviting him to her studio the next time he was in Los Angeles, which coincided with the Loyola game. And so he paid the starlet a visit in her MGM dressing room. She offered him ginger ale, coffee or tea. He said, "No, thanks." Then she said, "Well, how about some scotch?" That was his favorite libation. "Why, certainly," he said. He sensed that she was upset by the Gael-driven gossip. "All this publicity, I have no control over," she said. "I guess the world must think I'm an old bitch." She was all of 25. Brother Albert and Harlow made peace, and MGM decided not to sue, a huge relief for St. Mary's during its financial slide in the 1930s.

Loyola then self-destructed in a 19-7 victory for the Gaels as 55,000 attended at the Los Angeles Coliseum. The Lions fumbled the ball away four times in the second quarter alone, leading to a 8-yard touchdown sweep by Groux and a 1-yard scoring plunge by Floyd Maxham. Ferry scored in the same quarter on a 15-yard interception return. The Gaels' defense finally was scored upon after eleven quarters, when Billy Byrne threw an 11-yard pass to Jack Foley when it no longer mattered. St. Mary's suffered a key injury as Maxham tore a muscle at the base of his spine, reportedly costing him the rest of the season. "He is the greatest all-around fullback I have ever coached," said Madigan, forgetting his earlier comment about Dowd. Halfback Tony Falkenstein shifted to fullback, but the Gaels' injury list already was mounting, alarmingly.

St. Mary's record was 3-0 as it encountered the University of San Francisco, the Gaels having won the ten previous meetings between the two Catholic institutions. Dons coach Spud Lewis cared less about history: "We have a good chance against the Gaels. Because we stopped Santa Clara's offense, I believe we can stop St. Mary's. Whenever we get the chance, we'll throw the ball around, and maybe we'll click on a couple." The Gaels, a 3-to-1 favorite, would leave afterward for New York, and another matchup with Fordham. Lewis didn't get the win he sought, but he managed a scoreless tie in front of 26,000 at Kezar. The Gaels committed hari-kari, moving three times inside the Dons' 10, once to the 1-yard line, but failing each time to reach the end zone. St. Mary's had more yards, 130-29, and first downs, 12-2, but statistics can be meaningless. A fight broke out between St. Mary's and USF followers, injuring three people. Then seventeen balloons holding up a political banner at the stadium exploded when a fan put a cigarette to a balloon. Flaming clouds of gas shot twenty feet high, injuring seventeen more people. Ambulances rushed to the scene, and the injured were taken to Park Emergency Hospital. St. Mary's now had a new rival in USF, though the Little Big Game wasn't nearly this explosive.

Madigan once again scheduled two games on the same road trip: Fordham in New York and Marquette in Chicago on the way home. Plus the Gaels would attend the Notre Dame-Ohio State game in South Bend in between. En route to the Big Apple, the traveling party stopped off in La Junta, Colorado, and Chicago. On the way back, it would be Niagara Falls, Boston, and Quebec, along with visiting the St. Anne de Beaupre statue near Montreal—an 8,000-mile journey. Even NFL teams didn't travel this extravagantly. A party of 250 boarded the St. Mary's "honeymoon special" in San Francisco. On board were newlyweds Jack Cassidy and the former Alice Wilson.

This latest cross-country excursion wasn't devoid of breaking news. John R. Tunis, prominent sportswriter and novelist, proposed that colleges should cut in athletes on profits from games, claiming that most schools "conceal, they don't reveal" these profits. He listed California, Notre Dame, Harvard and Yale as semi-professional, and St. Mary's, Santa Clara, Stanford, USC, Oregon, Washington and Fordham as professional. He wouldn't reveal where he gathered this information, but the 210 "friends of St. Mary's" on the train paid $260 apiece for a total of $54,600, all of it directed toward the coffers of St. Mary's and Southern Pacific, but not the players who made it all possible. Madigan was against paying the players, pointing instead to their scholarships and free travel costs. Tunis' proposal died for the time being, though the concept of paying college athletes hasn't ever died.

Madigan also learned on the trip that bondholders who helped enlarge the St. Mary's campus were up in arms. Those bonds were issued in 1928, the same year as the move to Moraga, but no interest on the bonds had been paid since July 1, 1934. The $1,370,500 par value of the bonds now was outstanding. Of this amount, only $819,000 has been deposited. The bondholders demanded payment. St. Mary's, of course, was struggling during the Depression. But Madigan wouldn't be cowed. "Maybe they can foreclose," he told the traveling press, "but if they mean to put another of those bankers in charge to handle one more athletic setup, they can count me out. I will not remain under any condition but the present one." In Madigan's legally educated mind, a deal was a deal; his 10 percent of gate receipts was written into his contract. And if that deal was challenged, he just might speak out and claim that cut.

The "Slip Madigan Fordham Special Around America and Canada" finally arrived in New York City, to an unwelcoming reception. And all because Fordham won this time, 7-6, on Andy Palau's 45-yard touchdown bomb to Harry Jacunski, and Palau's PAT placement. The Gaels only managed two Lou Ferry field goals of 23 and 42 yards, with all the scoring completed in the opening quarter before 52,612 witnesses at the Polo Grounds. The Gaels were outgained, 180 yards to 127, and managed only 2 first downs to Fordham's 8. Fordham intercepted five passes—there went the Flying A offense—and recovered two fumbles to stay undefeated. "We lost to a better team," Madigan said, graciously, "and I'm glad it was Jim Crowley who got the break. A team making only two first downs cannot expect anything better than what we gathered. I knew it was one of those games that would be decided by a single touchdown. That's why I had Lou Ferry kick the first field goal. Had Ferry not been injured in the contest, we would have had a better chance to win." Ferry tore knee cartilage after his two field goals. Like Maxham before him, he was ruled out for the remainder of the season. Ten St. Mary's regulars now were sidelined with injuries—the harbinger of a difficult road trip, and a disappointing, already draining season.

St. Mary's and Fordham each paid $25,000 to rent the Polo Grounds. From the $112,000 gate, they split it, $56,000 apiece. The Gaels continued north to view Niagara Falls and the Old North Church in Boston, then journeyed to Montreal with the words of Notre Dame alum and current University of Detroit Gus Dorais ringing in Madigan's head: "Slip, you'll have an awful time trying to stop Marquette's Ray Buivid. He is the closest approach to Jim Thorpe, who is my favorite football player, the best I have ever seen, better than George Gipp. You'll forget about Ernie Nevers and all the other hard-hitting backs when you see him."

Buivid, one of the better passers in the nation, was a prime All-America candidate. Like Fordham, Marquette also was unbeaten. St. Mary's outweighed the Milwaukee-based school by fifteen pounds per man, that is if all the Gael regulars were healthy, which wasn't the case. To make a bad situation even worse, center Wally Garard was the latest Gael sidelined, with a peculiar stomach illness.

On the train trip to Chicago, Charlotte Madigan showed her husband memorabilia she had collected on the trip: Programs from Rockefeller Center, Radio City Music Hall, a "Tobacco Road" performance, and a Hollywood Night Club review featuring dancing girls from "The Great Ziegfield" movie. But the program cover that caught the Madigans' attention was from the Cotton Club, featuring sketches of nude black men and woman cavorting in a jungle setting. Quite shocking. She also had a menu from Jack Dempsey's restaurant, where most drinks were under a half-dollar, a filet mignon cost $2.20, and filet of sole $1.20. But the way Slip's delicate stomach felt after playing Fordham, he didn't feel much like eating or drinking.

The Gaels had practiced, but not scrimmaged, going east, but Madigan altered things going west. They practiced thrice in one day, with bodies colliding, while heading to Chicago. "I'm cracking the whip," said Madigan "because we've got to win one game before heading home." He even changed uniforms, packing up the green jerseys with the golden harp and green pants from the Fordham game, and changing to blue jerseys with white shoulders, red silk pants with blue stockings, and scarlet helmets. Madigan's coaching opponent at Marquette, Frank Murray, never played football, but taught himself the game by reading instruction books and attending coaching clinics. What mattered most in Chicago: Murray had a healthier roster than Madigan, plus the multi-talented Buivid.

On a Friday night at Soldier Field, before a gathering of 50,000, Buivid set a Marquette victory in motion with a 13-yard touchdown run and a 75-yard interception return of an O'Laughlin pass for a second score. O'Laughlin scored on a 3-yard run to cut the margin to 13-7, but Buivid put the game out of reach by uncorking a long pass that deflected off O'Laughlin and into the arms of Bill Higgins, who completed the 54-yard touchdown to give the Golden Avalanche a 20-6 victory—the Gaels' most one-sided loss in four seasons. Buivid truly played as advertised, though comparisons to Thorpe, Gipp and Nevers were debatable.

St. Mary's hadn't won in three weeks—its longest three-game drought since 1923—thus making it a depressing trip home. The team stopped off in South Bend to watch Notre Dame, Madigan's alma mater, beat Ohio State, 7-2. Madigan sat there a worried man, thinking of his Gaels giving up three scoring plays of seventy-plus yards in one year. Confidently, St. Mary's Hugh Sill told the traveling press corps, "I'm willing to bet nobody gets away from us again the rest of the season."

St. Mary's was reeling at 3-2-1 as it prepared for Idaho. The Vandals had beaten the same Gonzaga team, 18-7, that St. Mary's defeated, 26-13, in the season opener. Needing to right their season, the Gaels couldn't overlook the visitors from the potato state. Madigan needed a positive start, and Maxham, who wasn't lost for the season after all, carried two Vandals into the end zone on a 5-yard run and a 7-0 lead. Madigan threw down his Borsalino and kicked it as Idaho's Tony Knap grabbed a Falkenstein fumble out of the air and raced 85 yards to knot the score. Hugh Sill spoke too soon. Falkenstein made up for his miscue by catching a 27-yard pass from Groux at the 2, with Groux then squeezing over the goal line on his second attempt. Reserve back Frank Shock scored on a 6-yard run to give the Gaels a 26-7 triumph before a skimpy crowd of 7,500 at Kezar. Although the men of Moraga dominated in yards gained, 392 to 72, and in first downs, 19 to 3, they fumbled 10 times, losing five, and threw three interceptions. Turnover issues from the previous season had carried over, a clear sign, once again, of a careless football team.

Backfield regular Sill was ruled out of the Santa Clara game with a trick knee, thinning the Gaels' ranks further, and causing more rumbling inside Madigan's abdomen. "This year's injuries to important men before important games amounts to more than I have had in the total of my sixteen years at St. Mary's," he said. "I lost Floyd Maxham, Jerry Dowd, Vic Strub and Bob Timm in the early season, and from then on things have happened every week." The loss of Strub at end provided his backup, Jim Austin, with more playing time, although, more than likely, Jean Harlow wasn't paying attention in screenland.

A Santa Clara head-coaching change had occurred from the previous season: Clipper Smith moved on to Villanova, and his top assistant, Buck Shaw, replaced him. And Shaw, who would become the San Francisco 49ers first head coach in 1946, had the '36 Broncos undefeated when they engaged St. Mary's before 61,500 at Kezar. This time, they laid into the Gaels, 19-0, for their first win over St. Mary's since 1923. And for the first time since 1932, St. Mary's was shut out twice in the same season. The Broncos'

Manny Gomez scored on a short run and then tossed a touchdown pass to Norman Finney. The Broncos' last touchdown came on a blocked kick. Oddly, the Gaels only fumbled once, and led in yards, 185 to 93, and first downs, 10-4, yet produced zeros on the scoreboard. Madigan searched for something positive. "Nobody was hurt in the game," he said, finally. "It wasn't any one thing they did which bothered us. It was everything." The taciturn Shaw's appraisal of things: "I think the boys played very well." Very well, indeed.

The 4-3-1 Gaels went searching for their lost gallop against College of Pacific, the third meeting between Madigan and Stagg. Before their first meeting, in 1933, Madigan brought Stagg into the Gaels locker room, and respectfully introduced the iconic coach to his players. Coaching was different back then; imagine such a scenario occurring today between coaches. Madigan realized his mistake after squeaking out a 7-0 victory in '33. He wouldn't make that same mistake in '36, and the Gaels pounded the Tigers, 34-0, before a small audience of 12,000 in San Francisco. Maxham and Falkenstein tallied on short runs. Maxham found Joe Hurley all alone in the end zone for six more points. Lou Rimassa and O'Laughlin then scored, in order, on sweeps of 33 and 66 yards. "Those St. Mary's boys were rugged and quick," said Stagg. "Yes, indeed, they were quick." Madigan seemed imbued: "We're out of our late-season slump. We were on and Pacific was off, but I can understand how they held Loyola to 7 points and California to 14." The Gaels also held Loyola to 7, and Cal to zero, then let a promising season go poof.

In 1927, Pop Warner declared: "I'll never coach another team against St. Mary's," after the Gaels beat his Stanford team, 16-0, in a donnybrook at Palo Alto. Warner now coached at Temple, and guess which team he chose to face in 1936: None other than St. Mary's. How so, Pop? "No comment," he humph-ed in his usual humph-ing manner. "I'll just say that I'm feeling fine except for this hip, which means I have to use a cane. As for the game, I won't say that we can't win. We might, but St. Mary's has the better team." Madigan downplayed any animosity with Warner. "I'm very fond of the old boy," he said. "Despite one or two professional beefs, we have always been personal friends." Really, Slip?

Their rematch was a remake of '27, only at Kezar Stadium. And just like '27, Warner protested repeatedly that the Gaels were getting away with physical mayhem against his Owls. Plus, Warner added, Gaels assistant Red Strader was illegally signaling plays to a now uninjured quarterback, Ferry, by using a game program. The "Old Fox" sat on a shipping trunk, chain-smoking throughout the game, occasionally pushing himself up with the aid of his cane. Across the field, Madigan smoked nervously as he paced the sideline, crunching the Borsalino in his hands as the small group of Temple fans among the 15,000 spectators naturally yelled at him to take a seat.

Temple's only touchdown was a gift. St. Mary's center Wally Garrad had left school after the Fordham-Marquette trip, reportedly brokenhearted over a lost romance. Jerry Conlee replaced him, but a center snap of his against Temple sailed over the punter's head and into the end zone, where Temple's Edwin Walker recovered for a 7-0 lead. O'Laughlin saved a second Temple touchdown by catching Cliff Seaber from behind at the 11. O'Laughlin added yet another big play on the same drive, knocking down a fourth-down pass from Christian Pappas to Gordon Smith in the end zone. Later on, O'Laughlin carried the football three times for 30 yards to the 3, from where Maxham blasted into the end zone. O'Laughlin ended his finest performance by throwing a 22-yard touchdown pass to poster boy Jim Austin, giving the Gaels a 13-7 victory and a 6-3-1 final record. And just like '27, Warner promptly cut off ties with Madigan, this time permanently.

"Our Galloping Gaels," summarized Madigan, "played the hardest schedule on record, and only Santa Clara and Washington had better records on the Pacific Coast." However, the 19 points by Santa Clara and the 20 points by Marquette were the two biggest defensive yields by the Gaels in the same season since 1928. In a final poll, Minnesota ranked No. 1, California No. 9, Santa Clara No. 10, and St. Mary's No. 27, quite fitting with its tough schedule and injury onslaught. Jerry Dennerlein was the only Gael picked for the East-West Shrine Game.

A report surfaced that Madigan was pondering an offer to play unbeaten, once-tied Alabama on Jan. 2 at the Los Angeles Coliseum after the Crimson Tide was overlooked for the Rose Bowl. That report was nothing more than someone's imagination. The St. Mary's season was, indeed, over. But Gaels football still was in the news, because Madigan received a payment of $38,234.15 from St. Mary's; his 10 percent of gate receipts was collected, of course, after his wife leaned heavily on Brother Albert, who then paid off. A signed deal is a signed deal, but some critics, including at St. Mary's, equated Madigan to Pancho Villa.

Brother Albert offered a contrary view: "St. Mary's owed Mr. Madigan back salary and back percentage of the gate receipts for several years. After the Fordham game, I personally paid Mr. Madigan what we owed him, because I recognize a just debt, and because I recognize that he has brought certain assets to St. Mary's College. He is an outstanding figure on the St. Mary's campus. I will protect Mr. Madigan as I feel he is one of our greatest assets. He has a lifetime job at St. Mary's if he wants it."

Curley Grieve, *San Francisco Examiner* sportswriter, also defended Slip's largesse: "Madigan is worth his salary (of $25,000 annually). He has proved cheap at his price. Those with long memories recall that Madigan did not leap on the gravy train. He built it."

The graduating class in May 1937, by the way, included magna cum laude awardees Vic Strub of the Galloping Gaels and Joseph L. Alioto, a pre-law student and future mayor of San Francisco.

Whether Jean Harlow learned that her fictitious football leading man, Jim Austin, had won the 1936 season finale for St. Mary's is unknown. What is known is that there would be no future "romance" between the gridder and the glamour girl. Harlow died of a kidney disease on June 7, 1937. She was 26. Whether Austin mourned is also unknown.

13

Typewriter Kings

The two sportswriters removed their suit coats and loosened their ties. Their disagreement had gone too far, and now they would settle their dispute, in a manly fashion. Prescott Sullivan of the *San Francisco Examiner* and Tom Laird of the *San Francisco News* took off their hats, dropped them alongside the green at Harding Park, and assumed their fighting positions, with the combative Laird looking for an opening to land his "Iron Mike" right hand on Sullivan's chin.

They circled each other until the sun was in Sullivan's eyes, blinding him. And that's precisely when Laird unleashed Iron Mike, knocking Sullivan on his back, and rendering him nearly unconscious. Laird put on his coat and hat and drove away, feeling victorious, not cowardly. Sullivan, once revived, grabbed his coat and hat and drove back to the Examiner. He sat down at his typewriter, and wrote humbly about losing the fight. That heartfelt column made Sullivan an instant hero to his readers, a major reason why he became the most beloved sportswriter in San Francisco. Readers later awaited his traditional opening day baseball column, when he counted the number of peanuts in a bag, and compared their quality to past bags of peanuts on opening day. Sullivan wrote with character, and he was quite the character himself. There was little room for passengers in his car, with old newspapers, sandwich wrappers, bottles and cans piled everywhere. Recycling wasn't his thing. Neither was boring journalism. Not Sully.

The 1920s and 1930s were a halcyon, though primitive, time for Sullivan and other sports scribes in the San Francisco Bay Area. No major-league sports existed on the West Coast in those days, just minor-league baseball. College athletics ruled the roost, with a multitude of newspapers giving them blanket coverage. San Francisco had four newspapers: *The Examiner, Chronicle, News,* and *Call-Bulletin.* Oakland had the *Tribune* and *Post-Enquirer.* San Jose had the *Mercury* and *News.* Smaller papers, including the *Berkeley Gazette, Alameda Times-Star, Palo Alto Times* and *Redwood City Tribune,* added to the media mix.

It was a glorious era for newspapers, enjoying a rapt readership. There wasn't yet television, so radio was the only competition for news. Sullivan and Curley Grieve had huge followings at the *Examiner.* Frayne and Jack McDonald were readers' favorites at the *Call-Bulletin.* "Iron Mike" Laird was lead man at the *News.* Bill Leiser, Dick Friendlich, Will Connolly and Art Rosenbaum were emerging stars at the *Chronicle.* Art Cohn and Alan Ward were featured in the *Tribune,* Al Santoro in the *Post-Enquirer,* Louie Duino in San Jose, and Jack Clark in the *Times-Star.*

The acerbic Cohn made friends and enemies in Oakland. Readers lined up faithfully outside the *Tribune* building to get his daily column, "The Cohn-ing Tower." He so enraged the University of Washington's crewmen that they came looking for him. "The Boys in the Boat" were ready to "scull" him, but he escaped through a back entrance. Cohn nicknamed golfer Johnny Bulla as "Fulla Bulla" for no other reason than the rhyming aspect. Cohn later served as a World War II correspondent, upsetting Gen. Douglas MacArthur with his coverage. Post-war, Cohn wrote screenplays and the "The Joker Is Wild" about comedian Joe E. Lewis; Frank Sinatra played Lewis in the movie. Cohn was writing the biography of film producer Mike Todd, No. 3 husband of Elizabeth Taylor, when the two men were killed in a 1958 small plane crash.

The above sports scribes wrote eagerly, and often, about Slip Madigan in the 1930s. Also popular during that colorful era were local cartoonists, such as Jimmy Hatlo of the Examiner and Howard Brodie of the Chronicle. Hatlo, created "Senor Moraga," while Brodie sketched brilliant locker room scenes complete with texts. Madigan was readily available to be interviewed or drawn, and he became even more accessible when the Bay Bridge was built in 1936 and the Caldecott Tunnel opened in 1937. No longer did the San Francisco press have to drive by ferry to Oakland, and then motor over a mountain to get out to St. Mary's College in rural Moraga. The train was another mode of transportation, heading straight from Oakland to the campus. Madigan awaited the writers with a big smile and endless quotes. He was a sportswriter's dream.

Decades before newspaper consolidations and subsequent newspaper closings changed the Bay Area's media landscape, including the phasing out of sports cartooning, college football coaches owned the autumn months in terms of press coverage. Sis boom bah ruled! But even with that excessive coverage, the 1937 season signaled the demise of St. Mary's College football, and the unloosening of Slip Madigan's tight hold on St. Mary's College, which was, in literary terms, an unread manuscript that he personally turned into a national best seller. But on a balmy summer day, with Madigan preparing for his seventeenth season, an official of the Central Bank of Oakland, which represented the bondholders who had foreclosed on the Moraga institution, appeared in an Alameda County courthouse to announce that St. Mary's was for sale to the highest bidder—or, possibly, the only bidder. The latter was, indeed, the case: One bid, auction style, of $411,000. Going once, going twice, sold! St. Mary's had become the legal property of a San Francisco law firm. The future of the Gaels football program, and the college itself, was walking the plank, with sharks waiting hungrily down below.

San Francisco Archbishop John J. Mitty was a one-man rescue party. He negotiated with the new owners to buy back St. Mary's College, and return it to the Christian Brothers, but with several stipulations, including a closer scrutiny of Slip Madigan. To achieve that end, the Board of Athletic Control, initially a pro-forma body, was put in charge of all athletic expenditures. Demonstrating who's in control, Madigan's previous 10 percent of the gate receipts clause was excluded in his new contract. He had lost significant power, feeling the finger of the Board of Athletic Control poking him in the chest. Recruiting had fallen off, too, as Madigan's opposing coaches told high school prospects: "Why go to St. Mary's when the football program, and even the school, are in danger of closing down?" It was the big lie, but, then, the recruitment of athletes hasn't ever been based solely on truth.

And so Madigan launched the 1937 season with the first precarious hold on his coaching position, even though he ranked fifth among the nation's football coaches in terms of seniority at one school. Harry Hughes, starting his twenty-seventh year at Colorado State, topped the list, followed by Bob Zuppke at Illinois, twenty-five years, Ott Romney at Utah State, nineteen years, and L.A. Alexander at George Tech, eighteen years. Coaches don't coach forever, though, and Madigan's future in Moraga grew dim in '37. He now realized that fact of life himself.

"Standing in his galoshes," Prescott Sullivan wrote in the Examiner, "peering through the mist which seems never to have left Moraga this spring, Coach Slip Madigan cannot see a single Gael who, in any way, resembles Gipp, Thorpe, Nevers or any of the other standard All-America models." Madigan didn't have a Bettencourt, Frankian or an Ackerman who faintly resembled these past All-Americans. Madigan had lost eight starters from the banged-up 1936 team; such numbers during the age of single-platoon football were hard to replace. He would need to depend on sophomores, reminding him daily of his 1920s coaching roots. He crossed his fingers against another rash of injuries, because he faced a demanding schedule: Fordham, Cal, Santa Clara and the University of San Francisco. He had lifted those two Catholic schools to respectability through his own prowess and kindness. They felt a desperate need to catch up to St. Mary's. By 1937, they had caught up.

Madigan's carefully crafted reputation as "the nation's most popular coach" had the numbers to back that up when 850 people attended an April testimonial dinner in the fashionable Palm Court at the prestigious Palace Hotel in San Francisco. Crab Louie was served, also California olives, puree mongol, roast spring chicken au jus farci, green goddess salad, tutti frutti ice cream, petit fours and café noir. Fellow coaches Buck Shaw of Santa Clara and newly hired George Malley of USF attended. Even crusty Pop Warner sent a congratulatory telegram. And cartoonist Jimmy Hatlo entertained guests with several sketches of "Senor Moraga." Then the evening's honoree, Madigan, spoke: "We are proud of St. Mary's, and you have helped us to be proud. The loyalty of those who have helped us through the dark years and the bright years, it is that which I would have you honor tonight."

He was saluted in "The Brick Pile," St. Mary's campus publication, for "his daring, color, courage, gallantry and good sportsmanship. His magnetic personality, his fire, his charm as an orator, his unwillingness to admit defeat even when everything seems to be against him—all these things make us proud of him, that we haven't had a spineless automaton coaching our Galloping Gaels. The professional tormenters of the sob sister school of journalism have always found Edward P. Madigan a worthy object of their literary biliousness. . . . Slip has been too big to reply to all the attacks made against him. Slip Madigan has as many friends as enemies, even though the latter may have more innings than the former." Innings or quarters, the point was missed: Madigan had relatively few attackers among the "sob sisters," who generally admired and catered to him. If anyone was shouting for Slip to sit down, permanently, it was the increasingly bilious Athletic Board of Control.

The 1937 football season arrived as a relief for a nation in mourning. Amelia Earhart and navigator Fred Noonan disappeared after taking off from New Guinea, never to be found. The Hindenburg blimp burst into flames in Lakehurst, New Jersey. In happier aviation news, Howard Hughes set a record by flying from Los Angeles to New York City in seven hours, twenty-eight minutes, and twenty-five seconds. And the White House was keeping its eye on the unsettled situation in Germany, and the growing possibility of American involvement.

Madigan's inexperienced Gaels opened the '37 season on September 26 against what would be their toughest opponent, Cal's "Thunder Team," which was kicking off a 10-0-1 season that included a scoreless tie with Washington and a 13-0 Rose Bowl win over Alabama. The Thunder Team treated the Gaels as unkindly as Cal's Wonder Teams had in the early 1920s, romping to a 30-7 victory, the latest throttling of a Madigan coached team. St. Mary's made the task easier by fumbling eight times, losing half of them. But Cal dominated in yardage gained, 270 to 174. Vic Bottari threw a 29-yard scoring pass to Perry Schwartz, and the rout was on. Dave Anderson, off a fake reverse, burst through the Gaels defense on a 50-yard touchdown jaunt. Perry Thomas scored for Cal on an 85-yard interception return, Ted Hubert plunged over from the four, and Sam Chapman added a field goal. St. Mary's only touchdown came on a 63-yard, 11-play march, featuring Lou Rimassa's 23-yard cutback run, Harry Aronson's 14-yard reverse effort, and, finally, Whitey Smith's one-yard push for six points. Lou Ferry booted the PAT, anti-climatic for the thrashed Gaels.

The local press began promoting the running ability of the Gaels' Herbert Hoover "Whitey" Smith, taking literary license with his name. "My father's real name was Raymond Herbert Smith," said his son, Pat Smith. "But the writers dropped the 'Raymond' and added the 'Hoover.' Sportswriters were flamboyant back then. My dad didn't care." Clever Tom Tom Foudy was the one at fault, for creating Herbert Hoover Smith, even though Whitey Smith was the people's choice of Gael fans.

St. Mary's played Gonzaga seven times prior to 1937, winning five times with a tie. The Gaels only loss to the Bulldogs, along with the tie, occurred in the 1920s. But the '37 Zags held the Gaels to a scoreless tie at Kezar Stadium. The Masked Marauders of Moraga were once again unmasked. Each team had one scoring opportunity. St. Mary's defense, led by Karl Orth and Leo Scatena, snuffed out a Bulldogs drive in the shadow of the Gaels goal line. Orth then recovered a Gonzaga fumble at its 30-yard line. Rimassa's ensuing pass to Lavine Bettencourt moved the ball to the 15-yard line, where victory awaited St. Mary's. But Ferry's field goal from there was wide by inches. The Gaels' placekicking problems, much like their fumbling issues, haunted them in the 1930s.

Needing a win desperately, St. Mary's took it out on Nevada, whipping the Wolf Pack, 42-0. Madigan showed mercy, benching his regulars in the second half to hold down the score. Rimassa's passing, especially to Jack Crampton, proved effective. Crampton was becoming integral in the running game as well, breaking off a 39-yard run. Jerry Dowd blocked well from his center position, was equally effective on defense, and his punting was spectacular. It was "Bargain Day" at Kezar Stadium, a Depression-conceived scheme, and the 16,000 in attendance agreed the Gaels were quite the bargain that afternoon.

St. Mary's then headed south to take on Loyola before 40,000 at the Los Angeles Coliseum. Ferry provided the impetus for the Gaels' 13-7 win by blocking a Loyola punt in the second quarter that was recovered by a fellow Gael. Ernie Jorge then bulled over from a yard out. The Lions tied the score in the third quarter on Jim Rinaldi's quarterback sneak, climaxing a 66-yard drive in 10 plays. Another turnover factored into St. Mary's 13-7 triumph. Dowd recovered Harry Acquarelli's fumble at the Loyola 4. Smith scored from the one-foot line to send the Moragans home happy. Madigan was pleased with the performance of his sophomores, namely Smith and fellow back Dante Magnani.

The Gaels improved to 3-1-1 with a 6-0 victory over Idaho before 15,000 at Kezar in a rare Friday contest. The only score came in the second quarter. Starting from their 28-yard line, the Gaels marched 72 yards behind the running of Crampton, Harry Aronson and Lavine Bettencourt down to the 6-yard line. Crampton covered the remaining distance in one burst. The Gaels could have won by a larger margin, but a Whitey Smith touchdown run was called back, and Ferry missed a makeable field goal, giving the Vandals one last shot. They drove from their 32 to the St. Mary's 20, where a fourth down pass fell incomplete.

Then the ancient one, Amos Alonzo Stagg, pulled the rug out from underneath St. Mary's as his College of Pacific Tigers registered the second scoreless tie of the Gaels' season. The Stockton bunch clearly was the better team under a leaden sky at Kezar. Madigan smoked nervously as the Tigers mounted a last-gap drive. Al George threw a pass to fullback Joe Siegfried, who was end zone bound until Aronson caught up with him and drove him out at the Gaels' 21. Then using some razzle-dazzle, George lateraled to Benson Alexander, who passed to George at the 3-yard line, where he was tackled. There the Gaels braced, stopping COP four times short of the goal line to escape with a tie.

St. Mary's remained unbeaten in its USF rivalry with a 3-0 victory at Kezar. Ferry's 30-yard field goal in the first few minutes gave the Gaels a narrow advantage that held up the rest of the way. Tom-Tom Foudy boasted that Ferry was the only sextuple threat in college football: Kick, punt, block, run, pass, defense. Faced with impending defeat in the final period, similar to the COP game, the Gaels caught a break when it mattered most. USF's Alec Schwartz blocked Dowd's punt, and Hugh Malley recovered for the Dons at the St. Mary's 23-yard line. Johnny Swanson found halfback Lou Braga in the clear and hit him with a perfect pass in the end zone. But the Dons were ruled offside, nullifying the play. The Gaels dug in defensively at that point, and held off the Dons until the gun sounded, ending the game. The Gaels were 4-1-2, and very grateful, but their winning ways that season were over and done with. A sophomore-laden team had run out of success. Youth only can be served for so long. Pups tend to play like pups.

The Little Big Game was next, but Santa Clara had become a much tougher foe with Buck Shaw as head coach. The Gaels no longer owned the Broncos, who beat them for the second straight year, 7-0, at Kezar. Rubbing salt in the wound, that game marked the first time Santa Clara was favored to beat Madigan's men. You can only hold down a rival for so long. Jim Barlow's passing was the difference; he led the Broncos on a third-quarter drive to the Gaels' 17. Then gambling on fourth and 10, Barlow spotted King Fisher in the clear and hit him for the touchdown. The Gaels blocked the PAT try, but the Dons' George Locke picked it up and carried it across the goal line for a point, a legal play at the time. St. Mary's had two scoring threats, both in the second quarter. Two Rimassa passes, to Ferry and John Gianonni, brought the Gaels to the Santa Clara 41. There the drive bogged down, and Ferry's field goal fell short. Then the Gaels moved even closer as runs by Smith and Rimassa earned a first down at the Broncos' 32. Rimassa ran to the 21, Smith to the 16, and Rimassa to the 9. But the fumble-prone Gaels coughed up another one, right into the hands of the Broncos, who hung on to secure the win. Gaels agitator Norbert Korte was joyful that the Little Big Game rivalry he wanted quashed was still around, because his Broncos now were on top.

Sportswriter Alan Ward, no relation to a Gaels lineman of the same name, covered St. Mary's football in the 1930s for the *Oakland Tribune* prior to becoming its sports editor. He particularly remembered the Little Big Game battles with Santa Clara. "You can't imagine the enthusiasm, 60,000 people packed into Kezar," he said. "Those were the most hectic wild games, so far as the spectators were concerned, as I have ever seen in football." There was no brawl on the field this time, but St. Mary's left for New York City, and Fordham, in a fighting mood. They had fallen to the Rams on their previous two trips.

Those creative Gaels were the most "clever" everything in college football at the time. They had the cleverest coach, the cleverest uniforms, the most clever college band, made up of mostly union members, and the cleverest road trips. And they had the cleverest publicists in Will Stevens and Tom Tom Foudy. While heading east, and knowing that pre-game ticket sales were the lowest in Fordham-St. Mary's history, Foudy devised a plan to energize the gate. But, first, he needed Madigan's approval. "The only idea I can think of," he told the coach, "would be the possibility of St. Mary's firing you. It would make a great story." Madigan laughed at the idea. "Don't give them any ideas," he chuckled. But he played along, so Foudy put out a press release that Madigan was about to be canned. Foudy went so far in this ruse as to say that Brother Albert, the college president, couldn't do anything about the situation, because the decision belonged to the St. Mary's Athletic Board of Control. Foudy, stepping way beyond his authority, went even further by informing the New York press that Madigan was in a "win or be fired" predicament. Because Madigan was immensely popular in New York, his job "situation" became a big story. "Two days in a row," Foudy said, "I had the top line story, with Madigan's denial, and the reporters' reaction to it. We were supposed to have the lousiest sale ever, and we wound up with a sellout."

The capacity crowd of 52,000, partial to Fordham, saw the Rams win a 6-0 squeaker, even though they dominated throughout. The game's star was fullback John Locke, whose running and ball handling, was the difference in the outcome. After a scoreless first half, the Rams took over on their 41-yard line. Locke broke off runs of 11 and 31 yards to the Gaels' 17. He wasn't done yet, ripping off left tackle for 6 more yards. Then he took a center snap and handed it to quarterback Bill Krywicki, who lateraled the ball to Joe Woitkoski, who carried it into the end zone. St. Mary's had one scoring chance, but Fordham great Alex Wojciechowicz broke through to block Ferry's field goal. The Rams had two touchdowns negated by penalties. In the battle of Knute Rockne's alumni, Jim Crowley now had the edge on Slip Madigan, who didn't lose his job afterward. Foudy didn't lose his job either. Those were the days.

After St. Mary's seventh trip to play Fordham, the Gaels stood 4-3-2. The game seemed almost secondary to the "streetcar alumni" who tagged along at an arranged price. Sportswriters went for free, of course, with free cocktails. But in giving Madigan and St. Mary's free publicity, it was a tradeoff. Madigan made the trip more interesting with each passing year. Adieu, Montreal! Buenos Dias, Havana! The sportswriters who tagged along on these excursions never forgot them.

"After leaving New York, our next stop was Miami," said Alan Ward, "and from there we went to Havana. Remember, this was before Fidel

Castro, and Havana was a fabulous, wild, crazy, beautiful city in those days. We stayed at the finest hotel. We were there four or five days and had everything lain right in our lap. The season was over, and the boys could let their hair down, and they did. They had automobiles for the players to show them all over that part of Cuba. The whole group attended a reception with the President of Cuba. You will have to look up the name as they changed them pretty often in those days. Madigan so adroitly handled that presidential party. I noticed standing next to the President this heavy set military man, an army officer, who took it all in quietly, didn't have anything to say. I later learned that this fellow was the man Batista, and we all know what happened to him." Not good.

After leaving Cuba, the traveling party headed to Miami by boat. But a terrific storm, one of the worst in thirty years in those parts, made the water so choppy that many passengers became violently sick. Ward was proud that the sportswriters avoided sickness—"a little plug for my business"—even after hearing that the storm could have broken up the ship. Since this was Thanksgiving vacation for St. Mary's students, the Gaels footballers were in no hurry to get back home, especially with a three-day stopover in New Orleans, where Madigan was already a hero, for St. Mary's heroics had reached the bayou. "We had several feasts down there," said Ward. "I remember one in particular. The owner of a restaurant was this venerable Frenchman with a bristling mustache. He knew Madigan. The Frenchman got up on one of the tables to sing the Marseilles. We didn't know the words, but we sang. Madigan jumped up on a table with him. The old fella had his arm around Slip, and with his cane was leading the chorale singing."

Many years later, Ward reminisced about the "Slip Madigan Fordham Special Around the World," a world removed from the sports writing trips that succeeded it, almost like two different planets. "Of course, those trips are gone forever," Ward said, wistfully. "The era of the air stepped in and those marvelous trips ended. And pro football supplanted the independents. It's gone, although I want to say this: I traveled with the San Francisco 49ers for a long time. They were the closest approach to the old St. Mary's under Madigan. The 49ers reminded me so much of the old Madigan grand manner—first class or stay home. The difference in covering sports today and sports in those days is the difference between day and night, a jellyfish and an armadillo . . . in those days, there was fun; fun for the newsmen, coaches, players. There was empathy. Everyone seemed to be working towards the same end."

Then came the 49ers in 1946, followed by other big league sports in the Bay Area that shifted the spotlight away from the colleges, and the lifestyle that went with it. "All the camaraderie that we knew during those St. Mary's days disappeared," Ward lamented. "Commercialism came into it in a big way. There was a line of demarcation between players and reporters, whereas when we traveled on those overland trips, we used to visit the players in their compartments, or they'd come up and visit us. They trusted us. We trusted them. They knew that we would not drag up false stories for sensational release, and we knew that they were doing their very best. If a fellow had a bum leg, he had a bum leg. There was never any doubt about it. Nowadays, some of these athletes say they have ailments, and most of it is their imagination.

"It was great being a newspaperman in those days. When the pros came in, everything was cut off. Things were a little more leisurely in those days. We were comrades. Now so many athletes are afraid to talk to newspapermen. I know some athletes who want to be paid to have newspapermen talk to them. It was a transition from the old family style of one-for-all, all-for-one to a dog-eat-dog world. I would not trade my experiences during the grand old days of St. Mary's football for anything they have now. I had a taste of the contemporary game, but it wasn't for me. Things were great then, and they are "huh?" now.

And those grand old days became even grander when St. Mary's College reached the apex of the Slip Madigan era.

14

Let's Go Bowling

Slip Madigan had danced with bowl committees before, but those opportunities, as if having his feet stepped on, went to other colleges. Now in 1938, with St. Mary's facing financial hardships and Madigan's own future in Moraga in doubt, another bowl group began eyeballing the Gaels with interest. So how did Madigan coax movie siren Marlene Dietrich into closing the deal? With an alluring dance, what else?

At the start of the 1938 season, a bowl bid was hardly on Madigan's mind. After a 4-3-2 record in 1937, he was unsure what to expect in 1938. But Madigan, if anything, was an incurable optimist. His sophomores from the year before had survived their first varsity test, thereby carrying maturity and ability into their junior seasons. Madigan had two future professionals, juniors Dante Magnani and Andy Marefos, returning in the backfield. Adding depth there were two exciting sophomores: Ed Heffernan, equally adept at passing and running, and the explosive Mike Klotovich. Madigan compared Klotovich to 1920s star Red Strader as a runner. Klotovich would later draw comparisons to the great San Francisco 49er, Hugh McElhenny, in terms of faking tacklers out of their shoes. Maybe, just maybe, the Gaels might surprise everyone in 1938.

However, St. Mary's would need to get by Cal first, which certainly wasn't a given, as the Thunder Team still was in force. Following their Rose Bowl conquest of the previous season, the Golden Bears were poised for a 10-1-0 season in '38, blemished only by a 13-7 loss to USC in Los Angeles.

Led by All-America back Vic Bottari, Cal opened at home against St. Mary's. Gaels tackle Nick Katzmeyer recovered a fumble at the Cal 21-yard line late in the first quarter, and Klotovich quickly carried the ball to the 2. The Bears expected a dive up the middle, but Madigan called a time out and directed Klotovich on a sweep. He scored standing up and the Gaels led 7-0 entering the second quarter. Cal was back on its heels up until the fourth quarter when Bottari took control, marching the Bears down to the visitors' goal line, with Dave Anderson getting the final yard. George Cantwell blocked the conversion kick, and St. Mary's still led, 7-6. Then the Gaels got "booted" out of Berkeley's Memorial Stadium. Jerry Dowd was the country's leading punter in 1937 with a 44.5-yard average. He was averaging 40 yards against Cal in the '38 opener, but with seven minutes left, he shanked a punt of 14 yards, leaving Cal in great field position. From the 4-yard line, Bottari faked a line plunge and pitched to Louis Smith, who scored to give Cal a 12-7 win before a relieved partisan crowd of 60,000.

Madigan took that loss positively. The Thunder Team was one of Cal's greatest teams, yet the Gaels had it on the ropes. Madigan convinced his squad, and himself, that there were better days ahead. The following week, St. Mary's welcomed Gonzaga in wet conditions at Kezar Stadium. Even with slippery footing, the Gaels mounted a strong running attack. Klotovich scored from the 2 in the second quarter. Cantwell blocked a kick for the second straight week, Magnani recovering at the Lions' 14. Three plays later, Heffernan charged around the left side and into the end zone. Then Klotovich's short pass to Lou Rimassa turned into a 40-yard scoring play, and St. Mary's had a convincing 20-0 victory, pumping up its confidence in terms of bigger things ahead.

The Moraga marauders then unleashed their highest scoring output of the season, grounding the Portland Pilots, 32-7, in San Francisco. St. Mary's depth, its finest in several seasons, was evident throughout. Even its second and third strings played effectively before a fourth-string quarterback, Dave Nichols, scored twice on a short run and a 14-yard interception return. Whitey Smith got loose around end and scooted 54 yards for another score. The Gaels ended the rout when Heffernan found Jack Crampton uncovered in the end zone for a fifth touchdown. After the game, Madigan was so pleased by the number of reserves who contributed that he even hinted about revising his first unit.

USF hadn't yet defeated a St. Mary's team, dating back to 1926. But the improved Dons confronted the Gaels in 1938 with an unbeaten record. Nonetheless, it was the same outcome, a 13-6 victory for St. Mary's. Even the loss of quarterback Mike Perrie, who dislocated a shoulder in practice, didn't deter the Gaels as 50,000 looked on in a slight drizzle at Kezar. Their triumph required a come through effort; USF carried a 6-0 lead into the fourth quarter on a scoring pass from Cliff Fisk to Bill Telesmanic. Then Klotovich showed off his passing arm, connecting with Harry Aronson for a touchdown. The versatile Klotovich sealed the win by sweeping around right end and outdistancing Dons defenders on a 53-yard scoring run. It was too much Klotovich as the Gaels also won the ground game, 208 yards to USF's 95.

St. Mary's then departed on its latest two-game road trip, stopping first in Los Angeles to face Loyola. Before one of the Lions' largest home crowds ever, 48,000, the Gaels pulled out another nail-biter, 7-0. Heffernan's passing to Crampton set up the game's only touchdown, a 2-yard plunge by Smith. St. Mary's lost two other touchdowns when a Heffernan to Aronson scoring pass was called back for holding, and a Heffernan throw to Crampton was hauled in just beyond the end zone. The Gaels needed to dig in late as Loyola's Jack Lyons completed two long passes for a combined 79 yards to bring the Lions to the visitors' 21-yard line. On the next play, Smith intercepted Lyons to clinch the victory. Jerry Dowd may have cost St. Mary's a win at Cal, but he contributed largely to this triumph with a 42.5 average, including two punts beyond 50 yards. But his "longest" punt ever was just days away.

Riding a four-game win streak, the Gaels hopped on a train heading from Oakland to Los Angeles to New York. This time the Slip Madigan Fordham Special Around the World was a misnomer; the Gaels would stay within the contiguous forty-eight states (the annexing of Hawaii and Alaska was a ways off), and focusing on America's national parks. First stop: The Grand Canyon. The endlessly imaginative Tom-Tom Foudy concocted the idea of Dowd punting one into the history books. Thus he positioned Dowd at the rim of one of the "Eight Wonders of the World" and had him boot a football with a street shoe. Dowd's kick cleared the rim's edge, and a second ledge 2,000 feet below, and descended another 3,000 feet onto the canyon floor. Statisticians estimated that his punt traveled one mile. Dowd had made the Guinness Book of Records for the longest kick of a football, albeit downward.

What would a Slip Madigan trip think up next? While entering the Kentucky Caves, Joe Millett, a streetcar alumnus, was told he must choose between a lantern and a jug of moonshine, for he was carrying both items. He couldn't push his portly body through some narrow passages otherwise. Considering which item bore the most importance, Millett opted for the moonshine over the caves. The Gaels later stopped to practice at White Sulphur Springs, West Virginia, where a young unknown golfer, Sam Snead, watched the Gaels work out. Madigan showed Snead how to punt a football, and the golfer then tried it wearing street shoes, but he slipped and fell. "Slip, I don't want to ruin my golf career," said Snead, wisely choosing putting over punting. Traveling next to Baltimore, Madigan arranged for the traveling party to watch the ballyhooed match race between Triple Crown-winner War Admiral and Seabiscuit. Winning comfortably in an upset was the smaller, scrappier Seabiscuit.

There were more serious things to discuss, and to dissect, on the trip than kicking a football into the Grand Canyon. German troops occupied, and then annexed, Austria. Jews with Polish citizenship were evicted from Germany. Benito Mussolini was granted power over the Italian military. The Vatican recognized Francisco Franco's dictatorship in Spain. On the humorous side, Wrong Way Corrigan took off in a plane for California, he thought, but landed in Ireland. Joe Louis knocked out Max Schmeling quickly in their rematch. FDR established the March of Dimes. And Orson Welles' radio adaptation of "The War Of The Worlds" created panic across the land. The St. Mary's train reached New York with the non-playing, but ever-paying, "alumni" happy that they only had a football game to contend with.

Foudy convinced the New York press that this latest Fordham-St. Mary's game matched the country's two best sophomore backs, Klotovich and the Rams' Len Eshmont, who later played on the San Francisco 49ers' inaugural team in 1946. Foudy also invited New York's Jewish population to come see Gaels halfback Harry Aronson play, hiding the fact that Aronson wasn't Jewish. Sports publicity hasn't been quite the same in Moraga since Foudy stopped dreaming up outlandish schemes in the 1930s. Though Fordham and St. Mary's had each lost once, the Rams were the heavy favorite. But even the imaginative Foudy couldn't have invented the game's outcome.

Victory was in the Gaels' grasp that day, only they lost their balance. Heffernan hit Crampton in the clear, but he tripped and fell on his own at the Fordham 24-yard line. Aronson returned a punt 42 yards to the Rams' 48, where Harry Jacunski dropped him with a last-gasp ankle tackle. Ball-hawking Whitey Smith then intercepted a pass and was headed for the Fordham goal, but was run down by Jimmy Hayes. So the game still hung in the balance when the unbelievable happened. Rams placekicker Wilbur Stanton stood ready to kick a 20-yard field goal. But his placeholder fumbled the snap, and the football sat there on the turf. With the Gaels charging him, Stanton had no choice but to kick the ball, lying sideways off the turf, and it sailed crazily through the uprights. Madigan twisted his Borsalino into a pretzel at the very sight. Fordham scored a hard-to-believe-it 3-0 win that was Guinness worthy.

Win or lose, if Slip Madigan was in charge, the show must go on. Fordham, being the congenial host, threw Madigan a party at the popular Mamma Leone's restaurant in New York City following his third straight defeat to the Rams. Art Rosenbaum of the Chronicle was along for the trip, and recalled how Madigan kept the party going, and the trip moving, all at the same time. "After the game, the train was scheduled to leave at 1 a.m.," Rosenbaum said. "Slip, as tour director, warned everybody to be on time. Then he said he couldn't leave town without saying hello to a few people. He asked me, the boy reporter, to join him. First, it was Dinty Moore's, and as Slip entered, the M.C. stopped the show and called Slip to the stage for some impromptu singing of 'The Bells of St. Mary's.' Then it was over to Leon's and Eddie's for more singing. Next, it was the Cotton Club, or maybe the Stork Club; the names are vague now. But I remember reminding Slip at least five times that 1 a.m. had come and gone. Even so, I felt secure. No wheels could turn without Slip, and I was at his side. When we finally got there at 3:30 a.m., hundreds lined the depot, but the most indignant was a large man who said he was second vice-president of the railroad. Pointing a finger at me, he said, 'Why did you hold up Mr. Madigan? You've disrupted the entire line from here to Cincinnati.' " Rosenbaum had a good story to write, though.

The *Oakland Tribune*'s "Angry" Art Cohn, who tended to type with his fists, climbed on the same train from New York after sending his game column, transmitted by Western Union, back to Oakland. Cohn wrote: "The Gaels have been licked three years in a row by a team that, if it isn't mediocre, is not very good, either." Those three losses to Fordham were by a combined 10 points, yet Cohn made it sound as if the Gaels were finished for the season. On the contrary, they were merely warming up.

The Gaels returned to Moraga with a road split, and an overall record of 4-2. They needed to finish the season with a flourish after hearing that they were bowl timber once again. However, the Little Big Game was next, and Buck Shaw's Santa Clara Broncos, winners of back-to-back Sugar Bowls, had a 16-game winning streak that ranked them eighth in the country. Everything was stacked up against St. Mary's, including Santa Clara's being established as a 2-to-1 favorite. The Broncos had beaten St. Mary's twice in a row for the first time since the 1890s. After a scoreless first half, the Broncos stopped a St. Mary's drive at their 8-yard line. The Gaels resurged on Heffernan's accurate passes that deposited them at the 5-yard line. This time, Smith popped through left guard and darted into the end zone. Perrie, who played brilliantly that day with a tightly taped dislocated shoulder, booted the PAT. The Broncos moved into scoring territory twice, but were stopped once at the 4-yard line and a second time at St. Mary's 15. Defense and punting had carried the Gaels all season, and Dowd punted out of difficulty repeatedly against Santa Clara, thus enabling the Gaels to escape with a well-earned 7-0 victory at Kezar, ruining Norbert Korte's day.

Beating a formidable Bronco eleven was a huge step for the Gaels in terms of bowl ramifications. Cotton Bowl founder J. Curtis Sanford attended that Little Big Game. Madigan made sure, through Foudy, that Sanford's every needs were met throughout the game, and so he was treated as a visiting shah. After the Gaels won, Foudy hurried Sanford downstairs to meet Madigan, who invited Sanford to dinner. "I caught up with them later that night, having a high old time at Shanty Malone's bar," Foudy said years later. "Slip had taken Sanford to the Fairmont Hotel, where he introduced him to

Marlene Dietrich, who was performing there. How Slip knew Marlene, I'm not sure. But I understand that Sanford actually danced with the woman. We got the Cotton Bowl bid." How Slip knew all his celebrity friends, nobody knew.

Finally, after eighteen seasons, Madigan made it to a bowl game. Danke, Marlene. Unlike today's overly excessive bowl choices, bowl games were scarce in the 1930s. After the Rose, Cotton, Sugar and Orange, there was little else to offer. Thus Cotton felt like mink to the Gaels, who would face Texas Tech, led by their backfield star and campus hero, Elmer "The Great" Tarbox. He not only was an Eagle Scout, and president of Tech's junior class, but also voted the most popular football player in the state of Texas. "Great" in every way.

Texas Tech would be no easy pickin's for St. Mary's. The Red Raiders were unbeaten and untied after ten games, having defeated Montana, 19-13, Montana State, 35-0, Gonzaga, 7-0, Duquesne, 7-6, Loyola of New Orleans, 55-0, Marquette, 21-2, New Mexico, 17-7, Texas School of Mines, 14-7, Wyoming, 39-0, and Oklahoma City, 60-0. St. Mary's had scored 20 points once, 30 points once, while Texas Tech had scored 30 to 60 four times. Howdy!

Madigan wasn't impressed. "We'll be playing them blind," he said, "and I don't like to play teams blind, but there's nothing else to do. I'm glad we got the game because it gives the seniors another chance to play. But we'll give them a battle." Both teams took pride in their aggressiveness. However, Tech coach Pete Cawthon was often criticized for crossing the line between aggression and just plain dirty. Madigan wasn't worried. If it was to be a street fight, he knew his Gaels would be anybody's match. Tom Laird wrote in the *San Francisco News*: "Texas Tech always took their best shots—that is, elbow and knee fashion." Madigan said, "Our boys like nothing better than a real tough football game." All Pete Cawthon had to do was phone Pop Warner to concur.

Before the Cotton Bowl trip, Madigan gave his players some time off, which was a big mistake, because they ate like there was no ending. Smith ballooned from 196 to 216. Other Gaels added five pounds per man. Madigan was livid. Before the team traveled to Dallas to meet Texas Tech, he cut down on their training table portions. With only time for two full scrimmages, he made the Gaels pay for their overindulgence by working them extremely hard.

Then a disagreement arose between the two schools. Madigan heard that Tech had obtained film from the St. Mary's-Loyola game. He was furious. "If I find out who gave the Red Raiders those pictures, or sold them to Cawthon, I'll sue. I'll put him out of business." Only it wasn't Loyola, Madigan learned. "They sent me their copy to prove they still had it," he said. This was a time before teams exchanged game films before games. But Cawthon denied any chicanery: "We haven't looked at any movies of the St. Mary's-Loyola game. Madigan is just using that angle to steam up his players." Madigan denied doing any such thing. The film issue remained unresolved, but Slip's Irish dander was up, and it wasn't about to come down before the Cotton Bowl was decided.

After the Slip Madigan Cotton Bowl Express left the Fortieth and San Pablo station in Oakland at 10:30 a.m., it took two days and two nights to reach Dallas. Thirty-eight players were aboard along with Madigan and his family, assistant coaches Red Strader and Joe Ruetz, both of them future Gaels head coaches, trainer Frank O'Rourke, Dr. John Murphy, the team physician, comptroller Bill Milliker, Brothers Rafael and Cornelius of St. Mary's, and the usual streetcar alumni. Madigan hardly treated this bowl trip as a military invasion. If there was a football game to be played, regardless of its magnitude, and Slip Madigan was involved, there must be a party somewhere.

And so on New Year's Eve, Madigan invited twenty-seven people to the Dallas Variety Club. The revelry didn't stop there. Madigan ordered the group to follow him to a hotel where the Jimmy Dorsey Band was playing. Upon arriving, Madigan was told the event had been sold out for seven months, and there was not an inch of available space. Slip wasn't deterred. "Stand by your phone," he told the maître d', "it will be ringing in a few minutes." Madigan went to a pay phone, spoke to someone, and when he returned, the maître d's phone rang. "Yes, sir, of course, yes sir," he said into the receiver. Six waiters appeared, carrying tables and chairs over their heads into the main room, and then placing them on the dance floor, just before the Dorsey band played "Auld Lang Syne." "Everything is complimentary," the maitre d' whispered to Madigan. Who did Slip phone? He wouldn't say, but champagne was served, toasts were given, kisses were exchanged, and a brand new year brought with it Madigan's one bowl moment, and what a glorious moment it would become.

Although St. Mary's had lost twice, to Cal and Fordham, those two teams were stronger than any of the ten opponents on Texas Tech's schedule. So Madigan knew his Gaels could stand up to the Red Raiders, even in the state of Texas. Following the opening kickoff on Jan. 2, 1939, the Lubbock team broke off a 30-yard run, but the Gaels quickly stifled that drive and powered their way to Tech's 9-yard line. From there, Heffernan broke through a crease and crossed the goal line. Klotovich increased St. Mary's lead to 14-0 at halftime with some nifty running, followed by his 1-yard scoring plunge. The 40,000 mostly stunned Texans then watched Whitey Smith pick off a Bobby Holmes pass and speed 30 yards for a third Gaels touchdown. Down 20-0 in the fourth quarter, the Red Raiders finally caught fire. Tarbox gathered in a 33-yard scoring pass from Gene "Bubbles" Barnett. Tech got the ball back and Barnett tossed a 30-yard touchdown strike to E.J. McKnight, cutting St. Mary's lead to 20-13 as Madigan chewed on his Borsalino. The Gaels held on, though, and the game ended with no further scoring.

Elmer the Great was shut down on the ground, gaining eight yards in seven carries. Dowd's punting was a positive factor once again, averaging 47 yards. A significant play earlier in the game proved important later on—Marefos caught Tech end Forrest Webb from behind to prevent a touchdown. The Red Raiders, with a strong passing attack, gained 210 of their 309 yards through the air, but were intercepted five times along with losing two fumbles. The Gaels, remarkably, committed only two turnovers. Texas Tech might have obtained a St. Mary's game film, but, if so, still couldn't master the Gaels. The eminent sports journalist, Grantland Rice, wrote that St. Mary's was "equal with USC as the West's outstanding football machine." Rice, obviously, hadn't seen Cal play, but St. Mary's accepted the compliment.

Madigan, after realizing his one bowl opportunity, delivered, thus showing bowl committees that St. Mary's had been unjustly overlooked for too many years. Even with an enrollment of six hundred, St. Mary's was a gridiron match for schools with much larger student bodies. Though Madigan's stomach raged inside, he radiated the old Madigan charm at the

Cotton Bowl awards ceremony. He accepted the championship trophy, worth $5,000, a trophy that would be exhibited at the Treasure Island Exposition of 1939. Madigan, in turn, presented a rather tattered St. Mary's athletic blanket to outgoing Texas Governor James Allred. That blanket, conversely, wasn't ever exhibited in the governor's office, or anywhere else, as the state of Texas takes its bowl losses seriously. Madigan didn't seem to care. Texas could have the blanket. St. Mary's had the victors' trophy.

"We'll have a great team in 1939," Madigan promised on the trip home, one long, happy overland celebration.

15
The Curtain Falls

"St. Mary's College," bespoke Robert Maynard Hutchins, president of the University of Chicago, is "the country's most sensational football college." His words in 1939 sounded praiseworthy, but "sensational" in a Webster's dictionary contained a double meaning: "Arousing" and "superficial interest." Hutchins leaned toward the superficial. Sports, he warned, "attract boys and girls to college who do not want and cannot use a college education. They come to college for fun . . . athleticism, like crime, does not pay." He noted further: "St. Mary's, home of the Galloping Gaels, was sold at an auction."

Slip Madigan certainly heightened interest in St. Mary's College with his Cotton Bowl triumph. Regardless, he had stayed in one place too long, and his employer now regretted the gate receipts arrangement they agreed to long ago. The acclaim Madigan brought St. Mary's was wearing thin. He had become expendable, even though there would be no Moraga campus without the funds generated by his football teams.

The same year that St. Mary's College would dismiss Madigan, 1939, Hutchins discontinued football at the University of Chicago, just four years after the school produced the very first Heisman Trophy winner, Jay Berwanger. "The commercialism that characterizes amateur sport today," Hutchins reasoned, "would be sufficient to harden the purest young man." Hutchins then mentioned, though not by name, "one famous coach of a small college (who) was found, not long ago, receiving $25,000 between his salary and his percentage of the receipts." That coach he alluded to was possibly Madigan, who received that handsome check of $38,324.15 from St. Mary's in 1936.

St. Mary's College had reached the same financial crossroads as the University of Chicago. By 1939, Madigan was perceived by critics on his own campus as a money-stealing pariah, rather than a money-making visionary. "I don't think Slip was a dishonest man," said longtime St. Mary's professor Ron Isetti. "A clever entrepreneur with an eye open for a chance, yes, but I don't think he stole from the college."

Quite the contrary: St. Mary's entered into a contract with Madigan when it was a speck in the academic universe. He enlarged that speck into a planet. But his immense popularity was more than St. Mary's could tolerate. He had become too big for the school he had built up by himself. And so his walking papers were being prepared behind his back before the 1939 season even began. Such gratitude.

Sometimes it's difficult to identify one's executioner, if he exists. "My dad felt that Red Strader was working behind the scenes to get his job," Ed Madigan said of his father's first star player and later his No. 1 assistant, who would replace him in 1940. But what about another former player, J. Philip Murphy from the unbeaten 1929 team, who had become chairman of St. Mary's Athletic Board of Control? Was he undermining his old coach? Whomever the culprit, or culprits, Madigan's coaching longevity and his largesse had reached the finish line in a dead heat. References to "Slip Madigan College" could only last so long before it all boiled over, and his tenure was at its boiling point.

Strangely, the summer of '39 started out positively for Madigan. He was selected to coach in his second College All-Star Game in Chicago, along with Harry Stuhldreher of Wisconsin, Carl Snavely of Cornell, and head coach Elmer Layden. Snavely, a Lebanon Valley College alum, was the exception of the four; he hadn't played for Knute Rockne at Notre Dame. The New York Giants beat those All-Stars, 9-0. Back home, Madigan, a navy man to the core, walked the deck of the largest liner flying the American flag, the 666-foot U.S.S. Washington, when it appeared at the Golden Gate Exposition in San Francisco.

Then early signs of trouble appeared for the Gaels: Tackle George Cantwell fractured a leg in a motorcycle crash; guard Ray Ruddell broke a leg in an auto accident, and—the worst news yet—dazzling halfback Mike

Klotovich flunked out of school. Three regulars were lost before the season arrived, while additional Gaels were academically at risk. Madigan's players had, largely, done well in the classroom. He hadn't turned St. Mary's into an athletic factory, as Robert Maynard Hutchins implied. Madigan was an educated man, and he wanted no less for his players. But St. Mary's administration, looking at "those dumb football players," gathered more negative information against its "greedy coach."

Madigan was morose. His moon-shot expectations for the 1939 team fell dead at the launching site. "We had high hopes," he said, "but injuries and ineligibilities blasted those hopes somewhat." Klotovich could have become Madigan's greatest back. But Slip was Slip, publicly positive. "However, we are not pessimistic," he said. "Our greatest asset right now is the red-hot ambition of the squad. We have excellent spirit, perhaps the best in five years. Things, in general, are looking up here at St. Mary's." Maybe he was suddenly imbued after, once again, being named the West Coast's most popular football coach in a newspaper poll. Or, maybe, he just couldn't face the cold, hard truth.

Then this navy man went from drifting to sinking. Tackle Alan Ward broke an ankle. Injuries in the line forced Madigan to switch fullback Andy Marefos to center. That experiment lasted until backfield man Mike Mazaika broke his ankle in a scrimmage; Marefos shifted back to fullback. At that disjointed time, with the season still a ways off, plans for the latest Fordham trip were revealed. The Gaels would visit Balboa Island in California, then Acapulco and Havana: Madigan's last hurrah. He wondered, the way things were progressing, if he would have enough players to take along. "It looks like we will have a .500 season," he told the press. He had lowered his accustomed optimism, though maybe he was being too optimistic.

America was emerging from the Great Depression, yet fearing another World War. A Howard Brodie cartoon in the *San Francisco Chronicle* depicted Madigan saying: "Someone should hide the war news on the rear pages, and put that the 1939 football season up front. That's the kind of war we fight in the United States." Hide? Hitler had occupied Czechoslovakia, France had recognized Franco's government in Spain, and a gaunt Mahatma Ghandi fasted in protest of British rule in India. And across the Pacific, what are those rumblings coming from Japan?

Another cartoonist, Jimmy Hatlo, departed the *San Francisco Examiner* for employment in New York City. "See you at the Fordham game, Slip," he said. Madigan lost a trusted friend in Hatlo. Before the Gaels opener against Gonzaga, Postmaster General James A. Farley became the first Washington politician to visit the St. Mary's campus. Gael gridders gave him a shoulder ride, while whispering to one another, so the postmaster couldn't hear, that he felt heavier than a sack of Christmas mail.

A small crowd of 18,000 showed up at Kezar to see if Madigan's reduced roster had any firepower. And St. Mary's started off with a bang by humbling Gonzaga, 19-0. The Gaels were inspired by another defensive masterpiece—holding an opponent without a first down for the second time that decade—besides checking the Bulldogs with just 9 yards of offense. An amazing performance, considering that Gonzaga backfield star Tony Canadeo was a future Green Bay Packer and Pro Football Hall of Fame inductee. The Gaels offense wasn't nearly as efficient, fumbling five times and being held scoreless through the first half. Then Jack Guthrie's 6-yard swing pass to Jackie Sims turned into a touchdown. After that, Ed Heffernan plunged over from the 1, and Frankie Freitas threw a 23-yard scoring pass to Ken Sanders. Nick Katzmeyer missed two PAT kicks, while Marefos made his only attempt.

Publicist Foudy grew too positive over that opening win. "We're on our way to a national championship," he boldly predicted. "Who's gonna stop us? We'll win from bell to breakfast." Bell to breakfast? Madigan remonstrated his eager flak. "We'll be scrambling for every point," Slip forecast, from bell to breakfast, lunch, dinner, whatever. Ruddell rejoined the Gaels for their second game, against Cal, though lighter in weight. Future Cal coed Robin Orr, a 15-year-old high school junior, was chosen as drum majorette at all-male St. Mary's College. She high-stepped in front of the accustomed marching band comprised of Gael students and union musicians. Orr later became the *Oakland Tribune*'s society editor.

Prescott Sullivan of the Examiner wrote: "It's difficult to entertain much hope for California's Golden Bears in their game with St. Mary's this Saturday. Stub Allison's young men were pretty awful against Pacific last week." Cal lost 6-0 to Amos Alonzo Stagg's Tigers. To keep sportswriters' minds off the Cal game, the futuristic Madigan entertained them by talking about flying to games instead of taking the train, and playing in short-sleeved rather than long-sleeved jerseys. He wasn't too far off with his original idea, as jet travel was getting closer. He was so mind-blowing in general that the local press usually wrote whatever he said, and prayed that he wasn't putting one over them.

The nucleus of Cal's Thunder Team had graduated, and the Gaels defeated the Bears, 7-3, in Madigan's last game against his Berkeley nemesis. The game's signature moment, observed by the 60,000 in attendance, was a fight between tackles Dick Jones of St. Mary's and Lee Artoe of Cal. Jones blocked Artoe on a kickoff return, and Artoe took umbrage, getting Jones in a headlock and punching him in the face before banging his head on the ground. Though Jones didn't throw a punch, both players were ejected. Jones' lips were bleeding and the side of his face was raw from the abuse. Tony Firpo kicked a 17-yard field goal, giving Cal a 3-0 lead at halftime. Whitey Smith's game-winning 4-yard touchdown run in the third quarter left Madigan with a 5-12-2 record against Cal. "We had so few replacements, I had to use them sparingly," he said. After Jones was kicked out, Madigan sent in Ward, even with his injured ankle heavily taped. He blocked and tackled on "guts alone," said his impressed coach.

St. Mary's third scheduled opponent was Loyola, a road game in Los Angeles. But two Lions, tackle Robert Link and quarterback Burch Donahue, contracted infantile paralysis and were hospitalized. Teammate Jim Sullivan, a center, also came down with the disease and was placed under a physician's care in a private home. For health reasons, the game was rescheduled in early December. The Gaels were forced into a "bye" week before facing their next opponent, loathed rival Santa Clara. The Sugar Bowl committee was looking seriously at St. Mary's, based on its 2-0 record, and its successful Cotton Bowl showing. At that point, it all came apart in Moraga.

Santa Clara exposed the Gaels as unsuited for national honors with a 7-0 victory before 50,000 at Kezar. Jimmy Johnson got the Broncos rolling with a 40-yard pass to Ray McCarthy at the Gaels' 19-yard line. Johnson followed up with a 12-yard pass to Ray Roche, and a 6-yard pass to Joe Lacey in the end zone. Johnson kicked the PAT. Domination belonged to the Broncos: 214 to 63 in yards gained, and 11-2 in first downs, quite a showing for a 5-to-2 underdog. "It could have been over-confidence," said Madigan. "It might have been the layoff. I don't know what it was, but I do know we were up against the real goods today. Santa Clara outplayed us, and that's all there is to it." That was Slip Madigan, a gentleman to the very end.

Following the game, his secretary, 20-year-old Myrta Wohlwend, fractured her skull in an automobile accident, and was listed in critical condition. She survived, unlike St. Mary's season. The Gaels' fourth opponent was Portland, a team they humbled, 32-7, the year before. For the second straight week, a decided underdog knocked off the Gaels. The visiting Pilots won, 14-12, in the most shocking upset of the Madigan era. Frank Maloney put the visitors ahead on a 23-yard pass to Joe Blount, with Joe Enzer's PAT kick making it 7-0. Whitey Smith scored on a 6-yard run for St. Mary's, but Katzmeyer's PAT kick sailed wide. The Gaels took the lead, 12-7, on Guthrie's quarterback sneak, but Katzmeyer missed again on the conversion boot. Enzer then scored from two yards out, and converted his second PAT placement for a 14-12 lead. The Gaels, with seven minutes left, drove to Portland's 7-yard line, but were pushed back to the 22-yard line because of a substitution infraction. Katzmeyer's subsequent field goal attempt wasn't even close, and that's how it ended for the Gaels—three missed placekicks, leading to a two-point loss.

Afterward, Madigan launched a tirade against head linesman Ralph Coleman. "I'm talking for publication, and I'm protesting," he said. "He threw my boys into a frenzy of jitters against USF last year. He duplicated it this year in the Santa Clara game, and today he was the same whistler." St. Mary's was penalized 10 times for 98 yards, Portland 5 times for 34 yards. Madigan hadn't ever attacked a game official like that publicly. Herb Dana, head of the football officials on the West Coast, wouldn't honor his protest. Madigan continued his rant, regardless: "I have taken this officiating sitting down too long." His health had worsened through the decade, and now his emotions seemed frazzled. St. Mary's administration was watching, and listening, more closely, and beginning to believe that a coaching change might be in order.

Madigan shook up his team, replacing eight starters. "We never have shakeups at St. Mary's," he explained to the press. "We do have promotions." He was worried about the speed of his fifth opponent, Dayton.

"They're smaller, but quick," he said. Well, Dayton's nickname is the Flyers. He watched 168-pound Jack Radley bolt for 47 yards before Smith caught him at the 4-yard line. But Smith knocked himself out on the tackle. Radley scored from a yard away, but Tom Glick shanked the PAT kick. Then a comedy of errors arose. Guthrie took off running for an apparent Gael touchdown, but in shifting the ball between hands, he fumbled and Harry Jerina recovering for Dayton. Smith, having regained his senses, raced 21 yards to the Flyers' 1-yard line. From there, Dave Nichols dived into the end zone, only to have Katzmeyer miss another PAT kick. Marefos also had an 11-yard field goal try blocked by Larry Knorr, so the game ended, 6-6. "That's seven straight (conversion) misses by me," said Katzmeyer, counting them up for the writers. "And it looks like I'll set a new record if this keeps up." Madigan stayed positive: "The defense was OK, and that shows the boys are in their pitching." Pitching, but whiffing in the win-loss column.

The Bay Area press, strongly in Madigan's corner throughout his time at St. Mary's, now seemed to be throwing in the towel. "We have the paradox," wrote Don Glendon of the *Oakland Tribune*, "of finding the richest coach in America at probably the poorest school in America." Only Glendon didn't write that opinion in the Tribune; it appeared in a national magazine under the pen name Bert Dunn. It was a cheap shot, regardless, Glendon hiding behind an alias. What hurt Madigan even more: Foudy, his trusted publicist, had ghosted part of that criticism. Forces were building against an embattled Madigan from all angles.

St. Mary's remained winless for the fourth consecutive game—its worst losing stretch since 1902—as USF pinned a 7-0 loss on the Gaels, the Dons' first victory over them in thirteen attempts. Starting the second half, USF's Mel Reid kicked a low grounder that St. Mary's Ivan Pivaroff fumbled, with the Dons' Bill Telesmanic recovering at the Gaels' 22. Cliff Fisk then passed 16 yards to Marvin Mosconi for the game's only touchdown. The Gaels' closest scoring threats were two snuffed drives, the first at USF's 3, and a second time at its 16, where Katzmeyer, predictably, missed a field goal. The only bit of good news for St. Mary's that week was that its promising freshman team won again. Tom Meany of the *News* wrote: "Some good news for St. Mary's rooters: The Gaels had their best freshman squad in years." But would Madigan get to coach them as sophomores?

After losing to USF, the Gaels showered, dressed, and headed to the railroad station. They took off for New York City, and Madigan's last game against Fordham. He had scheduled another two-game trip, catching Loyola on the way home in a makeup of the earlier postponed contest. Somewhere in route, Art Cohn had this conversation with Madigan: "Have you noticed, Slip, how often a team goes undefeated the year it gets a new coach?" Slip responded, "No, I haven't, Art, but I've often noticed that a team never goes undefeated the last year it has an old coach." Cohn included that quote in his *Oakland Tribune* column.

How prophetic was Madigan, considering that he might be facing his first losing season in seventeen years. Cohn wrote this about Madigan: "A hard cold that aggravated bronchial trouble, which has been plaguing him all season together with his old stomach trouble, has flattened the Slipper. Last summer, he weighed 209. Today, he's down to 185 and still going down. This I know: Madigan is working on his nerves alone. His resistance has never been at a lower ebb. He needs a rest badly. Nor is the team in much better shape."

Madigan's health had reached its nadir. On a five-and-a-half hour stopover in Chicago, he didn't leave the train. Travelers were discussing the news of the time, the serious and the light: John Steinbeck's "The Grapes of Wrath," Billie Holiday's anti-lynching song "Strange Fruit," the new "Batman" comic strip, and the first Little League game. The travelers discussed Madigan, too. How bad was his health? How much longer could he hold on, with antagonism building toward him from St. Mary's administration? He had medical issues, and so did his Gaels, to the point where he ran out of fullbacks. End Frank Maderos was moved to fullback, a position he hadn't played since high school. On this trip, assistant Red Strader took greater control in running the team, for Madigan couldn't attend every practice.

Madigan, assessing his weakened condition, offered Cohn a rare opportunity for a sportswriter. "If Fordham wins, Art, you're the head coach against Loyola. What do you think?" Cohn, at first, didn't believe what he was hearing. "Are you kidding?" he asked. "I'm serious," Madigan emphasized. "Then you got a deal," said Cohn. Some writers think they know more than the coaches. Cohn was one of those writers; now he would have a chance to prove it.

Madigan thought of everything and everybody. And so the 207 travelers on this Gaels trip saw the Billy Conn-Gus Lesnevich light-heavyweight championship fight in New York City, won by Conn on a 15-round decision. Tom Meany of the *San Francisco News* was the first to write that the Fordham game could be pivotal to Madigan's future at St. Mary's. Bill Corum of the International News Service picked up on that theme. "Madigan is a figure that New York football would be poorer without," he speculated. Madigan, tormented by his stomach, observed his Gaels losing for the fourth straight year to Fordham, and by a larger score, 13-0, before 34,800 at the Polo Grounds. This wasn't the typical Fordham powerhouse, having lost twice that year, 7-6 to Alabama and 7-0 to Tulane. The Rams struck in the second half on Steve Kazlo's 40-yard touchdown pass to Alex Yudikaitis and Dominic Principe's 15-yard scoring run off a reverse. "Three missed blocks cost us as many touchdowns in the first period," Madigan said. "We could have scored 20 points in that period." That outcome wasn't the forty-third birthday present Madigan was expecting, but he didn't lack the strength, anyway, to blow out forty-three candles, even with three tries.

Whitey Smith's trick knee acted up against Fordham, and he was pronounced out for the year. Fullback Dante Magnani also was banged up along with a dozen other Gaels. So what kind of team would they put on the field against Loyola? Prescott Sullivan was tired of excuses. "Madigan, for our dough," he wrote in the Examiner, "has this year turned in the worst coaching of his long and distinguished career. Has he lost his grip?" Sullivan overlooked the uncommon number of Gael injuries, and Madigan's own health issues. Anyway, Cohn won his bet: St. Mary's lost to Fordham, so Cohn would coach the team against Loyola. On the train trip to Los Angeles, Madigan was bed-ridden much of the time with continued stomach issues. Strader conducted practice in Brownwood, Texas, before the team reached Mexico.

"My dad," said Pat Smith, son of Whitey Smith, "remembers Mr. Madigan in Mexico, throwing coins from a sack to the children outside the train. My dad asked him why he was doing that, and he said, 'They'll remember us when we come back.' " Madigan wouldn't ever come back, not as a coach. On that same trip, fourteen Mexican soldiers boarded the train and escorted the St. Mary's party to Mexico City. "Probably nothing would happen anyway," Madigan explained to passengers worried at the sight of military weapons, "but it was just a precautionary measure, a little added protection. You know, they do have revolutions down here, and bandits, too." Only Slip Madigan would arrange a trip with bandidos on his mind. Viva, Zapata!

Madigan didn't coach his final game for St. Mary's College. Art Cohn was in charge, or thought he was, until Red Strader took over. For Madigan was too sick to make it to the Los Angeles Coliseum. St. Mary's won easily without him, 40-7. Cohn was on the Gaels sideline until halftime, before heading up to the press box. Only 10,000 attended the blowout. Smith and Magnani managed to play, not at 100 percent, but effectively. Ed Heffernan threw scoring passes of 41 and 26 yards to Magnani, Smith broke off a 63-yard touchdown run, and Lavine Bettencourt picked off a Ray Elsey pass and returned it 77 yards for another score. Loyola actually scored first, on Tony Delellis' 60-yard interception return of a Freitas pass, which lit a fire under St. Mary's.

"Art Cohn, the only major undefeated and untied football coach on the Pacific Coast, today retired from the profession," Cohn, the *Tribune* sports editor and columnist, wrote of his "victory" debut. "It's too easy. I have resigned as head coach of St. Mary's and have recommended that Slip Madigan be given another chance. After all, the poor man has a wife and three kids to support."

The Gaels accumulated 224 yards to Loyola's 163, and piled up 12 first downs to 3, but even Cohn couldn't correct the team's miscue problems. St. Mary's turned the ball over five times. Cohn was wise to give up coaching and return to skewering others. A few days after the season he wrote: "It is true that two St. Mary's regulars—both of whom scored against Loyola Sunday—quit college two weeks before they left with the Gaels for the Fordham game. Now that the season is over, several more plan to drop out of school quietly and are in a receptive move for any job."

Fourteen Gaels in 1939 did leave school, eleven for academic reasons and three—tackle Dick Jones, quarterback Dave Nichols, and halfback Whitey Smith—to get married. Three of the dropouts were seniors: Smith, tackle-placekicker Katzmeyer, and guard Pete Sedar. Madigan expressed surprise at the number of players departing, the largest exodus during his tenure there. St. Mary's administrators looked at that number with a jaundiced eye, furthering their case against Madigan, including his 3-4-1 record, his first losing season since 1922.

Whitey Smith explained to his son, Pat, why he dropped out of school in December 1939. "They didn't have a decent season, Slip was sick, and my dad was in love," the son said in 2016. "He got married to my mom for the rest of his life, and they had six children. He died in 1987, but he always regretted not getting his sheepskin, even though he wasn't the most academic student. He didn't know his real dad, and coach Harry Shipkey at Salinas High School and Mr. Madigan became his father figures. They baptized him at St. Mary's, and he kept a strong Catholic faith the rest of his life. He owned a gas station before becoming a letter carrier in Salinas. He always was proud of scoring the touchdown against Santa Clara that got St. Mary's the Cotton Bowl bid. One more thing about Mr. Madigan: My dad broke his nose three times at St. Mary's. Mr. Madigan told him, 'Don't worry, Herb, I'll take care of it after you're done playing.' In 1940, my dad's nose was fixed. Mr. Madigan took care of it, just as he said."

The biggest story of 1939 was Germany's invasion of Poland, and the start of World War II, with the United States declaring itself, initially, as neutral. Three months into 1940, Slip Madigan still was St. Mary's football coach. Health-wise, his condition hadn't improved. But with rest, diet and medication, he was convinced that he would be strong enough to resume coaching. On March 5, the *Call-Bulletin* ran a headline: "Madigan Will Stay! Coach Denies He'll Go to Loyola or Retire Temporarily." Mike Pecarovich had been fired as Loyola's coach. Clipper Smith had left Villanova and returned to the West Coast, but denied interest in the Loyola job. Strader conferred with Loyola officials, the *Call-Bulletin* reported, but "Strader was playing a John Alden role for Madigan, and that the latter may go to Loyola, leaving the Gael position to Strader."

Madigan denied, emphatically, that he was going anywhere. "There's nothing to it," he told the *Call-Bulletin* regarding the Loyola rumor. As for his health, Dr. John Murphy told the *Call-Bulletin* (likely Pat Frayne, though the story had no byline): "That Madigan illness and operation rumor is six years old. Madigan is well enough. I would change places with him today. The X-rays showed nothing seriously wrong with the Gaels coach, certainly nothing that would interfere with his work."

A *Post-Enquirer* headline read: "Slip Angered Over False Reports." But Madigan, who likely was quoted by Al Santoro before the latter left for a sports writing job in Los Angeles, said, "I don't know how such rumors get started. Why don't people come to me before they print things like that? I was available all last night, and could have been reached by anyone who tried." The *San Francisco Examiner* didn't reach out to him before writing that Strader, in speaking with Loyola, was "merely acting as good old Slip's agent. . . . Madigan, not too happy at St. Mary's these past few years, isn't averse to moving on if the price is right."

Suddenly, it became a question of whom to believe. Bill Leiser implied that he phoned Madigan before quoting him thusly in his *Chronicle* column: "I got back from the hospital a few days ago, but must stay home for a while. There's something still wrong, and I'll have to be operated on sometime reasonably soon." That's exactly the opposite of what Dr. John Murphy had said about Madigan's physical condition. "I hope, however," Slip continued in Leiser's column, "that I can go through the usual spring work and let the doctors take care of me during the summer. They seem to think I can work it out this way."

Two weeks later, Leiser offered a contrary opinion: "We rather think that, with head coach Slip Madigan in somewhat questionable health, St. Mary's simply will not let Red Strader get away. Madigan has made himself to the effect that he would vote to release Strader if Red wanted to take a new job, but both Madigan and the Board of Athletic Control want Red to stay. The best bet is that they will arrange it that way."

Madigan had a profound sense of what was coming. "My dad told us that when you stay in one place too long, and say no to too many people too many times, you create too many enemies," said Ed Madigan.

How sick, exactly, was Slip Madigan? A phone call came from Ottawa, Illinois, saying that Patrick Madigan, 83, had passed away. It was first reported that Slip would leave Oakland for the memorial service honoring his father in Ottawa. Then it was reported that Slip would be unable to attend the service because of his illness. If a son is too sick to attend his father's funeral, the public surmised, he must be very sick.

St. Mary's took Madigan's health into full consideration, but that didn't factor into its decision to fire him on March 11, 1940. Bay Area steel magnet and bridge builder J. Philip Murphy, Slip's former player and now a member of the school's Athletic Board of Control, released a succinct statement that Madigan's time at St. Mary's College was over. "But my dad felt that Andy Burke, who was also on the Athletic Board of Control, was out to get him," said Ed Madigan. "Dad had said no to Burke too many times."

And so Slip Madigan's nineteen defining seasons at St. Mary's, and his impressive 116-45-12 coaching record, now were history. He would be paid through 1940 as his contract, drafted in 1938, stipulated. But it was a renewed, drastically cut, contract, eliminating his receiving 10 percent of gate receipts. St. Mary's had gotten cheap with the man who had enriched its image.

Madigan sacrificed a great deal, and not only his health, to grow St. Mary's into what it became. He coached football, basketball, baseball, track and field, and boxing, while also serving as athletic director. He nailed cleats onto football shoes to save money. He dragged the practice field, and mowed its grass, for that same reason. He worked around the clock with limited assistance. And with all that on his plate, he won. Only he didn't just win; he won plenty.

Through his success and charisma, he won converts to St. Mary's College who wouldn't otherwise have been converted. He was solely responsible, because of his football teams, for St. Mary's move to Moraga and for a good share of the construction that occurred on that campus. He certainly deserved that 10 percent, for it's hard to conceive of a football coach who had a greater influence on a college. Slip Madigan didn't found St. Mary's College. But he was, and is, St. Mary's College.

16

The Final Years

Slip Madigan left one legacy behind him, and immediately constructed a new legacy. If he could create one football empire, why not create a second empire? Upon leaving St. Mary's, or upon St. Mary's leaving him, he filled in briefly as University of Iowa head coach as a wartime favor to a coaching friend. He served as general manager in a new professional league that eventually merged with the National Football League. But being a builder at heart, he set out to build something new, something more permanent than a coaching career. He built homes, built them into an empire.

He built them in Contra Costa County, where St. Mary's College is located. He had majored in architecture and law at Notre Dame. He was a businessman as well as a coach at St. Mary's. He then merged that acumen and background into his becoming a millionaire homebuilder. Because he was Slip Madigan, could anything less be expected?

Ed Madigan, his son, oversees his father's two legacies. The football part is stored in tome-like scrapbooks, but is also visible in photographs lining the walls of the rumpus room of the Oakland home his father purchased in 1932, and which the son lives in today. The son manages the housing part, and on September 9, 2016, one month and one day before the fiftieth anniversary of his father's passing, the son discussed Slip Madigan's transition from his first legacy into his second legacy.

"He was hurt when he left St. Mary's, mostly hurt by the way it was handled," said Ed Madigan. "But he wasn't a man who dwelled on things for long. He didn't hold grudges. He had an Irish leprechaun's personality. He loved the media, but he loved playing with them. When he got into the construction business, he named one street 'Sullivan Way' after Prescott Sullivan, 'Ward Way' after Arch Ward of the *Chicago Tribune* and Alan Ward of the *Oakland Tribune*, and 'Frayne Lane' after Pat Frayne. Pat and my Dad were very close; Dad hadn't forgotten that it was Pat who re-named St. Mary's as the 'Galloping Gaels.' My dad also had streets named 'Notre Dame Avenue' and 'Rockne Street.'

"My dad's feeling, though, was that his leaving St. Mary's could have been handled better. Other people felt the same way, but there was a lot of jealousy at that point. But he wasn't a grudge-carrier. During World War II, when one of the brothers at St. Mary's asked dad for his help in establishing a pre-flight school at the college, dad used his influence with President Roosevelt, Postmaster General James Farley, and the Democratic Party, and it was done in 1942 or 1943. And the brothers paid my dad for it."

So even though Slip Madigan departed St. Mary's in 1939 not on the best of terms, St. Mary's still paid him into the next decade, well beyond the final year of his contract in 1940. "He liked the brothers there, and was willing to help them," said the son. "He was a generous man, and optimistic, and always looking ahead. That's how he got into the racetrack business. Golden Gate Fields was built, and he was its general manager. Then it rained for forty days and forty nights, making the track muddy. The war came along and our government stopped all racing on the West Coast. My dad said it was biblical that he wasn't supposed to be in the horse racing business."

As the final act between St. Mary's and Slip Madigan, when he passed away in 1966, J. Philip Murphy was among the pall bearers. This is the same Phil Murphy who suited up for Madigan in the late 1920s, and who issued the official statement when St. Mary's fired him. "My dad never held Phil accountable; he was just the messenger from the Athletic Board of Control," said Ed Madigan. "When dad went into the building business, Phil, a builder himself, signed the application for dad's contracting license. Dad had no animosity toward Phil. Andy Burke was the thorn in dad's side. And dad held Red Strader accountable, too."

Slip Madigan's coaching was passed down to the son, only in a matrimonial way. Ed Madigan found himself courting Carol Ann Nichelini, the niece of the great St. Mary's running back of the 1930s, Al Nichelini, who was coached by Slip Madigan. "We were at a party in San Francisco on a Blue and Gold boat under the Bay Bridge," said Ed. "Carol belong to the Spinsters organization, and I belonged to the Bachelors organization. She fell into me, and when I told her that her uncle was my boyhood hero, that started the relationship right there. When we got engaged, it was announced in Art Rosenbaum's column in the *San Francisco Chronicle*. Art covered my dad's teams at St. Mary's. I invited Uncle Al Nichelini to the wedding, and he came."

Notre Dame's influence on Edward Patrick "Slip" Madigan was passed down to Ed Madigan, and then onto his son, also named Edward. "I was at my sister Pat's wedding reception, right here in this house," said Ed Madigan, "and attending the reception was this priest, James Doll, who played football for Notre Dame. He started working on me to go to Notre Dame. I was attending St. Ignatius High, a Jesuit school in San Francisco, and thinking of going to Cal, not St. Mary's. I don't want to say anything bad about St. Mary's and the Christian Brothers, but my dad always thought the Jesuits were better educators. Notre Dame is a Holy Cross institution. Dad was very pleased that I decided to attend Notre Dame.

"And I'm still 'attending' Notre Dame. I've had season tickets for Notre Dame football for forty years, and I go back two or three times a year for games. It goes back to my father going there, and my mother being a 'townie' in South Bend. I have relatives from both sides of my family around there, and dad really loved Notre Dame. He went back for Rockne's funeral, and took his St. Mary's teams through South Bend several times.

"When dad coached at Iowa, the Big Ten was squeezing Notre Dame, and wouldn't schedule them. Dad scheduled them for the next several years, and that started the relationship between Iowa and Notre Dame. Whenever dad went back to Notre Dame, it was like old home week. All the priests knew him. Notre Dame is like a family; it never stops. When my two sons went back to South Bend for a game, they went inside a bar where there was a team picture with dad and George Gipp. My sons said, 'That's my Granddad.' The bartender bought them free drinks all night."

Wherever Slip Madigan traveled, even internationally, he'd run into Notre Dame alumni or followers. The same thing was true of his St. Mary's influence. Son Ed recalled being in Rome with his father, and hearing "The Bells of St. Mary's" played in a restaurant in honor of his dad. In Germany, Ed's cousin, Bill Madigan, was in charge of a military depot. When Slip Madigan visited, he met the town's mayor, and "they were the best of buddies within a matter of hours," said Ed. Then there was the Ronald Reagan connection. "My Notre Dame classmate, Ron Mazzoli, became a Congressman in Kentucky," said Ed Madigan. "Ron and another Congressman, Michael Madigan from Illinois, were traveling with President Reagan on a political trip to the Midwest. The President asked Michael Madigan if he was related to Slip Madigan. He wasn't, but Reagan mentioned that he was a great fan of my dad. They both grew up in Illinois; dad was born in Ottawa and the President in Tampico. I believe dad was an advisor on the movie about Knute Rockne, in which Reagan played George Gipp.

"Dad was on Bing Crosby's radio show a lot; Bing attended Gonzaga; dad coached against Gonzaga. Bob Hope liked my dad, too; Bob and Bing were friends. Dad also was a good friend of Pat O'Brien, who played Rockne in that film. When dad went into the Helms Athletic Hall of Fame, there was a big dinner in San Francisco. Dad was sitting at one end of the table, and Pat O'Brien was at the other end. Pat told my dad to shut up because Pat was supposed to be the star that evening, and dad was taking over the party. He had the kind of personality that when he walked into the room, everyone gravitated toward him, and it didn't take long to get to know him.

"He didn't criticize people too much," the son continued, "but he had his enemies. Some sportswriters used to take shots at him. Those shots never bothered him. In the building business, contractors and sub-contractors would come over to a job, and he'd sit and talk to them for hours about business and pleasure. He had the kind of friendly, easy-going personality that everyone liked. He also had this hard line, saying: 'Shirtsleeves to shirtsleeves in three generations.' Here's what he meant by that: The first generation of shirtsleeves was poor, the second generation of shirtsleeves made money, and the third generation of shirtsleeves blew it all.' That's how smart he was about business, and how cautious, too. He never lost his perspective from the beginning."

In Slip Madigan's final years, he shared new stories with his son. "Dad told me he got the idea for a variation of the Notre Dame Shift from watching the Rockettes dance." Slip saw some connection between choreography and pulling guards. "He also brought up the incident involving Dante Magnani and Bronko Nagurski, who played together on the Chicago Bears. They were drinking at Shanty Malone's in San Francisco, and Dante told Bronko he'd give him a 50-yard running start, and he would tackle him. We're talking Bronko Nagurski! Well, they went to Golden Gate Park, Bronko got his running start, and Dante dropped him with a perfect tackle. Dante was my dad's player, and dad always taught proper technique.

"When dad coached at Iowa, he said his ulcers didn't bother him, because there was no pressure. He could have stayed at Iowa as athletic director, but he wanted to get back home. One of his Iowa players wrote me years later, saying that dad's coaching helped get him through difficult combat situations during World War II, by my dad's teaching him courage and integrity."

St. Mary's College's strongest effect on Slip Madigan, sadly, was his failing health. He had ulcers as a coach, and then suffered his first heart attack in 1960, six years before his death. Did coaching shorten his life? "I'm sure it did," said Ed Madigan. "The smoking, the stress, the hard work, it affected his health. Even in the contracting business, the light would be on, and he'd be working late at night. Then he'd be up the next morning and off to work. He always had a lot of energy. Then I noticed his shortness of breath. I persuaded him to go see his doctor, and dad had a heart attack right there on the table. He didn't know he had a bad heart until then, 1960. They rushed him to the hospital, but that heart attack saved his life."

But that attack was a reprieve, not a reversal. Slip Madigan's life ended just shy of his 70th birthday on October 10, 1966 with this fitting tribute written by the *Oakland Tribune*'s Joe Shea: "Edward Patrick (Slip) Madigan, the man who introduced the Jet Set concept into football when there were no jets, and at the same time molded little St. Mary's College into one of the nation's top football powers, is dead."

Even without the benefit of jet travel, Madigan didn't miss anything on his coaching journey. "I never heard him say that," his son said. "He seemed to enjoy whatever he was doing. He loved coaching, and he loved the contracting business. Just loved it, the contracting and the people, who loved him back. He was very handy with his hands, and he'd always be fussing with electrical wires. He'd be up there high, playing with those wires, and I'd say, 'Dad, be careful.' And he'd reply, 'Don't worry.' If something needed to be done, he'd jump in and do it.

"Dad also was a generous man. He gave a lot of money to Notre Dame for its library, and he contributed to Boys Town in Nebraska. He was a strong Catholic who went to church. He was a great man, but also a good man. Oh, he had his flaws. He had a hot temper, but it would blow over. He could get on me pretty good, but it never lasted long."

Did Slip Madigan foresee his own death in 1966? "Dad must have had a premonition," said his son, "because he picked out his plot at St. Mary's Cemetery a short time before he passed away." But his larger-than-life presence remains. "I think about him all the time," said the son. "I worked with him from the time I got out of Notre Dame in 1954. I told him after graduation that I would be home in three weeks, because there was a party in New York and another party in Chicago. He called me Ed or Eddie, but it was Edward when he was serious. He said, 'Edward, if you want to work for me, you'll be home in three days.' I had my next vacation three years later. I worked right along with him, seven days a week. Like in coaching, he'd say, 'Don't lie down, get up and fight.' He was always on the go. I'd be right there with him. He'd tell me from his own experience: 'Fame is fleeting, don't take yourself so seriously.'

"But he was very good to me, and to his family. He loved us, and he was generous to us. He bought a house for one of my sisters, and built a house for my other sister," the son noted. "One sister had a son who was partially sighted. My dad was a man of faith. He gave up smoking so that the boy's sight would return, and it did. When I'm back at Notre Dame, or at St. Mary's, or at a sub-division we own, I feel my dad around me. Besides being a flamboyant coach, he was a great teacher. He taught me about business, about finance. I started with him as a laborer and carpenter as a kid, and I knew then that I wanted to go to work for him. I was living in his house, like I'm doing now, and he'd used this old Navy term on me: "Come on, Ed, rise and shine, let's go.'

"There was separation between my two sisters and me for years, going back to when dad was alive. That made him distraught, and mad as hell, and he'd show his temper. He was a strong family man, but he wasn't able to heal that breach. That might have been the biggest misgiving in his life. I think it was."

Slip Madigan was only used to winning.

EPILOGUE

The drama that was St. Mary's College football in the 1920s and 1930s—the Slip Madigan era—was relived again in the den of his Oakland residence. Ed Madigan turned on the projector and the 1988 documentary, "Brickpile to Broadway," was shown, containing interviews with Slip's son, Slip's players, and others who helped the inimitable Slip forge a dynasty that seemed more like a fairy tale.

"They're all gone," Ed Madigan said in September 2016 of the film's participants, save himself and narrator Bob Fouts. Ed sat down with his wife, Carol, and Slip Madigan's biographer to watch the one-hour, twenty six-minute film, capturing a special, but forgotten, time in football history. Suddenly, they appeared again: Angelo Brovelli, Bill Fischer, George Canrinus, John Giannoni, Vic Strub, Andy Marefos, Lou Ferry and Marty Kordick, the Galloping Gaels whom, together with their dynamic coach, transformed little St. Mary's into a college football giant.

College football in the 1920s and 1930s belonged to the Fighting Irish of Notre Dame, but as Canrinus pointed out on film, "St. Mary's was just like Notre Dame." Except St. Mary's, unlike Notre Dame, came off as the underdog, perfectly suited for a nation gripped by a Depression. But, in truth, St. Mary's acted like the bourgeois, not the proletariat. Madigan made sure his Galloping Gaels stayed in plush hotels and even a country club on its Eastern swings. Slip Madigan always went first class.

"Slip was one of the most dynamic individuals you could ever know, full of enthusiasm," Paul Hungerford, who played on Madigan's earliest teams at St. Mary's, said on camera. "Slip was intelligent. A lot of these coaches were like barbarians. He always told us that the perfect practice makes for the perfect game. Needless to say, our drills in spring practice were very meaningful. It was dog eat dog."

The black-and-white documentary featured game film footage. St. Mary's, with its signature white shoulder epaulets and operating out of the Notre Dame Shift, moved through opponents with ease. Gael halfbacks ran freely as their blockers cut down three, four and five defenders. Perfect execution, perfect preparation. Just like recruiting.

"Slip would sit down in the kitchen and sell what St. Mary's has to offer,'' said Fischer, recalling a recruiting visit from Madigan. "He sold the parents and the student. He'd also talk to the high school principal, who appreciated it."

Madigan left nothing to chance, especially the basics. "First of all," said Giannoni, "Slip took care of the kicking game; no bad centers, no bad kickers. Slip said if you punt a ball 60 yards, and you hold them, and they punt it back to you 40 yards, you've gained 20 yards for doing nothing." Giannoni smiled at the memory.

Madigan believed blocking and tackling gave the Gaels the edge they needed. "He spent all of his time with the line, not the backfield," said Fischer. An edge meant everything to Madigan; he was so competitive, he wanted to be the first in anything. Thus St. Mary's became the first mainland team to play in Hawaii, in 1922. "It was so hot, you could hardly breathe. People were lined up on the sideline, but no one knew where the sideline was," Hungerford recalled. "They had luaus in our honor. They served a punch that was spiked, but you couldn't taste it. I remember Slip trying to give a speech after his third one . . . it was one of the funniest things I ever saw in my life."

Three years after Madigan came to St. Mary's, the Saints, as they were known in 1924, "scored the upset of the season," narrated Fouts, a 1943 St. Mary's graduate, referring to a 14-10 victory over USC. "They hit our line four times inside the 5-yard line, and we stopped them," said Hungerford. "But they called defensive holding; can you imagine that? Well, they hit the line four more times and didn't score."

Then in 1928, after a fire destroyed The Brickpile, St. Mary's moved its Oakland campus to rural Moraga, or cow country. "Football put St. Mary's on the map, and that's how we were able to move out to Moraga, because the football team was making money," Brother Jerome said on film. "God is a Gael." St. Mary's player Bob McAndrews found the new campus "to be paradise. You're out there in the hills, with no flowers, no trees, and no paved roads. We had a standard uniform of jeans and high boots to go through the mud." From the mud grew the lotus. St. Mary's became one of the loveliest small college campuses in the country.

In 1929, St. Mary's, with 300 students, took on a high-powered schedule and fashioned an 8-0-1 record for its first undefeated season. Then Madigan "thought about the theater of New York" and the bright lights of Broadway in making his Gaels nationally known, said Jack Henning, a student secretary to Madigan. And so St. Mary's, in 1930, went east to play unbeaten Fordham with high hopes and an expensive budget, authorized by Madigan. "We're staying in this fancy New York hotel, and we ordered a case of scotch and some expensive cigars," said Owen Duffy, a St. Mary's publicist at the time. There were New York writers to entertain, but Fordham still to beat, which the Gaels did, 20-12. "I still remember the announcer, Ted Husing, saying that St. Mary's is going through Fordham like a dose of salt," recalled Henning. By then, it wasn't Brickpile to Broadway, but cow pasture to Broadway.

Bill Fischer, a Catholic, hadn't forgotten the post-Fordham celebration after the Gaels returned home: "I ate fish three times in one day, and it was a Friday." The next year, 1931, St. Mary's traveled to Los Angeles and beat national champion USC, 13-7. "One of St. Mary's greatest victories, and one of the greatest upsets of all-time," said Henning. "Slip made the gates. He gave St. Mary's great influence through football, and while there were later periods of decline, there never was a season where Slip lost money."

"Slip was called the P.T. Barnum of college football," said Bob McAndrews. "He not only was a brilliant entrepreneur, but he knew football. But he had this other ability as a showman." Henning noted: "Slip knew what was dramatic. He moved from the old drab uniforms to red pants, blue jerseys." Plus "they were real silk, nothing synthetic," said Bill Beasley. No college team dressed like the Gaels, who then outdid themselves with green pants and jerseys with golden harps. "We walked out of the dressing room onto the field, and the whole stadium went, "Ohhhhh," said Giannoni. "Talk about flashy." Only the harp jerseys were made of satin, not silk. "They were spectacular," said Ferry, "but when we played Cal, it was 100 degrees, and those jerseys wouldn't breathe. Steam was coming out of them. I told the fellows to come on, let's go, but we actually wilted."

Madigan's relationship with sports writers was unlike most coaches. "He had no inhibitions; he dealt openly with the press," said Henning. "He treated them as equals, rather than as ink-stained wretches. He had ability with words, and so he was often quoted. He was an ideal coach for the sports writers. He was very often news." The press went along with St. Mary's on its junkets to New York and elsewhere. "Two, three thousand would watch us practice in Lubbock, Texas," said Giannoni. "They hung banners on the street: 'Welcome Slip Madigan and the Galloping Gaels.'" In Alva, Oklahoma, "a band was there to greet us," said Vic Strub. "We'd change into our uniforms in the stands, we'd practice, and then we'd get back on the train."

Madigan introduced his players to a world beyond their wildest expectations. "I was just a poor kid from the sticks," said Giannoni. "I'd see those structures, and the places where we stayed, and it was just beautiful, mind-boggling." Strub enjoyed staying at the Westchester Country Club in New York, "with two golf courses and a polo field. Imagine, practicing on a polo field. After we played Fordham, we had a night on the town. With some Fordham people, we went down to the Cotton Club, where Cab Calloway was just coming into his prime. You can imagine what a thrill that was."

When the St. Mary's train got stuck in a snowstorm in Moose Jaw, Saskatchewan, on the way home, "the town threw a party and a dance for us," said McAndrews. On another eastern trip, the Gaels came home through Havana. "Slip met the president of Cuba, and then Slip sent out a Christmas card which read, 'The president of Cuba sez to me, and I sez to you, Merry Christmas,' " said Henning, who later served as undersecretary of labor during the Kennedy administration before becoming ambassador to New Zealand.

St. Mary's fumbling habits became a topic of controversy during the Madigan era. "They'd say that we fumbled on purpose," said Strub. "To intrigue the press, Madigan would have us fumble in practice down at the goal line, and then have someone fall on it in the end zone. It was ruled, eventually, that you couldn't fumble forward on purpose." Did the Gaels, indeed, fumble on purpose? Madigan kept the press guessing. And he enjoyed out-foxing coaches.

During the 1934 St. Mary's-Santa Clara game at Kezar Stadium in San Francisco, the wind howled and the rain came down hard, soaking the field.

Madigan was setting up Broncos coach Clipper Smith. The Gaels wore practice uniforms in the first half, before Madigan had them change into red-and-white silk uniforms. "We had nice, dry uniforms in the second half, while Santa Clara was soaking wet," said Bill Beasley. "We backed them up, blocked a kick, recovered it in the end zone, and that was the ball game (St. Mary's, 7-0). We just took the spirit from out of them."

En route to cover the 1936 Olympic Games in Berlin, Madigan, who was Irish to the core, stopped to kiss the Blarney Stone in Ireland. The "Brickpile to Broadway" documentary captured that moment: Slip, held by the ankles, bent backward and down in order to kiss the rock. Slip's filming of the track and field events showed Jesse Owens winning the 100-meter dash. But the moment Madigan dreamed of, a bowl game, finally occurred during the 1938 season, when the Gaels were chosen to meet Texas Tech in the Cotton Bowl. "Slip told us that he had just received a phone call from his mother, that she was in very bad condition," said Marefos. "Her last wishes, he said, was that St. Mary's win this Cotton Bowl for her. We won the game, and afterwards, one of our players asked Slip, 'How is your mother?' And Slip said, 'She's fine. Why do you ask?' "

Eventually, the end came for Slip Madigan at St. Mary's. The breech between academia and athletics, big spending and cost cutting, celebrity and jealousy, became too big for any thought of healing. Madigan produced a 116-45-12 (.718 winning percentage) record at St. Mary's, but it was draining, emotionally and physically on the man, and, eventually, financially on the school. It had to end, and it did in 1939 after nineteen incredible seasons.

"I remember his taking every phone call from the media; he never turned anyone down," said Bob McAndrews. Marty Kordick added, "He should have been an actor. He was a great entertainer." John Giannoni rhapsodized: "I happened to play for him, but what a guy." George Canrinus noted: "Knute Rockne, Pop Warner, Amos Alonzo Stagg, Howard Jones: These four men wrote football history. But if you put Slip Madigan up against them, he'd have to be a fifth man, and I might consider putting him right at the top." Madigan defeated Warner, Stagg and Jones, but didn't get to face Rockne. Could there be five faces on college football's Mount Rushmore? "What he did, with what he had to do it with, you just had to admire the man," said Angelo Brovelli. "We could beat anybody, and usually we did."

Ron Isetti, St. Mary's professor and historian, summarized that glorious era perfectly on film: "It was a school that beat the odds. During the Depression, when the odds were against people, it was wonderful to see the little guy or the little school win, and not only win, but win with color, with panache, with style. The thing with Slip Madigan is that he was more than an individual. He was a cultural phenomenon, expressive of the decade. He was the perfect man at the perfect time."

INDEX

D

E

F

G

L

M

T

U

V

W

Y

Z